REVOLUTIONARY ANGLICANISM

Revolutionary Anglicanism

**The Colonial Church of England Clergy
during the American Revolution**

Nancy L. Rhoden

NEW YORK UNIVERSITY PRESS
Washington Square, New York

First published in the U.S.A. in 1999 by
NEW YORK UNIVERSITY PRESS
Washington Square
New York, N.Y. 10003

This book is printed on paper suitable for recycling and
made from fully managed and sustained forest sources.

Library of Congress Cataloging-in-Publication Data
Rhoden, Nancy L. (Nancy Lee), 1965–
Revolutionary Anglicanism : the colonial Church of England clergy
during the American Revolution / Nancy L. Rhoden
p.   cm.
Includes bibliographical references and index.
ISBN 0–8147–7519–5 (alk. paper) .
1. Church of England—United States—Clergy—History—18th
century.   2. Anglican Communion—United States—Clergy—
History—18th century.   3. Episcopal Church—Clergy—History—18th
century.   4. Episcopal Church—History—18th century.   5. United
States—Church history—18th century.   I. Title.
BX5881.R48   1999
283'.73'09033—dc21   98–31403
                                                                    CIP

Printed in Great Britain

To Raymond Harold Porter and
to the memory of Maud Christina Porter

Contents

Acknowledgments

With great pleasure, I acknowledge the many people who assisted in the research and writing of this book, at its various stages. In many centers, the library staff aided my search for materials. At Firestone Library, the staff of Interlibrary Loan, Microforms, and Reference were particularly helpful, especially Mary George. I also wish to thank the staff at many other research facilities, including Alderman Library at the University of Virginia, the Archives of the Episcopal Church, the Episcopal Archives of the Diocese of Connecticut, the Episcopal Diocesan Library of Maryland, the Historical Society of Pennsylvania, Maryland Historical Society, Maryland State Archives, North Carolina Archives, South Carolina Historical Society, South Carolina Library, Swem Library at the College of William and Mary, the Virginia Historical Society, and the Virginia State Library and Archives. I am also grateful for a doctoral fellowship from the Social Sciences and Humanities Research Council of Canada and other financial support from the Department of History at Princeton University. A Faculty Research and Creative Work Award from the University of Southern Indiana financed a later research trip to the Archives of the Episcopal Church in Austin, Texas.

Formally or informally, I have shared my research with a number of generous scholars. As a graduate student at Princeton, many colleagues provided practical suggestions, including the members of the Dissertation Writers' Group, especially Jacob Cogan, Gary Hewitt, and Geoffrey Plank. At formal conferences or presentations, including the Institute of Early American History and Culture First Annual Conference at Ann Arbor, the Newberry Seminar in Early American History and Culture, and the Canadian Society for Eighteenth-Century Studies, commentators and other interested scholars offered persuasive criticisms. On these occasions, I especially appreciated the valuable comments of Jon Butler, Alfred Young, and Margaret Kellow. At a late stage in this project, I also shared my findings with members of the NEH Summer Seminar 'Social Historians Write Biography' at the Newberry Library. Additionally, Ian Steele and Thad Tate each provided a careful and timely reading of a chapter in progress.

For his early and continued encouragement, I would like to thank Ian Steele, for it was in his undergraduate seminar at the University of Western Ontario that I first became interested in the trials and tribulations of these Anglican ministers. At Princeton University, Professor John Murrin proved an excellent teacher and dissertation supervisor. His insights into this project and the colonial world were always thought-provoking. It was both a privilege and a delight to work with him. For their thorough advice and interest, I also thank my dissertation readers: the late Eugene R. Sheridan, John F. Wilson, and Peter Lake. The suggestions of these readers improved both my clarity of thought and my prose. Any errors or omissions which remain are, of course, entirely my own.

To my husband Brian I owe a special thanks. His constant encouragement and practical assistance has made a great difference to both my work and my life. Other family members also shared in this project in their own way, including my sister, Linda, and my parents. To my father, Raymond Harold Porter, and to the memory of my mother, Maud Christina Porter, this book is lovingly dedicated.

List of Abbreviations

AEC	Archives of the Episcopal Church, Austin, Texas
AEH	*Anglican and Episcopal History*
AHR	*American Historical Review*
AL	Alderman Library, Special Collections, University of Virginia, Charlottesville, Virginia
Appletons' Cycl.	J. G. Wilson and John Fiske, eds, *Appletons' Cyclopaedia of American Biography*, I–VII (New York: Appleton, 1894–1900)
CH	*Church History*
DAB	Allen Johnson and Dumas Malone, eds, *Dictionary of American Biography*, I–XX (New York: Charles Scribner's, 1956; orig. publ., 1928)
Doc. Hist.	Francis L. Hawks and William Stevens Perry, eds, *Documentary History of the Protestant Episcopal Church, in the United States of America. Containing Numerous Hitherto Unpublished Documents Concerning the Church in Connecticut*, I–II (Hartford, CT: The Historiographer, 1959; orig. publ., 1863–4), II
EADC	Episcopal Archives of the Diocese of Connecticut, Hartford, Connecticut
EDLM	Episcopal Diocesan Library of Maryland, Baltimore, Maryland
Fulham Papers	Fulham Library (Lambeth Palace) Papers, Microfilm, Firestone Library, Princeton University
Hist. Coll.	William Stevens Perry, ed., *Historical Collections Relating to the American Colonial Church*, I–V (New York: AMS Press, 1969; orig. publ., 1870)
HMPEC	*Historical Magazine of the Protestant Episcopal Church*
HSP	Historical Society of Pennsylvania, Philadelphia, Pennsylvania
JAH	*Journal of American History*
JEH	*Journal of Ecclesiastical History*
Lambeth Palace Misc.	Lambeth Palace Library Miscellaneous American Material, 17th–18th Centuries, Microfilm, New York University, New York

MHS	Maryland Historical Society, Baltimore, Maryland
MSA	Maryland State Archives, Annapolis, Maryland
NCSA	North Carolina State Archives, Raleigh, North Carolina
SCHS	South Carolina Historical Society, Charleston, South Carolina
SL	Swem Library, Special Collections and University Archives, College of William and Mary, Williamsburg, Virginia
SPG Journals	Society for the Propagation of the Gospel in Foreign Parts Journals, Microfilm, Firestone Library, Princeton University
SPG Ser B, C	Society for the Propagation of the Gospel in Foreign Parts, Series B and Series C, Microfilm, Firestone Library, Princeton University
VHS	Virginia Historical Society, Richmond, Virginia
VMHB	*Virginia Magazine of History and Biography*
VSLA	Virginia State Library and Archives, Richmond, Virginia
WMQ	*William and Mary Quarterly*

1 Introduction

As a civil war, the American Revolution polarized residents of the rebelling American colonies, who faced complex decisions of loyalism or patriotism, but perhaps Thomas Paine's famous commentary on the Revolution, '[t]hese are the times that try men's souls,' applies most fittingly to the colonial clergymen of the Church of England.[1] As the ministers noted themselves, the American Revolution was a particularly 'trying' or 'troublesome' time.[2] In deciding between loyalism and patriotism, Anglican parishioners often faced a difficult decision, but the church's colonial clergy truly found themselves in dire straits. At ordination, Church of England clerics pledged allegiance to the king and promised to defend him against any threat, foreign or domestic. Furthermore, they swore an oath to conform with the Book of Common Prayer and thereby maintain the church's liturgy unaltered. For revolutionaries, such promises tainted the Church of England's clergy with grave suspicions of loyalism. After the Declaration of Independence, prayers for the king and the royal family, which were required parts of the liturgy for the Eucharist and Morning Prayer, became offensive to patriots. Consequently, Congress demanded that such royal prayers be omitted and replaced with comparable prayers for Congress, and in many states the clergy also were required to take oaths to Congress which contradicted previous ordination oaths. Despite their professional affinities with England, these men had also forged ties of affection, of varying degrees, with the colonists. A rising proportion of the ministers on the eve of the Revolution had been born in America, and after years of service even those British-born clergy had established regional friendships or married into local families. Arguably, no other group of individuals during the revolutionary period faced more contradictory demands of conscience, duty, and allegiance. Their collective story illustrates the complex political, social and private issues which surrounded decisions of political affiliation.

Practically all ministers who remained in the colonies found these revolutionary years filled with personal tests of endurance, patience, and spiritual fortitude, although loyalists or suspected loyalists faced the harshest treatment. According to the report of a colleague, Rev. Daniel Batwell of Pennsylvania had been dunked several times in a river with 'savage cruelty' and then made to ride over 12 miles to get dry clothing.[3] In Virginia, Christopher MacRae's parishioners allowed him to continue preaching, despite his loyalism, but in the fall of 1779, after being called away on a

1

pretext, MacRae was seized, bound to a tree, beaten, and left naked in the woods. His attackers were later tried and fined.[4] Jonathan Boucher of Maryland had sufficiently angered his patriot parishioners that he preached with a pair of pistols on a nearby pillow. Like a number of other ministers, Boucher reported that one Sunday a body of armed men had prevented him from even assuming his place at the pulpit.[5] Contemporaries believed that James Herdman risked a coat of tar and a surplice of feathers, for he refused to swear a new oath to the revolutionary government in Virginia, declined to preach on a Congressionally-ordered fast day, and reportedly denied the authority of both the County Committee of Culpeper and the Continental Congress. Likewise, Thomas Johnston, also of Virginia, found himself with serious problems after drinking to the success of the king's forces.[6]

Legal or extralegal intimidation could provoke both fear and despair. While fellow ministers frequently attributed the deaths or illnesses of their colleagues partially to rebel mistreatment, the plight of Ephraim Avery of Rye, New York, encouraged additional speculation. Like fellow loyalists in the community, Avery had welcomed the king's troops, and later local rebels retaliated by driving away his cattle. Samuel Seabury Jr reported in March 1777 that one Tuesday morning, Avery had asked his maid to serve his children breakfast and went outside. Later he was found on his property with his throat cut. While some neighbors suspected murder by local rebels, Seabury noted that many believed that Avery's fears and disappointments had driven him to extreme desperation.[7]

The tumultuous events of the Revolution and demands of rebel authorities frequently endangered the livelihood and personal safety of colonial Anglican ministers. Patriot ministers also faced hardships, especially when British troops moved through their parishes, or when they accepted more dangerous duties. Although they did not face revolutionary committees or local mobs, Anglican chaplains in the Revolutionary army risked their lives by aiding rebel forces. At least ten Church of England chaplains, or more than half the total number of Anglican chaplains in the Revolutionary army, came from Virginia.[8] Serving in the Continental forces or the militia, these ministers provided spiritual and moral inspiration for patriot soldiers. The famous 'Fighting Parson' John Peter Gabriel Muhlenberg became a major-general in the Continental Army. Tradition has it that he preached a rousing sermon in his Anglican parish church at Woodstock, Virginia, in early 1776, after which he dramatically threw off his vestments to reveal a colonel's uniform. His selected text from Ecclesiastes 3: 1, 'To every thing there is a season, and a time to every purpose under the heaven' emphasized the timeliness of military action against the British, and his personal example resulted in substantial enlistments.[9] In its examination of the plight of the colonial Anglican clergy and their reactions to the American Revolution, this study may be considered both a collective biography of the church's ministers and a Revolutionary history of the denomination. Traditionally, Anglican ministers have been depicted as the arch-Tories of the event, in part because of the notoriety of loyalists, such as Charles Inglis, Thomas Bradbury Chandler, Samuel Seabury Jr, and Jonathan Boucher, who produced a large share of the loyalist literature. To depict the full range of clerical experiences, including loyalism, patriotism, and neutrality, this project tracks the careers of more than three hundred Church of England clergy who lived and worked in the 13 original American colonies anytime between 1775 and 1783.

Anglican ministers in the colonies occupied a range of social and economic positions. The office of Church of England clergyman conferred a degree of respectability, as did certain customs by mid-century, including the wearing of a wig and the fashionable lawn sleeves of the surplice. By the end of the eighteenth century in England, more gentry were entering the Church of England, resulting in a general rise in the status of all clergy, even if the church continued to admit many non-elite candidates.[10] The social status or public reputation of colonial ministers may have been affected by these English trends, even though most colonial parishes on the eve of the Revolution preferred American-born candidates. These ministers shared a profession with increasingly standardized entrance requirements; many had university degrees from British institutions or colonial colleges. All had experienced ordination in England. In America, the clergy were spread unevenly throughout the colonies, although the largest number enjoyed relative fiscal stability in Virginia and Maryland, at least before the Revolution. The wealthiest ministers of the colonial south were tobacco planters and slaveholders who lived in a genteel manner, but their economic situation depended upon many factors, including region, parish wealth, manner of payment, provisions for a glebe, age, or experience, and formal position as curate, rector, educator, or missionary. In the northern and middle colonies, missionaries of the Society for the Propagation of the Gospel usually had only modest incomes and frequently complained of poverty.

In addition to providing a denominational history of the Church of England during the Revolution, this study aims to consider broader issues of patriotism and loyalism. In debating the formulation of a distinctively 'American' identity, one might point to such events as the Great Awakening, the Seven Years' War, the American Revolution, or the deification of the

Constitution as indicative of a budding sense of 'American-ness.'[11] A study of the Church of England during the Revolution casts light upon issues of political allegiance and the process through which self-identification with a particular nation changed. Anglican clergymen may be considered representatives of the colonial population and members of the empire; this group consisted of native-born Americans as well as recent British immigrants. Their relationship to Britain, however, was crystallized and formalized more concretely than that of their parishioners or the dissenter population, due to ordination oaths and professional affiliations.

While historians have long been interested in the religious dimensions of the American Revolution, the contributions of evangelical Protestantism to both American patriotism and the moral dimensions of the Revolution have received most of the attention.[12] Denominational histories first focused on the victors of the Revolution, such as the Baptists or Presbyterians, whose evangelical patriotism won them religious toleration, and correspondingly historical accounts neglected rationalist and loyalist denominations. Of course, the fact that the Episcopal Church today is not one of the most populous American denominations does not accurately reflect its past significance. Established in six of the 13 colonies before the Revolution, the Church of England wielded considerable political power, especially in the Chesapeake which had the highest concentration of Anglicans. Although the church did not keep abreast with immigration and the proliferation of dissenters in the back country, the decade before the Revolution witnessed substantial growth within the colonial Church of England. It was truly an intercolonial church on the eve of the Revolution.[13]

Despite reduced church attendance during the war years, Anglican clergymen wielded considerable influence among their parishioners as the chief conveyors of information in their community. From the pulpit, colonial ministers of all denominations provided their parishioners with the only regular (weekly) medium of public communication.[14] In many regions, church attendance, court days, and other public rituals also reinforced and perpetuated the class structure or other social divisions.[15] Presumably, sermons possessed less influence in rural areas where dispersed settlement patterns prohibited such regular church attendance, but in settled areas of the south, gentry mansions and parish churches functioned as important communication centers. Despite the proliferation of rival forms of information exchange by 1776, including newspaper articles, printed pamphlets, and revolutionary meetings, church gatherings continued to provide an opportunity for members to discuss events and share information. By the late eighteenth century, clergymen no longer functioned as the main purveyors of public information, but by keeping a watchful eye on those suspected of loyalism, revolutionary committees acknowledged the potential influence of the neighborhood minister.

Since the eighteenth century, historians have asserted a strong connection between the pulpit and the Revolution, specifically by emphasizing the patriotic messages emanating from New England's Congregationalist pulpits. In a speech to Parliament on 22 March 1775, Edmund Burke attributed America's peculiar spirit of liberty to its temper and character, particularly its history of religious dissent in the northern colonies.[16] From the pulpit, Congregationalists had been taught that if the king seriously violated God's commands and broke his compact with the people, the people then had a duty to resist in order to assure their religious covenant.[17] In the jeremiad, a type of Puritan sermon which lamented lost virtue and warned of divine retribution, American revolutionaries found a language of unity. Colonial boycotts aimed for the repeal of offensive Parliamentary Acts, but they also encouraged positive Puritan traits of virtue, simplicity, and frugality.[18]

Baptists and Presbyterians also shared an overwhelmingly patriot point of view. Under the Presbyterian cleric, John Witherspoon, the College of New Jersey functioned as a 'seminary of sedition.' Its graduates were overwhelmingly patriot. As an official pronouncement of the Presbyterian church, the pastoral letter drafted by Witherspoon at the synod gathering of 19 May 1775 endorsed the cause of American revolutionaries.[19] Later, Witherspoon became the only clergyman to sign the Declaration of Independence. Other New Light patriots, such as the Baptist leader Isaac Backus, contributed to the revolutionary movement by campaigning for the moral reform of American society. By employing arguments similar to those that patriots used against Britain, Backus objected to ecclesiastical tyranny in New England. The evangelical movement in Virginia, which coincided with the climax of the patriot movement, also challenged the hegemony of the Anglican gentry class.[20] To a certain extent, Baptist and Presbyterian opposition to the prevailing religious establishments, whether Anglican or Congregationalist, predisposed its members to embrace the colonial cause.

Other colonial religious groups such as Quakers, Mennonites, and Moravians never developed a theology of armed resistance to monarchs. Although the Continental Congress exempted religious conscientious objectors from required military service, neighborhood patriotic sentiment was often less tolerant, and Quakers, as well as members of smaller peace sects, were accused of hiding behind conscience to avoid military service or to disguise their loyalism. The Philadelphia Yearly Meetings of 1775 and 1776 warned Friends throughout the colonies to avoid participation in the Revolution, or else they risked potentially serious disciplinary measures. The religious pacifism of German-speaking groups, including Mennonites, Amish, and Moravians, also offended patriot sensibilities, although as farmers in rural counties, they were a less obvious target than groups of urban-dwelling, cosmopolitan Quakers.[21] Conflicts over oath-taking, the payment of war taxes, and principles of religious pacifism fostered misunderstandings between various peace sects and those patriots who assumed that non-participants were enemies.

Although the loyalist perspective existed most consistently in the Church of England, Methodists, Roman Catholics and some Old Light Calvinists (Congregationalists, Baptists, or Presbyterians) also harbored a continued affection for the king and Britain. Because of the widely publicized views of Charles and John Wesley on the impropriety of the American Revolution, Methodism in the colonies had a strong loyalist element.[22] To many colonial Catholics, Britain appeared to offer more security (especially after the Quebec Act) than the more intolerant colonial Protestants, at least until the French alliance of 1778. Subsequent and deliberate cooling of anti-Catholic sentiment encouraged more colonial Catholics to support the patriot cause.[23]

In recognition of this tremendous variety, one might present a spectrum of Revolutionary political affiliation along denominational lines. Congregationalists, Baptists, and Presbyterians often demonstrated a patriot response to the Revolution; Quakers, Mennonites, and Moravians are usually characterized as pacifists; and Anglicans (especially clergy) might be depicted as loyalists.[24] Likewise, colonists could be divided into two camps: evangelicals who embraced the Revolution and liberal anti-evangelicals who largely resisted the patriot movement. Nonetheless, only the first part of this equation has gained wide acceptance. Evangelicals tended to be overwhelmingly patriot, but non-evangelicals filled both extremes of patriot and loyalist leadership.[25] The political views of Anglican clergymen, one such non-evangelical group, illustrates the range of this spectrum. Although Anglicanism was associated closely with loyalism, this study describes how several strains of political thought, such as loyalism, patriotism, and pacifism/neutrality, existed within the Anglican clerical community.

The Church of England contained a strong loyalist element, and its connection with England rendered it suspect from the beginning of the Anglo-American disputes. Other religious groups in the colonial period had maintained connections with their European mother-church (Methodists also looked to England, Presbyterians to the Scottish Kirk, the Dutch Reformed Church to Holland, and the Lutherans to Germany), but independence had especially dramatic repercussions for the Anglican church (and the associated Methodist movement) since the British monarch functioned also as the head of the Church of England. Ultimately the colonial church suffered from its continued association with the Crown. American revolutionaries, particularly in the northern colonies, directed their disaffection for Britain toward the colonial counterparts of the king's church. Patriot troops desecrated colonial Anglican churches by quartering troops and stabling horses in church buildings, although British forces also damaged these ecclesiastical edifices. American patriots tried to make an example of the Church of England clergy by forcing them, as visible and sometimes influential public officials, to declare openly their allegiance to Congress. A similar fate befell the clergy of France at the time of the Civil Constitution of the Clergy in 1791. Policies initiated through this document generated considerable discontent among French Catholic clergy and parishioners, which in turn produced a leadership class for the forces of counter-revolution.[26] In contrast, the many prominent loyalists who fled to England in the early years of the American Revolution did not provide lasting leadership for a counter-revolutionary movement.

Ultimately, depictions of colonial Anglicans as fervent loyalists prove insufficient. Rather, a certain paradox exists in this equation of loyalism with the colonial Church of England.[27] Anglicanism furnished more than its share of patriot leaders; at least (very) nominally, many of the famous revolutionaries were Anglicans – including Patrick Henry, Thomas Jefferson, Alexander Hamilton, and George Washington. Also, the Church of England contributed the largest number of signers of the Declaration of Independence. To explain this paradox of Anglicanism's association with loyalism and yet the patriotism of some of its most famous members, one must first distinguish between the clergy and laity. Although Anglican clergymen shared certain views with their parishioners, a unified Church of England reaction to the Revolution never existed. Institutionally, the church lacked the infrastructure of other denominations' synods or presbyteries which formulated church policies. Consequently, the laity's attachment to the church could be more easily broken by the events of the Revolution. Unlike their ministers, lay members had not taken any oaths to support the king; nor were they bound by solemn declaration to a strict fidelity to the Book of Common Prayer.[28] In contrast, the clergy's political and liturgical commitments both distinguished them from their parishioners and influenced their decision to side with the loyalists or the patriots. The clergymen's special circumstances do not negate a significant interplay between lay and clerical opinion, but they do justify a study of the clergy as a group distinctive from their lay brethren.

At various times and with slightly different meanings, I have used the following terms: Church of England, churchmen, Anglican, Episcopal, and the (American) Protestant Episcopal Church. The plethora of labels results, in part, from the church's long history in the Old World. The Church of England followed colonists across the Atlantic where ministers and parishioners continued to identify themselves as 'churchmen' or 'conformists,' meaning members of the established English church. Not until the independence of the United States and subsequent creation of the American Protestant Episcopal Church did its clergy and parishioners cease to call themselves members of the Church of England. The Episcopal Church, or more formally the American Protestant Episcopal Church, then emerged officially. Because of the church's historic insistence on the importance of episcopacy and the colonial pamphlet war of the eighteenth century over the validity of presbyterian versus episcopal ordination, the term 'episcopal minister' preceded the official founding of the American Episcopal Church in 1785. References to 'Episcopalians' or 'American Episcopalians' can be found in the colonial era.[29] The more general term 'Anglican' actually dates from the nineteenth century, but is used here somewhat anachronistically (but not unusually) as a synonym for the Church of England.

While most studies of the Church of England in America have focused on either the colonial era or the early nineteenth-century origins of the Episcopal Church, this book focuses on the formative revolutionary period to examine the clergy's experiences as well as the church's role in the Revolution and the Revolution's impact on the church. The following chapter depicts the state of the church before the outbreak of the Anglo-American disputes, by assessing measures of institutional growth and decline. Throughout the eighteenth century, the Church of England acquired a stronger foothold in the colonies, but growth did not keep pace with demography, nor compensate for the church's weak institutional infrastructure and sagging public image. To amend this situation, several Anglican ministers campaigned in the 1760s and 1770s for the appointment of a colonial Anglican episcopate which, they believed, would remedy the institutional deficiencies of their church, improve their professional reputation, and strengthen Anglo-American relations. This movement for an American episcopate, orchestrated largely by colonial ministers, provides the focus of the third chapter. The next chapter concerns the political philosophies of the partisan Anglican clergymen, and explains how both loyalist and patriot philosophies of government emerged from Church of England teachings. Despite the notoriety of a few Anglican ministers who were also influential Tory pamphleteers, clerical political

affiliation should be considered a spectrum. By tracing the careers of all
Anglican clergymen who ministered in the colonies during the Revolution,
this study depicts how a series of political and military crises produced a
variety of ministerial reactions, including loyalism, patriotism, and neutrality. Neutrality played an important role for the majority of clergymen
who remained in the colonies but gradually withdrew from politics to
focus exclusively on spiritual concerns. Whereas the Revolution brought
about a dramatic growth in popular politics which extended beyond
Revolutionary committees to the community at large, the Anglican clerical
community experienced an opposite but parallel process of depoliticization. Chapter 5 examines the depoliticization of the group throughout the
Revolution and assesses the extent of neutrality. Lastly, Chapter 6 addresses
the divided allegiances of the clergy and their reactions to the prevailing
shift from an establishmentarian model of church–state relations towards
an acceptance of denominationalism, the new religious paradigm of the
post-revolutionary republic.

2 The Pre-Revolutionary Colonial Church of England

By most standards the colonial world of the eighteenth century retained an essentially religious character. Church spires of colonial seaboard towns reached towards the heavens, church bells announced services and sang God's praises, and at least in areas of considerable population, a neighborhood church stood usually only a short walk away. If religion is defined broadly as a resort to superhuman powers, the prevalence of a belief in magic and the occult serves as evidence for the strong religious sensibilities of the American people. Until 1765 and even during the American Revolution, the largest category of printed matter consisted of religious literature. Institutional churches also prospered; compared with the unsettled state of religious belief and practice in the seventeenth century, the eighteenth century witnessed consolidation for many denominations. The period 1680 to 1760 can be depicted as an era of both religious renaissance and reassertion of the English state church, rather than decline.[1]

Whereas considerable energy has been spent on the question of the alleged decline of religion in the eighteenth century, a similar query may be asked of the Church of England specifically. Did this particular denomination witness patterns of growth or decline in the late eighteenth century? In many respects, the story of the colonial Anglican church is a tale of mixed successes and failures with tremendous intercolonial differences. This chapter evaluates four measures of the Church of England's strength in each colony: the character of its legal establishments; patterns of church construction, recruitment of clergymen, and conversion of parishioners; the development of the denomination's institutional infrastructure; and lastly the public image of the church and its clergy in the years preceding the Revolution.

To assess the character and relative strength of the colonial establishments, one must first define the term 'establishment.' A church establishment involved an intermingling of religious and political realities, since the official status of an established church conveyed certain privileges and immunities, and its members often gained access to higher education or political power denied nonconformists. Within England, the eucharistic sacrament became a political test since only Anglican communicants could aspire to hold governmental office or graduate at the universities. Furthermore, public taxes paid the salaries and other expenses of the church.[2]

In England, 'establishment' clearly referred to the Anglican church officially supported by the government, which excluded non-Anglicans from
positions of power and social influence. It also referred to a national communion rather than a voluntary body of members; Anglican political theo-
rists explicitly rejected Lockean contractualism. The church provided
order, which helped to sustain the state and, like two sides of a coin, each
required the existence of the other. According to traditional orthodox
Anglican political theology, the church-state united the spiritual and temporal dimensions of the body politic, both of which were derived from
God and embodied in the monarch. By theorizing that English churchmen
were the true patriots and by reasserting Trinitarian orthodoxy, High
Churchmen provided an ideology to explain and justify monarchical and
aristocratic power.[3] To preserve the existing social distinctions and hierarchy, Anglican ministers preached obedience to God, the king, and their
agents. Furthermore, the use of a national liturgy, the Book of Common Prayer, permitted comprehensiveness and uniformity in worship and
doctrine.[4]

The English church's intimate connection with the state, as well as its
theological rationalism, has led many historians to de-emphasize matters
of Anglican spirituality and theology. Studies of the rise of American
evangelicalism also have pointed to the church's spiritual decrepitude
as a factor which aided evangelical ascendancy, but religious rationalism may be interpreted as an alternative form of spirituality, or 'practical Christianity,' rather than an indication of its absence. The Church of
England's formal creed was embodied in the Thirty-Nine Articles, but a latitudinarian spirit emphasized reason within the context of a 'broad' or comprehensive church. Clerical candidates affirmed their belief in the Articles
at ordination, but without a 'detailed interpretation.'[5] High Churchmen,
including a few SPG missionaries in colonial New England, opposed the
prevailing latitudinarian trends in the English church. In delivering a funeral
address for Rev. Timothy Cutler, Rev. Henry Caner paid the deceased the
highest compliment by commending his

> attachment and perseverance in the true faith and principles of the christ-
> ian religion … at a time when so many sit loose to the fundamental articles
> of it … and if they stop short of barefaced infidelity, plunge into the gulph
> or dead sea of latitudinarianism, under the specious name of morality.[6]

Despite differences between High and Low Church interpretations,
Anglicans generally defended the role of reason in religion, the importance of free will, and their perception of God as both a rational deity and
a model of moral perfection. Theologically the Church of England walked

the middle path between the strict predestinarianism of Calvinism and the alternate Arminian extreme of emphasizing good works.[7] The moralistic theology of Anglican divines certainly emphasized men's need to live according to the gospel, but Anglicans also insisted upon the importance of the sacraments to salvation. When administered in the true church (one whose ministers have been episcopally ordained according to apostolic succession), the sacraments served as a means of salvation. In this manner, the church affirmed the doctrine of justification by the grace of God through faith, but considered that salvation should be mediated through the institutions of the church.[8] Anglicans explained spiritual regeneration as a lifelong process and therefore stressed the importance of public worship and regular participation in the church's sacraments.

In ministering to their colonial charges, Anglican clergy believed that their church offered particular liturgical advantages over its rivals. The majority of colonial Anglicans attempted a union of beliefs, behaviors, and forms of worship through their use of the Book of Common Prayer. While they generally denounced revivalism's tactics of enthusiasm as indicative of irrationality and weak theology, Anglican ministers adhered strictly to the forms of services articulated in the liturgy and presented the Church of England as a bastion of orderliness.[9] Henry Caner described the character of Anglican services to be the 'most perfect Form ... of publick Worship' in its majesty and simplicity, but also because its language contained 'no affectatious Expressions, no Flights of Fancy, no enthusiastick Rants, nor superstitious Follies ...'[10] In 1771, Rev. John Tyler similarly asserted that 'the liturgy of the Church of England is the best collection, both of prayers, and rules for public worship, that can be found among all human compositions,' and that it agreed exactly with both reason and the commands of the Scriptures.[11] These ministers asserted the perfection of the church's liturgy as one of its finest qualities.

Although Church of England establishments in the American colonies shared many traits with their mother church, the characteristics and even the meaning of the establishments could not be identical. The ideal model for a religious establishment required a fairly homogeneous society, but in their scattered and varied beginnings, colonial societies could not emulate the English-style establishment. In part, the need for settlers rendered such exclusivity unachievable.[12] Many colonies had been founded as a haven for dissenters: New England as a bastion for Puritans, Maryland for Roman Catholics, and Pennsylvania for Quakers. Despite later Anglican resurgence, Restoration colonies founded after 1660 also provided generously for dissenters. The prevalence of colonial dissenters mitigated against the creation of any homogeneous Anglican establishment.

In fact, English society also fell short of the ideal establishment model. Over the seventeenth and eighteenth centuries, Englishmen gradually came to realize that a truly comprehensive national church was an impossible goal. In many respects the Act of Toleration of 1689 admitted that reality, although the Test Act continued to deny full political freedom to non-churchmen. High Churchmen, however, defended establishmentarianism and, with varying degrees of success, sought acts of establishment in the North American colonies. Colonial Anglicans, for their part, recognized the religious diversity of the colonies and so may have rejected the principle of uniformity which undergirded English establishmentarian thought, but many continued to expect tax support and other privileges.[13]

Colonial establishments differed most significantly from the English church due to the absence of colonial bishops. An episcopal church without a bishop is a contradiction in terms, but under such circumstances the colonial Church of England labored until after the American Revolution. Without bishops, colonial legislatures and governors assumed many of the civil functions of English bishops, while some episcopal responsibilities remained unfulfilled. English bishops performed ecclesiastical duties relating to the discipline and government of the church, the confirmation of communicants, and the ordination and suspension of ministers, but also a second class of functions which was in part civil, such as the probation of wills, issuance of marriage licences, and collation of ministers to benefices.[14] In most colonies where the Church of England was established, the governor exercised this second group of powers, and colonial legislatures enacted laws relating to the governance of the church. Confirmation, as a rite of the church, ceased to be performed, while the Bishop of London ordained colonial ministerial candidates as deacons and priests.

In addition to the lack of bishops, the relative strength of the colonial laity as embodied in the vestry differed from its English counterpart. Without colonial bishops, ecclesiastical courts, or centers for theological direction, the colonial laity by default had to manage church affairs. Whereas the English vestry consisted of an annual and open meeting of parishioners without substantial powers, colonial vestries often acquired significant areas of jurisdiction.[15] Where Anglicanism was not established, colonial vestry functions remained confined to narrowly spiritual matters, but in southern establishments, colonial vestry duties included a mixture of civil and ecclesiastical tasks: levying the parish tithes and providing poor relief, selecting and paying the rector, recording parishioners' vital statistics and lists of taxables, maintaining church buildings, and presenting individuals to the county courts for moral offenses (such as drunkenness, fornication, profanity, or absence from church services). In the south, the government supported the vestries; in the middle colonies it often left them alone; and in New England the vestries frequently found themselves at odds with the Congregationalist establishment, particularly in their attempts to win the right to tax themselves or to have the church rate turned over to their own ministers.[16]

Perhaps the most significant vestry power at variance with English custom concerned the selection of ministers. In the English system, patronage of church livings, called *advowson*, belonged generally to large landholders or to an institution such as a college at Oxford or Cambridge, which made the appointment of beneficed clergy (those with tenure for life). The bishop, who could reject a nominee, inducted the candidate, thereby formally signifying his placement in the cure and granting him tenure for life or good behavior.[17] The system of clerical selection which emerged in colonial Virginia reveals the increasing strength of the parish vestry. When the vestry presented a candidate, the governor, empowered by the Bishop of London, inducted the minister into the cure of the parish. Many parishes preferred to fill a position in an acting capacity without induction (which conveyed security of tenure) since, without a colonial ecclesiastical court, no mechanism existed to remove a minister who later proved unworthy.[18]

Despite the objections of the clergy and several royal governors, the maintenance of a cleric on a year-to-year basis gained widespread support in Virginia. North Carolina vestries, which also claimed the right of presentation, attempted to copy this practice. In early Maryland, the proprietor, instead of the vestry, appointed clergymen to specific parishes, and consequently the vestry's functions remained more financial and secular than its Virginia counterpart. In the middle colonies and New England, the Society for the Propagation of the Gospel assumed the initiative for the supply of clergymen early in the eighteenth century, although gradually vestries made their preferences known. In a few larger parishes, such as King's Chapel and Trinity Church in Boston, financial independence conveyed to the parish a legal right to choose its own clergy.[19]

By the eve of the Revolution, the character of the Church of England establishments in the colonies differed not only from England but also from each other, in part since each colony found itself at a different stage of development. In Virginia the church had existed for almost 175 years and had been legally established since the middle of the seventeenth century. The establishments in other southern colonies dated from later periods and often followed in the wake of royal government. With the exception of New York City and some surrounding counties, no denomination in the middle colonies experienced the privilege of establishment;

there the Church of England competed with rival dissenting denominations. In New England, where a Congregationalist establishment reigned until the nineteenth century, the Anglican church found itself in the position of a dissenting church as it sought toleration for itself and criticized the existing establishment.

With the founding of Jamestown in 1607, the Church of England gained a foothold in the New World, but a legal establishment did not exist until the charter was revoked in 1624 and Virginia became a royal colony. What then existed can be characterized as only a partial establishment since it lacked a resident bishop, canon law was unenforced, and nonconformity was widespread, but the law guaranteed the church's support, and parishes had been created. From its inception, the House of Burgesses had confirmed the authority of the Church of England, requiring attendance at services and furnishing ministers with a glebe and a fixed salary of corn and tobacco.[20] An Act of 1641 required vestries to govern the church affairs of the local parish, and a 1662 law fixed the number of vestrymen at 12; by the 1660s vestries had become self-perpetuating.[21] By 1696, the Virginia General Assembly had fixed ministers' salaries at an annual rate of 16 000 pounds of tobacco, which remained in force until the Revolution. Consequently the long-standing church establishment of Virginia, although subject to dissenter criticism later in the eighteenth century, was the most fully articulated one in the colonies by the 1760s.

Maryland's original charter, granted to a Roman Catholic proprietor, did not promote Anglican establishmentarianism, and few Anglican clergy resided there in the 1600s. With the Glorious Revolution of 1688 and the corresponding revolt in Maryland against the proprietor, Maryland became a royal colony for a generation, and the assembly, consisting largely of Protestants, then attempted to establish the Church of England by dividing the province into parishes, organizing vestries and legislating tobacco taxes for the support of the clergy. Although the articles of establishment of 1692 and 1696 both met with disallowance in England for political reasons, the Maryland act of establishment finally passed in 1702. It provided for the election of vestry members and churchwardens, and fixed ministerial salaries at 40 pounds per poll.[22]

Although the charter for Carolina granted by Charles II in 1663 called for the toleration of dissenters, the 'Fundamental Constitution' provided that only the Anglican church was entitled to public support. In the early years the establishment clause did not become a central issue, but in 1698 the assembly passed an act for the support of the Anglican minister in Charleston, and six years later the assembly agreed to an act of establishment, which, with some revisions, secured English support by 1706. This act differed from other colonial establishments in that clergymen did not have to be certified by the Bishop of London, a vote by parishioners rather than the vestry selected the clergymen, and the government paid for ministerial salaries. Unlike Virginia, in South Carolina disagreements about the Anglican establishment resulted in compromise with dissenters, who won broad religious toleration.[23] When South Carolina became a royal colony in 1719, Anglicanism received additional support.

The development of a church establishment in North Carolina, which after 1729 became a legally separate royal colony from its southern namesake, faced stiff dissenter opposition. Only in 1765 did an act of establishment meet with the approval of British authorities. Previous acts passed by the colonial assembly had been disallowed by the Crown because of dissenter opposition in the colony or because the legislation gave too much power to the vestries. This last attempt passed London's scrutiny since it remained silent on the question of presentation, a right many vestries continued to claim for themselves since it was not explicitly given to the governor.[24] Nonetheless, the Vestry and Orthodox Clergy Acts established legal support of the Church of England in North Carolina, created parishes, and made provisions for taxation, clerical salaries, and glebe lands. Thus legal establishment provided a beginning, albeit a shaky one, for the church in North Carolina.

The proprietors of Georgia, which was founded as a haven for the English poor in 1732, did not concern themselves with the establishment of the Church of England. Rather, they granted religious liberty to all Christians, except Roman Catholics. When the proprietary charter expired in 1752 and Georgia became a royal province, concerted efforts succeeded in passing a bill of establishment, which finally gained approval in 1758. By 1760 the assembly had divided the colony into eight parishes and had appropriated funds for the support of the clergy which supplemented SPG stipends.[25] In this case, the legal establishment of the church erected only a framework for later growth, since in 1769 only two Anglican ministers resided in the colony.

In the eighteenth century, the state–church principle reasserted itself in southern colonies outside of Virginia, in part due to the missionary zeal of the Society for the Propagation of the Gospel in Foreign Parts (SPG). A British organization founded in 1701, the SPG was an offshoot of the Society for Promoting Christian Knowledge (SPCK). These organizations became involved in overseas missions by providing parochial libraries in England and abroad, supplying and financing missionaries for the plantations, and establishing colonial schools and churches. Although the Society sent clergy to the Carolinas and Georgia in the colonial period, the middle colonies and New England benefitted most from their extensive labors.[26]

North of Maryland, only in New York did the Church of England make any claims to an established status, albeit a limited and contested one. Successive governors interpreted the assembly's law of 1693 as having established the Church of England in New York City and the counties of Richmond, Westchester, and Queens, although the law technically provided only that the parishes be served with a 'good sufficient Protestant minister' without mentioning the Church of England by name. English legal usage implied precisely that meaning, although the predominantly non-Anglican assemblymen may have intended a more flexible, regional interpretation. This act fixed ministerial salaries, ordered that 12 vestrymen and two churchwardens be elected by the freeholders, and provided that clergymen be chosen by the vestry and wardens. Nonetheless ambiguity lingered about the exact terms of the establishment act, specifically whether dissenting ministers could be selected as incumbents. In 1694 when Trinity Church in New York City elected a dissenter as their pastor, the governor intervened and substituted William Vesey, an ordained minister of the Church of England.[27]

The religious scenario of the Jerseys and Pennsylvania closely paralleled each other; neither colony had any kind of religious establishment. Although Governor Edward Hyde, Viscount Cornbury, received instructions from Queen Anne in 1702 to ensure that worship was conducted according to the practices of the Church of England, the colonial assembly never passed an act of establishment. No sustained work of the Church of England took place until SPG missionaries George Keith and John Talbot toured the province in 1703. The original charter of Pennsylvania declared that Anglican worship could be organized in any community when desired by 20 or more people, but not until 1695 did parishioners organize the first Anglican parish, Christ Church of Philadelphia. By granting religious freedom to all, William Penn awarded the Church of England no particular advantages, while Quakers maintained political control of the colony.[28]

Despite the continued potency of the Congregational state–church alliance, Anglicanism in Massachusetts benefitted from the advent of royal government, and in Connecticut chiefly from the apostasy of 1722. Late in 1686 Governor Sir Edmund Andros, a friend to the Church of England, arrived in Massachusetts. He immediately planned for the erection of King's Chapel, and in the meantime commandeered a Congregationalist church in which to hold Anglican services for part of each Sunday. In Connecticut, the earliest travels of Anglican missionaries did not threaten the Congregationalist establishment, but the surprising defection of some of its key members shook its foundation. In 1722, the president of Yale College, Timothy Cutler, and two other professors, Samuel Johnson and Daniel Brown, declared their determination to seek ordination in the Church of England. Upon their return to America, Cutler and Johnson became leaders in the phenomenon of New England Anglicanism, which grew despite its lack of local governmental support.[29]

In this manner, the colonial Church of England persisted in a wide range of situations throughout the seventeenth and eighteenth centuries. As an established church in many southern colonies and parts of New York, the church possessed a framework for development. In the middle colonies, particularly New Jersey and Pennsylvania, where no church–state relationship existed to give preference to one denomination, development hinged upon many other factors. Where Congregationalism thrived officially in more northern latitudes, Anglicans found themselves in a difficult, but not impossible, position from which to encourage denominational growth.

As a framework for colonial church growth, an established status conferred certain benefits, but during the American Revolution these privileges became liabilities. Revolutionary values, including egalitarianism and popular sovereignty, not only promoted religious voluntarism, but also denounced privilege generally and the Church of England specifically, as an aristocratic branch of the English state. By the end of the Revolution, the Church of England found itself disestablished in every colony where it had been the established church before the outbreak of civil war.

Since a legal establishment did not assure the prosperity of the Church of England in the colonies, denominational vitality in the eighteenth century may be measured by assessing patterns of church construction and the recruitment of both clergy and parishioners. Statistics on church-building demonstrate significant growth in the latter part of the eighteenth century; consequently the period 1680 to 1760 may be characterized as a time of 'Anglican renaissance' and 'sacralization of the landscape.'[30] Church construction followed in the wake of various colonial acts of establishment and the creation of the SPCK and SPG at the turn of the century, and often occurred in regions which previously had never seen Anglican buildings. Where churches already existed, in New England urban centers or long-settled Virginian communities, a process of 'resacralization' tore down the church buildings of the seventeenth century to erect larger, more opulent buildings with fine pews, decorative carvings, and elaborate church bells. Church construction expanded even faster in the 15 years following 1760, during which no less than 100 colonial churches were built; in the longer 40-year period between 1720 and 1760, only 130 had been constructed.[31]

By the time of the American Revolution, the Church of England's influence had expanded into every colony, although the rates of growth varied tremendously. Anglican churches multiplied most rapidly in Connecticut, which had 30 churches in 1761 and 47 by 1774, with an additional 20 congregations that met in neighborhood schools or other public buildings. The middle colonies experienced the lowest rates of church extension; New York acquired six more, Pennsylvania four and New Jersey two. Maryland constructed nine new churches and five chapels of ease between 1761 and 1775. In the hundred years before the Revolution, Virginia had doubled the number of parishes; the colony had 48 in 1680 and by 1786 there were 95 organized parishes and a dozen more nominal parishes.[32] South Carolina acquired four new structures, and Georgia gained a second Anglican church in Augusta by the late 1760s.[33] Of course, statistics on church construction provide only one measure of denominational strength.

Another vital sign of prosperity may be found in the changing number and origin of clergy licensed by the bishop of London for service in the American colonies. In the 30 years between 1745 and 1775, 409 men were so certified: 156 between 1745 and 1760 and 253 in the next 15 years.[34] Since the supply of colonial clergymen originally depended upon the number of English, Irish, or Scots the Bishop of London sent to the colonies, the rise in the proportion of American-born clergy seeking orders indicates to what degree the colonial church was becoming self-sustaining. Until 1716, American-born clergymen accounted for less than 2 per cent of those licensed for the colonies, but by 1744 that number had climbed to 22.6 per cent. In Virginia, there had been no native-born ministers at the beginning of the eighteenth century; by 1748 two-thirds of the clergy were English or Scots, but the remaining third consisted mainly of Virginians. Finally, by 1775 over two-fifths of Virginia's Church of England ministers had been born in Virginia, and an additional tenth were from other colonies.[35]

Many Anglican communities declared a preference for native sons in their petitions to the SPG. Speaking of a trend with which he did not agree, the English-born Rev. Matthew Graves wrote that in Connecticut '[a]ll Europeans, especially ministers, meet with a very ungrateful Reception.'[36] Thomas Dawson, a Virginian commissary, approved of the practice of favoring American-born clergy; in fact, many contemporaries believed the ranks of immigrant clergy included those who had been unsuccessful in the Old World and so emigrated out of necessity 'to retrieve either lost fortunes or lost Characters.' Like the Bishop of London who noted that many Scots and Irish clergymen were sent to the colonies who could not find employment at home, colonial Anglicans often tied their estimation of a minister's worth to his national background in a way which reflected existing social and ethnic prejudices.[37] Unlike the bishop, they had begun to distinguish between colonial and English clerics, giving preference to the former.

The Revolutionary War temporarily ended the ordination of new colonial candidates for the Anglican ministry, and many clergymen were lost to the colonial church because of loyalty or death. Nonetheless, the American Episcopal Church reorganized after 1783 and secured ministerial replacements so that the number of clergy in 1789 in some states almost matched their prewar total in 1774. Figures from the General Convention of 1792 indicate that recovery was slower in Virginia.[38] During the war, many churches also suffered damage at the hands of the rebels or the British, but between 1783 and 1789 heroic efforts encouraged a rapid recovery. In addition to repairing many existing churches, former Church of England members erected at least ten new buildings in the 1780s. By 1789, 80 per cent of the prewar parishes continued to operate, having adapted to the new system of voluntary support.[39]

Since a vital church requires not only buildings and clergymen, but also a thriving audience, lay membership remains a crucial dimension to church vitality. Since colonial Anglicanism at least partly accepted the English imperial vision of a church–state establishment, its ability to be a comprehensive church was an essential trait. With varying degrees of success, the church attempted to bring non-English European colonists, as well as Indians and slaves, into the fold.

The SPG charter declared one of its objectives to be the evangelization of Indians and African American slaves, and various ministers wrote of their attempts to include these groups in Anglican services and instruct them in the catechism. Early in the eighteenth century, Rev. Francis Le Jau found the Indians of South Carolina to be virtuous, moral people, thereby confirming his belief that they were descendants of the sons of Noah.[40] John Ogilvie, SPG missionary in New York, reported that the Mohawks possessed a serious sense of religion. Indian attacks on settlers on the Pennsylvania frontier had convinced Thomas Barton of Indian 'savagery,' although later in the 1760s he advocated the education of a few Indian boys that they might return to their people as missionaries.[41] In addition to humanitarian motives, Anglicans advocated the potential political and strategic advantages of converting Indian tribes. As the SPG noted, French Jesuits who understood and spoke the Indian languages acquired not only Catholic converts, but also French allies.[42] Without discrediting the intentions of missionaries, humanitarian motives merged with an implicit imperial agenda.

Historians, looking toward the abolition of slavery in the nineteenth century, largely have accepted that the Anglican church, in comparison with more evangelical denominations, accomplished very little for African American peoples. Although the majority of black Christians were Anglicans in the colonial period, missions to African American populations enjoyed only limited success, reaching perhaps two or three thousand blacks out of the half million living in the colonies on the eve of the Revolution.[43] In letters to the SPG, many local parish ministers specifically noted the small number of slaves they had baptized since their last correspondence, and several seemed especially interested in their education and conversion, but they did not advocate manumission (and in fact many clergymen owned slaves). A host of social and cultural values impeded their work, including white attitudes about the innate intelligence of black slaves, the priority given to labor over education, language barriers, the disparity between Christianity and native religions, and the lack of qualified teachers. Most notably, slaveholders feared that the baptism of slaves might lead ultimately to their emancipation.[44] The belief persisted that slave literacy would produce unruly laborers, even though colonial schools for Negroes had opened at Williamsburg, Philadelphia, Charleston, and Newport. In New York City, Elias Neau enjoyed moderate success with, at one time, more than 100 slaves in his classes until the 1712 slave uprising in New York caused a backlash against his educational efforts.[45]

While the colonial Church of England attempted to civilize and christianize Indians and blacks, additional efforts aimed at the conversion of non-English speaking colonists. In this project, churchmen enjoyed more success than in the conversion of African and Native peoples. Throughout the eighteenth century, Anglican relations improved with French Huguenot, Dutch, Swedish, and German groups; ministers of the Church of England hoped that such unions would strengthen colonial Anglicanism.

In the process of assimilating to American culture, the Huguenots and, less categorically, the Dutch found in the colonial Church of England a new home. Friendly relations with Huguenots sometimes led to the assignment of SPG missionaries to French congregations, as in the case of Rev. Moreau who was working in a French community in Nova Scotia by 1750. Overwhelmingly, colonial Huguenots preferred the Anglican church (or Dutch Reformed Church) to Congregationalism or Presbyterianism as they assimilated into American society in the eighteenth century.[46] Disturbed with divisions in their church and the turmoil surrounding the Great

Awakening, many Dutch found refuge in the Church of England. The decline of the Dutch language, increase in intermarriage, spread of English schools, schism in the Dutch Reformed Church and the lack of Dutch ministers, all lowered the traditional Dutch resistance to Anglicanism. Acceptance of the Church of England sometimes accompanied the more general process of anglicization, although both trends may have been upset by the Revolution.[47]

Anglican commentators claimed that an Anglican–German Lutheran union and an Anglican–Swedish union in the colonies might be possible, especially in Pennsylvania. In a letter to the Bishop of London, William Smith of Philadelphia recommended Mr Bryzelius for Episcopal ordination, explaining that Bryzelius was ordained among the German Lutherans. Because of the 'extreme good disposition among the Lutheran Clergy here to be united to our Church,' Smith asked if some provision could be made so that candidates like Bryzelius did not have to be re-ordained.[48] Richard Peters believed that a careful examination of the liturgies, church offices and articles of religion revealed a near resemblance of the Swedish church and the Episcopal church, such as 'may well entitle us to the Name of Sister-Churches.'[49] Of the Dutch Calvinists and the German Lutherans, Thomas Barton wrote in 1764:

> The German Lutherans have frequently proposed an Union. A large & respectable body of Dutch Calvinists in Philadelphia have already drawn up Constitutions, by which they oblige themselves to Conform to the National Church, & to use her Liturgy & forms, & none else, provided they be approved of & received at Home, & that the Lord Bps of London will grant Ordination to such Gentlemen, as they shall present to him. The Germans in General are well Affected to the Church of England, & might easily be brought over to it.[50]

Barton displayed less generosity toward the Presbyterians or the other 'multitudes of Dissenters of every kind who are all brought up in such narrow principles that they can be no friends to the National Church ...'[51] In this manner, the respect and friendship accorded the Huguenots, Swedes, Dutch, or German congregations depended directly upon their acceptance of Anglican liturgy, government and imperial vision which included a national church.

Relations with dissenters, particularly Congregationalists, did not approach the level of amicability which Anglicans shared with French, Dutch, Swedish, and German peoples who came to embrace Anglicanism. Nonetheless, SPG missionaries in New England, many of whom were former Congregationalists, seriously considered both the desirability and possibility of improving relations with these nonconformists. With joy, Rev. Samuel Peters, missionary at Hebron, Connecticut, noted that '... the dissenters behave much better than they used to do, & a good friendship seems at present to subsist between him & their Teachers.'[52] In February 1763, Matthew Graves, missionary at New London, Connecticut, declared that his church was 'held in greater esteem,' and all denominations attended his services. By visiting dissenters in sickness and in health, he had 'gained their Love and laid the foundation of a most perfect harmony.'[53] In some respects, such an era of good will with one's neighbors would have to precede any substantial integration of dissenters back into the Anglican fold. Revealing his belief that church growth might be measured, in part, by the conversion of dissenters, Rev. Bass reported that some 'Dissenters of repute & substance' had been regularly attending Anglican services, and so he held great hopes for the church's growth.[54]

In their correspondence and other writings, colonial Anglican clergymen often elaborated on the situation of their local church. In their *notitias parochialis*, a biannual report required by the SPG, clerics discussed matters of church growth, specifically including the numbers of baptisms and communicants as well as the number of inhabitants and dissenters residing within the parish. Very often the tone of such accounts remained positive, as individual clerics asserted, modestly or not, their own contributions to the community. As one minister proclaimed in 1762, 'Religion and virtue gain ground in this Mission. The people committed to my care have shewn [*sic*] a remarkable spirit in finishing, enlarging and ornamenting their Churches, which in a little time will certainly vie with any Country Churches in America.'[55] Such optimism about growth frequently was tempered with a plea that SPG financial support be continued since the community could not adequately support their ministers without such assistance.

Despite a prevailing tone of hope about the church's ultimate success, many Church of England ministers declared their belief that the church in the colonies was losing ground to the dissenters. This phenomenon was particularly evident in Virginia, which in its early history had enjoyed a high degree of Anglican homogeneity. In the second half of the eighteenth century, the church found itself negotiating with increasingly numerous groups of dissenters. Commissary Thomas Dawson, having been informed that dissenters were complaining of persecution in Virginia, exploded that the local government had been quite indulgent in the licensing of non-Anglican houses of worship. He believed that dissenting ministers, including Samuel Davies, would not be satisfied, but rather encroached on the colonial establishment.

[S]ince Mr. Davies has been allowed to officiate in so many places (an allowance I humbly conceive, inconsistent with our duty to favour and protect the Church of England), there has been a great defection from our Religious Assemblies. The generality of his followers, I believe, were born and bred in our Communion.[56]

Spreading Anglicanism became harder as dissenting groups prospered, and for this reason Church of England clergy not only praised Anglican growth, but also worried about advances made by rival denominations.

Relative concepts of growth and decline require a comparative approach. While this realization did not escape Church of England clerics, understandably they did not always have sufficient and suitable information to evaluate the gravity of their collective situation. Without complete census data, vital statistics, and church records, the modern historian also faces difficulties in trying to assess matters of interdenominational growth and decline. Nonetheless, reliable evidence on the rates of colonial church construction and ratios of clergymen to population demonstrate that the eighteenth-century Church of England did not keep pace with many of its rivals.

The expansion of colonial Anglican church construction in the period before the Revolution may be considered an indication of its vitality, but an interdenominational analysis reveals that the rate of dissenter church construction greatly surpassed Anglican growth. Between 1700 and 1780, the number of Congregationalist churches grew by five times its original number, Roman Catholics by 2½ times, and more substantial growth occurred among the Baptists, Lutherans, and Presbyterians. In this period, the number of Baptist churches increased by almost 14 times, Presbyterian churches by 17½ times, and by 1780 each denomination had more churches than the Anglicans. The colonial Church of England, which had 111 churches in 1700, 246 in 1740, and 406 by 1780, enjoyed a growth rate between 1700 and 1780 of only 3½ times its 1700 figure. At the beginning of the eighteenth century, Anglicans had the largest number of churches after the Congregationalists, a position which they barely maintained by 1740, but by 1780, Anglicans had fallen to fourth place, behind Congregationalists, Presbyterians and Baptists.[57] Even if Church of England church construction matched the increase in its own church membership between 1700 and 1750, the church fell behind other denominations in drawing new parishioners. In 1700, Anglican churches served roughly one-fourth of the colonial population, in 1750 one-sixth, and in 1775 one-ninth.[58]

Geographic factors inhibited the ability of the colonial clergy to attract large numbers to their churches. A perennial complaint of the colonial

Anglican clergyman detailed his long, laborious journeys over rough terrain to minister to the various areas of his frontier parish, large southern county or his scattered New England congregations. Compared to an average English parish, which often consisted of less than five square miles, southern parishes of 60 to 100 miles seemed especially daunting. Rev. John Beach found his parish at Reading, Connecticut, too extensive; as he often reminded the SPG it measured 20 miles in length and 12 in breadth. As they described their own usefulness and indefatigable efforts, missionaries focused on the great challenges posed by such a large geographic area, realizing that too great a territory would reduce the frequency of their visits and so diminish ministerial effectiveness.[59]

A mountain-top view of eighteenth-century demographic trends reveals more serious problems of the colonial church. By determining the number of Anglican clergymen ministering in the colonies and comparing these figures with those of other denominations, one can produce interdenominational ratios of clergymen to population.[60] As Benjamin Franklin and T. R. Malthus both recognized in the eighteenth century, the American population increased at an unprecedented pace. Modern estimates claim an average increase of 34.5 per cent per decade between 1700 and 1790.[61] While this rate posed a challenge for all denominations attempting to expand their membership, Anglicans met with less success than some of their rivals. In the Chesapeake, the total white population per minister (of all denominations) climbed from 1200 in 1700 to well over 2000 by the eve of the Revolution. The figures for Anglican clergymen tell a bleaker tale as the total population (white and slave) per Anglican minister in 1770 reached 5698 souls, or 3493 for whites only. The population per minister ratio had not been under 1000 since 1635. In the Lower South (North Carolina, South Carolina and Georgia), there were over 1500 whites per minister in 1770, but the number of whites per Anglican minister exceeded 6000. In the middle colonies and New England, Anglican clergy formed a smaller percentage of the total number of clergymen, and there the number of people served by ministers of all denominations enjoyed more stability. Particularly in New England, the number of people per minister remained most stable between 1680 and 1760, and in Massachusetts and Connecticut the number per minister did not exceed 1000 before 1770.

Just as rates of church construction and ratios of clergymen to population differed, interdenominational success varied in the recruitment of parishioners. Anglicans often underestimated the success of dissenting ministers in the backcountry from Pennsylvania to South Carolina, where Calvinist Scots and Ulstermen and German Lutherans had flooded. These frontier communities, containing a larger proportion of youth, immigrants, and marginal persons than long-established areas, provided an especially fertile ground for the intercolonial revival of mid-century, and one lasting contribution of this first Great Awakening consisted of its innovative support of lay preachers who continued to encourage religion on the frontier. Meanwhile, colonial Anglicanism, which remained concentrated in coastal towns and long-settled tidewater vicinities, did not avail itself of the opportunity to proselytize among this new source of potential parishioners.[62] Governor Arthur Dobbs of North Carolina recognized dissenter strength in the expanding western regions when he asked the Society to support Anglican clergy in the 'back Western Counties where numbers are daily arriving.' William Smith also discussed the pressing need for more frontier missionaries with English officials; Smith believed that instead of sending missionaries to New England, the SPG should have sent them to backcountry Germans and Indians, especially to prevent alliances with the French.[63]

The Church of England enjoyed considerable stability by mid-eighteenth century, including an improved occupancy rate in its Virginia parishes. No longer did it suffer from vacancies which had plagued its long history. Nonetheless, the improved occupancy rate at existing parishes cannot disguise the fact that the Anglican church did not possess an effective plan for the conversion of arriving immigrants, and in those regions where the birth rate was highest, the Church of England was weak.[64] In the race for souls, Anglicanism appeared to be falling farther and farther behind.

The limited achievements of the colonial Church of England, when compared with other denominations, may be explained, in part, by differing institutional constructions. What growth the church did experience tended to disguise significant institutional deficiencies which British and colonial authorities did not remedy in the course of the eighteenth century. Like a house built upon sand, the colonial Church of England grew without strengthening its traditional hierarchical foundations. Perhaps the two most significant institutional elements essential to the development of a self-sustaining Church of England, but absent in the colonial church, were bishops or surrogate officials having colonial jurisdiction and a sufficient pool of clerical candidates from local seminaries or colleges. Although the proportion of American-born Anglican clergymen improved substantially in the eighteenth century, the numbers of candidates continually fell short of the large demand created by soaring population growth.

In an inventive manner, the English church attempted to cope with the predicament of having no colonial bishops by granting royal governors authority over some civil matters and by extending the jurisdiction of the

Bishop of London to include the plantations. From the time of William Laud, the Bishop of London was assumed to be responsible for the colonies, although between 1607 and 1776 only two of the 15 Bishops of London, Henry Compton and Edmund Gibson, actually held royal commissions for this purpose.[65] After becoming the Bishop of London in 1675, Compton both asserted and arrogated his power over the colonial church; the Bishops of London previously had licensed candidates for the colonial ministry, but in 1675 the English government informed colonial officials of the necessity of such certificates. In 1725 Crown lawyers claimed that only a royal patent could give the Bishop of London authority in America. This patent, granted to Bishop Gibson two years later, provided him with limited powers over the clergy, but virtually none over the laity.[66]

Bishop Compton also took the initiative by sending commissaries to the colonies to solve those problems caused by the Bishop of London's distance and indirect management of colonial church affairs. Thomas Sherlock, subsequent Bishop of London, wrote in 1751 that his office had jurisdiction over the colonial church, but that 'care is improperly lodged, for a Bishop to live at one end of the world, and his Church at the other.'[67] In England, the office of commissary had emerged because of the wide range of episcopal duties; consequently commissaries acquired the power to exercise episcopal functions, with the notable exception of confirmation and ordination. As the agent or deputy of the bishop, commissaries could call conventions, supervise clergy and preside over ecclesiastical courts. James Blair, the first commissary of Virginia, advocated reforms to raise clerical salaries, induct ministers, and establish a college to train divinity students. In securing the charter for William and Mary College, Blair provided a lasting legacy. Another significant commissary, Thomas Bray, helped in the founding of the SPCK and SPG, and assisted the establishment of the Church of England in Maryland. Likewise, Alexander Garden served as commissary to the Carolinas and the Bahamas for two decades after 1729.[68] Although a commissarial system existed in New England, it may not have functioned as well as its southern counterpart; Roger Price, rector of King's Chapel from 1730 to 1748, wrote reports as the commissary but claimed that he was unable to act in a supervisory capacity beyond his own parish.[69] While commissaries Blair and Bray improved the situation of their colonial church, the office of colonial commissary, which was largely discontinued by mid-century, did not solve all the problems of hierarchy which the infant churches faced. Commissaries could never effectively replace colonial bishops as long as they were prohibited from ordaining candidates for orders.

The colonial church's inability to recreate English bishoprics in America, or to provide a suitable surrogate official, proved detrimental since bishops were not only required to sustain the hierarchical system of the traditional Church of England; they also served vital sacramental functions by confirming the faithful and ordaining candidates for the ministry. The colonial church ran the risk of appearing hypocritical, for its ministers labored with difficulty to convince people of the centrality of the sacraments, especially infant baptism and communion, while no bishop existed to administer other important church ordinances, namely confirmation and ordination. The lack of confirmation may have concerned some individuals, but the inability of clerical candidates to be ordained without a dangerous and expensive journey to London remained an issue of continual discussion and perpetual anxiety for colonial Anglican ministers.[70]

In the field of education also, dissenters may have enjoyed institutional advantages unknown to the Church of England. Particularly those sects which had minimal education requirements could enlist clergymen quickly and 'with but little expence and forthwith dispatched ... [them] ... to any part of the Continent.'[71] With a tone which mixed a little envy with much contempt, Anglican clerics noted the facility with which dissenters could become teachers. Despite an evangelical outlook on religion, Devereux Jarratt of Virginia shared the Anglican belief that no one should presume to preach the Gospel before he had the necessary education and was duly ordained.[72] Even the Congregationalists and later the Presbyterians, who valued an educated ministry, had the advantage of long-standing institutions of higher learning, particularly Harvard and Yale Colleges and, after 1746, the College of New Jersey. British ecclesiastical authorities, including the SPG, did not challenge Congregationalist control of either Harvard or Yale, or Presbyterian dominance of the College of New Jersey, but colonial Anglicans continued to worry about the influence of these institutions. Anglican attempts to infiltrate the pedagogical fortresses of Congregationalism met with only limited success; between 1725 and 1748, only 5 per cent of Yale graduates and 2 per cent of Harvard graduates became Anglican ministers.[73] At such a rate, these institutions could not function as educational centers for colonial Anglicanism.

Church of England clergy, in New England and elsewhere, feared the collapse of Anglicanism for want of missionaries, and attributed this phenomenon, in part, to the substantial influence of dissenter colleges. Henry Caner petitioned for an Anglican church in Cambridge to counterbalance Harvard's corrupting influence, in particular its spreading of 'bad principles.'[74] The President of Yale in the 1750s did not allow Anglican pupils to attend services at New Haven's local Church of England, causing complaints from Samuel Johnson and others. In fact, the sons of Rev. Ebenezer Punderson, rector of the church in New Haven, had been fined at Yale for non-attendance in the Hall or for attending Church of England services.[75] In addition to bemoaning the corrupting influences of these colleges, Anglican ministers worried about their efficiency as producers of dissenting clergymen. As Thomas Barton of Pennsylvania feared, 'the Sectaries are likely to overrun us. Their Colleges in New England and the Jerseys are continually sending out preachers; who are always not Men of the most Catholic principles. I believe no less than eight or nine have been licensed in this single province within this twelvemonth…'[76] If only to combat the effects of dissenter colleges, Anglicans needed to develop their own educational facilities.

Until the middle of the eighteenth century, the extreme weakness of Anglican educational institutions was a glaring problem which limited denominational prosperity. From the beginning of Anglican settlement and particularly with the founding of the SPCK and the SPG, education received the attention of British authorities and colonial clergymen.[77] Clergymen taught school and instructed the youth of their parish in the catechism, but such individual efforts did not correspond with equivalent institutional achievements. The College of William and Mary, chartered in 1693, remained the only Anglican-affiliated college in the colonies until the founding of the College of Philadelphia in 1749 and King's College, New York, in 1754. James Blair, founder of the Williamsburg college, hoped the associated divinity school would attract sons of the gentry to the ministry and revitalize the colonial church, but in the 47 years that the divinity school operated, only 32 of its graduates became Anglican churchmen.[78] While many of these graduates proved valuable additions to the Virginia church, Anglicanism in the northern and middle colonies did not benefit. Since the educational record of the colonial Anglican clergy is incomplete, difficulties arise in assessing accurately the proportion of colonial-educated and English-educated clergymen. What does remain clear is that the numbers of graduates produced by colonial institutions and by English schools, principally Oxford and Cambridge, did not keep pace with the demands of the colonies.[79] Between 1690 and 1790, the overall rate of population increase for the North American colonies was a daunting 34.5 per cent per decade. Without an incredibly innovative system of educational expansion, including additional facilities to increase dramatically the numbers of graduates, the fixed numbers of existing colleges could not match this geometric population growth.[80] Although a bishop could have tapped into that portion of the colonial population which displayed a reluctance to travel to England for orders, a solitary bishop soon would have proven insufficient without substantial educational innovations.

The founding of the College of Philadelphia and King's College addressed the paucity of colonial Anglican seminaries in the middle colonies, but as a result of dissenter strength in New York and Pennsylvania, these schools were not 'church-related' in the same direct manner as were Harvard, William and Mary, Yale, and Princeton. Of the two new schools, Anglican connections remained weaker in Philadelphia. Richard Peters wrote to the Archbishop of Canterbury in 1763 that the College of Philadelphia, in its plan, was not confined to the Anglican church but 'founded upon a coalition of all religious Societies' and so it would please him to be able to say that there was a 'proportional number of Churchmen [among its masters], but the truth is that at present we have only one professor, Dr. Smith, one tutor ... and one writing master ... out of five Professors.'[81] Hugh Neill, an SPG missionary in Pennsylvania, lamented that in America his church was declining and the dissenters gaining. They even benefitted from the College of Philadelphia, for 'Dissenters ... are bred there, and thus they get instead of mechanics persons of Learning for their ministers.'[82]

Anglicans also provided the impetus for the chartering of King's College, which dissenters feared would be the first step in the forceful extension of an Anglican establishment throughout the colony. Anglicans formed 10 per cent of the population, but seven of the ten trustees of the college were Anglicans, Anglican liturgy was compulsory in the college's services, and the College President, Samuel Johnson, simultaneously held the rectorship of Trinity Church, which had donated a valuable tract of land to the college. Johnson believed that the college promoted generous toleration for other denominations, but its creation spawned a series of newspaper and pamphlet attacks on the colonial Church of England.[83] Instead of strengthening the church's stature in the community, the beginnings of this college created a storm cloud of suspicion and fear which mitigated against church growth and threatened the church's reputation.

The College of Philadelphia and King's College served, in part, as Anglican seminaries, but even those two notable institutions could not rectify the prevailing hierarchical deficiencies of the church. They did not manage to supply great numbers of clerical candidates. Nor did they obviate the primary structural deficiency of the church's hierarchy: ordination in the colonies remained impossible. As the Philadelphia clergy put it, '[t]he inconvenience of passing & repassing the dangerous Atlantic, being added to these difficulties will we apprehend induce many to Educate their Children to the Dissenting Ministry rather than ours, so that our Church will not have such full advantages from these Seminaries of Learning as she otherwise might have.'[84] Similarly, Governor Dobbs of North Carolina wrote of the numerous 'Sectaries of all Denominations ... These Evils cannot be removed till there are proper Schools erected for the Education of Youth and qualifying them for holy Orders, and Bishops appointed in America to confer them.'[85] Of these two tragic institutional flaws of colonial Anglicanism, its lack of bishops and educational centers, the former perhaps proved the most fatal. In the course of the 1760s and 1770s, the campaign for a colonial Anglican bishop encouraged traditional dissenter fears about episcopacy and, in the minds of many revolutionaries, linked Anglican ministers to the English state and crown even before the firing of the first shot.

While denominational growth and decline may be measured in terms of church construction, recruitment of clerics and laity, or the development of its institutions, matters of public reputation may be just as critical to sustained development. In the two or three decades preceding the American Revolution, several issues brought the Anglican church and its clergy into the spotlight. In addition to the creation of the College of Philadelphia and King's College, scandals of clerical immorality, salary disagreements, and open disputes over episcopacy all gave publicity to the church and its clergymen in this period. While these issues had surfaced intermittently, the years preceding the Stamp Act crisis were particularly virulent. As a result, the collective image of Anglican clergymen became tarnished.

Scandals involving the alleged immorality of colonial Anglican clerics occurred periodically throughout the colonies, but by the time of the Revolution, the reputation of clerical immorality in Virginia and Maryland had grown more pronounced. From 1692 to 1776, as many as 35 (or one in six) Anglican ministers in Maryland prompted complaints, although perhaps ten of these cases were unsubstantiated or erroneous.[86] In Virginia, charges (including unproven ones) were brought against 15 per cent of the clergy, and perhaps two-thirds of those had merit. These figures may not depict widespread degeneracy, particularly since some indictments were fierce and others frivolous.[87]

The actual number of cases scattered throughout the century cannot explain fully the reputation of Anglican clergy in Maryland and Virginia, but an increase in the number of accusations in the 1760s served to intensify the malignant image of Maryland ministers. In Virginia the actual pace of accusations about clerical immorality may not have quickened noticeably in the 1760s. From 1723 to 1743, the character of 20 Virginian ministers was disputed, and perhaps 11 of these seem serious. Between 1743 and 1776, 14 cases appear legitimate.[88] Of the 35 individuals accused of irregular conduct in Maryland, almost one-third were accused of some offense in a single decade, the 1760s. In fact, in 1768 Rev. Richard Brown was accused of murder.[89] Contemporaries must have witnessed these events as indicative of a general cancer among the ranks of Anglican clergymen. As Rev. Thomas Cradock described the situation, enemies of the church

> go about to ruin us, and join us all together: they distinguish not the *Person* from the *Profession*, but fall foul on an Order, that by all good men has been held sacred and necessary to Society; they separate not the *good* among us from the *bad*, but say, we are all alike, and call the best of us only more cautious Imposters than the others.[90]

Although Cradock delivered this sermon on the governance of Maryland's established church in October 1753, its message must have continued to ring true in the 1760s.

The reputation of Anglican clergymen did not depend exclusively on the pace of such accusations, since even a few incidents of improper behavior consistently gained more notoriety than the more numerous cases of the conscientious. Unfortunately for the clergy as a whole, the problems created by just one aberrant minister would continue to fester indefinitely since, without spiritual courts, no mechanism existed for dismissal or other disciplinary action once he had been formally inducted into his parish. Charges of immorality also became better publicized; in the early years such activities had an exclusively local focus, but with the proliferation of newspapers later in the eighteenth century such stories could reach an intercolonial audience. In part, the Great Awakening gave this phenomenon added emphasis by encouraging the denunciation of unregenerate ministers.[91] Devereux Jarratt, an Anglican minister who favored an evangelical approach, criticized his Virginian colleagues for not opposing 'fiddling, dancing, and such like.'[92] Although public reputation also depended upon other factors including the politics of the clergyman and his national origins, some subsequent histories of the eighteenth century internalized this evangelical position and replicated unfavorable characterizations of some Church of England ministers.[93]

Accusations of immorality and ineptitude could succeed not only in maligning the character of an individual, but also in striking a blow against local Anglicanism by driving away parishioners. Criticism of Anglican clerics, especially when it came from within the church itself, proved quite damaging and divisive to their collective reputation. Thomas Cradock's sermon of 1753 against his colleagues gained a wide circulation and undoubtedly caused considerable havoc in Maryland. Regional prejudices also existed as many northern clergymen assumed the moral laxity of their southern counterparts. Thomas Bradbury Chandler's often-quoted assessment of the Maryland clergy provides evidence of such antipathy; he reported that the general character of the clergy was 'most wretchedly bad. It is readily confessed that there are some in the province whose behaviour is unexceptionable and exemplary, but their number seems to be very small in comparison, they appearing like here & there lights shining in a dark place.'[94] Echoing Chandler's views, the governor of New Jersey, Francis Bernard, expressed concern to the SPG in 1759 that ministers from Virginia and Carolina had applied for positions in his colony. Believing that the situation in the midst of Presbyterians required 'a greater strictness of Morals than is generally practiced in the Southern Provinces,' the governor asked for a minister from England or Ireland.[95] Such suspicions mitigated against intercolonial cooperation during the 1760s and 1770s movement for a colonial bishop, or during the American Revolution.

In addition to scandals over their public reputation, Virginia and Maryland clergymen also experienced disputes over their salaries. It appears no coincidence that these phenomena coexisted since the triangular struggle among clergymen, governors, and the vestries could only harm clerical reputations. In Virginia, a 'combative corporate spirit' among the Anglican clergymen may have originated with the resolution of Rev. William Kay's law suit of 1748, which gave the clergy security of tenure, whether or not they had been inducted.[96] To the clergymen, the Kay victory for clerical independence appeared to be challenged with the Twopenny Act passed by the Virginia General Assembly in 1758, which provided that the 16 000 pounds of tobacco owed to ministers as their annual salary be commuted into a money payment at the rate of two-pence per pound.[97] Anglican clergy objected since they had been forced to receive money in lieu of tobacco in 1755 and considered that a repetition of this Act constituted a violation of their legal rights. But the tobacco crop had failed in 1757, and the proposed clerical salary would have amounted to approximately £144, a salary larger than the ministers had previously received. If paid in tobacco, the clergymen would have reaped a considerable financial windfall, given that scarcity had driven up the price; they stood to make a tremendous profit from the community drought.[98] Outraged and selfish Virginian clergymen convened and unofficially empowered Rev. John Camm to launch an appeal in London for the disallowance of this Act. In this successful appeal to Britain, in subsequent colonial suits after the Twopenny Act was declared void, and in the anti-clerical polemics written by orthodox lay churchmen Richard Bland and Landon Carter, colonial Anglican clergymen were depicted as clear enemies of the colony. Popular opinion against the clergy may have even prohibited them from utilizing the colony's presses, since John Camm published some of his material in Maryland.[99] In any event, these salary disputes and the ensuing pamphlet war contributed to heightened suspicion and mistrust of the established clergy.

Similar salary disputes focused attention on the Anglican clergymen of Maryland and further maligned their reputation. In 1763 Maryland legislators reduced the clerical salaries by one-quarter; previously they had not challenged the total value of the 40 pounds of tobacco per poll, although permitting one-quarter of it to be paid in other products. This Act, however, directed that 30 pounds of tobacco per poll be the entire tax for the support of the clergy. Great influxes of immigrants had made many older parishes extremely lucrative since clerical remuneration depended on the number of ratepayers, and the 1763 revision was probably justified due to the increased population in most parishes. For instance, the income of Bennet Allen of All Saints, Frederick County, was nearly ten times that of the average SPG minister. In part, Marylanders lashed out at a system which they could not control; they had built and endowed Anglican churches entirely at their own expense, but the proprietor claimed the sole right of patronage and had inducted individuals into Maryland parishes without the approbation of the parishioners. Allen, who proved an ill-tempered sort, had been inducted into his post contrary to the desire of his parishioners who had petitioned for the division of the parish upon the demise of the previous incumbent.[100] Despite clerical objections, both houses of the colonial assembly passed legislation to authorize the governor, three clergymen and three laymen to exercise visitorial jurisdiction over ministers accused of immoral behavior, but Governor Horatio Sharpe refused to sign the bill. Like the tumult which followed the Twopenny Acts in Virginia, popular rage swelled against the Anglican clergy, the proprietor and the governor, all of whom found their positions supported by law but scorned by popular opinion. When the Act of 1763 expired in 1770, some parties claimed that the 1702 Act then came back into force, which would have raised the clerical stipend from 30 to 40 pounds of tobacco per poll. Several clergymen initiated lawsuits to regain the previous rate, but juries refused to grant their demands.[101] On balance, litigious clergymen succeeded only in alienating popular opinion and encouraging anticlericalism.

In the northern and middle colonies, salary disputes also arose periodically between clergymen and parishioners, but unlike Virginia and

Maryland where salary rates were fixed by law, northern clergymen enjoyed far less financial security. SPG stipends to clergy averaged about £50, and additional funds from parishioners remained uncertain.[102] Given the poverty of their charges, many clergymen excused their non-compliance, noting that they would willingly pay more if circumstances allowed. Henry Caner's relationship with his parishioners did not seem to have been strained, despite the fact they did not contribute as much to his support as the SPG expected.[103] Rev. Mr Browne, missionary at Portsmouth, New Hampshire, claimed that for over 23 years his congregation had never met the Society's terms; he had to find himself a house, his annual allowance never exceeded £24 sterling, and still his parishioners did not support him adequately. Browne's situation deteriorated due to inflation which accompanied the Seven Years' War, and his patience grew quite thin with the spending habits of his flock. As the SPG recorded, his parishioners owed him 23 years of house rent, which they could afford to pay as evidenced by their recent purchase of a Boston organ worth £200 sterling.[104]

Although these clergymen found themselves in a poorer financial state than their southern counterparts, they appeared less willing to take their parishioners to court. With no fixed legal salary, their suit would have been harder to resolve through the courts, but also SPG missionaries realized that their litigious behavior could harm the delicate state of religion in their community. As Rev. Isaac Browne of Newark, New Jersey, put it, 'in many provinces there is no other provision for the clergy than their people's voluntary Contributions, or Obligations ... which are a perfect Cheat in too many instances.' Browne simultaneously realized that if clergy should have 'recourse to Law, after all other Methods have been tried in Vain, he is sure to break up his Congregation & to be most desperately maligned himself.'[105] Although the veracity of this statement appears self-evident, the incongruity of the Rev. Joshua Bloomer's situation also seems apparent. As the minutes of the SPG recorded, 'it is his strenuous indeavor to cultivate peace and harmony among all persuasions, & he avoids all personal difference, tho' he is at law for the recovery of his salary ...'[106] That litigious clergymen damaged their reputation and that of the church appeared to be a lesson which many Maryland and Virginia clergymen did not learn.

Salary disputes, particularly in Maryland where the clergymen possessed adequate wealth by most standards, tended to display the baser, self-serving motives of Anglican ministers who fought colonial legislation to adjust their incomes. In these circumstances, popular opinion characterized these clergymen as insatiable, whining creatures. Appeals to British courts and officials not only associated colonial Anglicanism further with England, but also made the ministers appear as lackeys of the British crown and generated discussion about the desirability of a church establishment which permitted ministerial profligacy in the name of privilege. The collective reputation of the Anglican ministers became tarnished as they focused more energy on their own privileges and less upon matters of spirituality.

Throughout the eighteenth century, colonial Anglicanism faced a number of challenges. The legal establishment of the church in six American colonies had facilitated growth, although ultimately the foundation proved precarious and subject to revolutionary censure. Particularly in the decades before the Revolution, patterns of church construction and clerical recruitment contributed to a colonial Anglican renaissance, although growth did not always match the pace of rival denominations. Postwar recovery also may be described as rapid, given that Anglicanism suffered more than any other denomination. In its ability to recruit parishioners and expand into African-American and Native American populations, the Church enjoyed less success. Nor did the Anglican church of the eighteenth century actively seek new members among frontier immigrant communities. It concentrated its efforts in older, coastal centers. Significant institutional deficiencies and a sagging professional image among Anglican clergymen proved formidable handicaps during the American Revolution, but also left great opportunities for renewal in the postwar formation of the American Protestant Episcopal Church.

3 The Bishop Controversy

Considering the origins of the American Revolution, John Adams wrote in 1815, 'the apprehension of Episcopacy contributed fifty years ago, as much as any other cause, to arouse the attention ... of the common people.'[1] Indeed, significant religious forces helped to shape the American Revolution, including eighteenth-century revivalism, controversy over the possible creation of colonial Anglican bishops, and Parliament's enactment of the Quebec Act in 1774.[2] To one pamphleteer, the Quebec Act, in conjunction with the other Coercive Acts, demonstrated that Britain was implementing 'a settled fix'd plan for *inslaving* the colonies, or bringing them under arbitrary government.'[3] A decade earlier, rumors proliferated that the British government intended to undermine religious and civil liberties by establishing a colonial Anglican episcopate. When interpreted as part of the general imperial reorganization which followed the Seven Years' War, Anglican growth and proselytizing caused dissenters to fear that the British government might impose bishops, like taxes, upon unwilling colonial communities. Since the creation of American bishoprics would be accomplished most likely by an Act of Parliament, the issue added to pre-existing concerns about Parliament's legislative rights over the colonies and so contributed to the coming of the American Revolution.[4] For many churchmen, bishops were an essential (although historically a missing) part of the colonial establishments, but from a dissenting-patriot perspective of the late 1770s, the bishop controversy had been an early instance of British and Anglican treachery.

Dissenting interpretations of the colonial bishop controversy in the 1760s and 1770s are well known, in part because prominent historians have defended dissenters' assumptions by arguing that colonists believed British officials deliberately aimed for the subversion of English liberty. This conspiracy thesis, articulated clearly by historian Bernard Bailyn, has focused mostly on political matters, even when it admitted that fear of an ecclesiastical conspiracy coexisted with concerns of a civil plot.[5] By claiming to substantiate the existence of a political conspiracy of New England SPG missionaries who functioned as subversive sleuths or lackeys of the British government, historian Carl Bridenbaugh provided religious perspective on conspiracy.[6] In reconsidering colonial Anglican views on episcopacy, this chapter proposes an alternative solution. While many Anglican ministers did share British imperial values, the notion of conspiracy has exaggerated political considerations and given inadequate

37

attention to the religious or spiritual motives for advocating episcopacy. Like colonial dissenters who greeted Anglican arguments for episcopacy with a mixture of scepticism, incredulity and horror, many historians (particularly those writing denominational histories of dissenting churches) have regarded the religious aspects of Anglicanism in an unsympathetic manner.[7] Furthermore, the general treatment of Anglicanism reflects not only the thesis of an Anglican conspiracy, but also a predisposition to focus on evangelicalism and diminish the spiritual dimensions of rational religion.[8] Religious opinions have been considered of secondary importance, or (in the vein of a conspiracy thesis) only a disguise for real intentions.

A few scholars have considered whether Anglican goals in promoting colonial episcopacy can be traced to theology, rather than political collusion. Decades of theological controversy influenced both Anglican and dissenting views on the appointment of a colonial episcopate, and internal divisions, largely between High and Low Church perspectives, further divided the colonial Church of England on this question.[9] Certainly a thorough reading of the pamphlet literature of the eighteenth century reveals religious arguments of both colonial Anglicans and dissenting ministers.[10] Nonetheless, the full range of arguments, religious and political, published and unpublished, must be re-examined. Of course, the approximately three hundred ministers of the church did not share a single, monolithic opinion. Although some zealous advocates from northern and middle colonies claimed to speak for the collectivity, considerable diversity of opinion existed, and in the southern colonies, many Anglican clergymen opposed petitions for a resident colonial bishop.[11] Consequently, this chapter provides an intercolonial account of the bishop controversy of the 1760s and 1770s, an explanation for the failure of the movement to appoint a colonial Anglican bishop, and lastly, an analysis of their various arguments. An evaluation of the relative importance of the historical, theological, political, and religious arguments utilized by colonial Anglican ministers, either to support or oppose colonial episcopacy, provides an alternative perspective to those conspiracy theories which focus more exclusively on matters of politics.

That English authorities of the King's Church never sent a resident bishop, or even a visiting prelate, to the colonies was quite amazing given the strong links between church and state in the mother country. Considering those interpretations of the English state in the eighteenth century which insist upon a High Church Anglican and aristocratic hegemony in the political culture, the underdeveloped colonial church appears an anomaly.[12]

The Anglican experience in America also contrasts with the Roman Catholic example, since New France had a bishop by the late seventeenth century and Mexico first acquired one earlier in the sixteenth century.[13] With some annoyance, colonial Anglican ministers noted that a Catholic bishop resided at Quebec after the English conquest of New France.[14] Why then did colonial Anglicanism continue to labor without a head?

Intermittently throughout the colonial period, individuals and agencies on both sides of the Atlantic campaigned for the appointment of one or more resident bishops to the American plantations. As early as 1638, Archbishop William Laud proposed to send a bishop to the New World. Although no plan secured a bishop for America until after the Revolutionary War, within the eighteenth century three distinct campaigns can be distinguished. The first, initiated by the SPG almost immediately upon its founding in 1701, consisted of a letter-writing campaign by early colonial missionaries and Society members in England. In 1713, the SPG plan for a colonial episcopate gained the support of Queen Anne, and a bill was prepared for submission to Parliament, but her death in 1714 ended the issue. Although the SPG renewed their petition to George I, the new king and his Whig administration did not share the Society's goals.[15] Petitions for a bishop continued to arrive from the colonies, but the second campaign may be dated from 1741 when Thomas Secker, then Bishop of Oxford, preached before the SPG a sermon advocating the creation of a colonial episcopate. The appointment of Thomas Sherlock to the See of London in 1748 and the translation ten years later of Secker from the bishopric of Oxford to the archbishopric of Canterbury both raised churchmen's hopes that an episcopate would be established in the colonies.[16] These ecclesiastical leaders, however, failed to persuade the king and his ministers of the necessity of a colonial bishop.

Petitions continued throughout the 1750s and 1760s, but by the mid-1760s the campaign for an American episcopate assumed a more public profile, and the initiative passed to the colonial ministers individually and as assembled in their clerical conventions. The publication of pamphlets and articles on episcopacy intensified in this period, far exceeding previous campaigns and matching the volume of material printed on the Stamp Act dispute.[17] This third phase both exacerbated dissenter–churchman tensions in New England and heightened internal conflict among colonial Anglicans since most southern Anglican ministers opposed the proposals of their northern colleagues.

Unable to convene official clerical conventions without the authority of an English bishop, many colonial Church of England clergymen had adopted the practice of holding informal gatherings. At such a meeting at

Elizabeth Town, New Jersey, in October 1766, 19 clergymen from Connecticut, New York, New Jersey, and Pennsylvania gathered under the leadership of Thomas Bradbury Chandler and agreed to petition the Archbishop of Canterbury and the English bishops about the appointment of a colonial episcopate. Collectively they sent letters to colonial governors and the Anglican clergy of Maryland and Virginia, and individual ministers did their part by penning letters to colleagues. Members of a subsequent Anglican convention at Elizabeth Town in 1767 authorized Chandler to prepare a pamphlet, *An Appeal to the Public, in Behalf of the Church of England in America*, to articulate their arguments for episcopacy and thereby convince opponents of the necessity of an American bishop.[18]

Instead of dissolving opposition, the *Appeal* caused the eruption of voluminous pamphlet and newspaper warfare. Incredulous, Chandler himself had to accept that his publication had caused a great 'Out-Cry.'[19] As Rev. William Smith put it, the Jersey Convention and Chandler's *Appeal* 'tho in the Main well done, have raised a great Flame. There is nothing but Writing in every News Paper.'[20] Beginning in March 1768 'The American Whig' which appeared first in Parker's *New York Gazette* ran weekly for over a year. Reprinted in the *Boston Gazette* and the *Pennsylvania Journal*, the series popularized the debates over the American episcopate. In Philadelphia, 'The Centinel' appeared in the *Pennsylvania Journal* only a few days after the reprinting there of the path-breaking New York series. Chandler and a few Anglican clergymen from New York, including Samuel Seabury and Charles Inglis, responded to the 'Whig' by publishing 'A Whip for the American Whig,' and in reaction to 'The Centinel' William Smith countered with 'The Anatomist.' While newspaper battles raged fiercely, pamphlet exchanges proliferated too. Chandler's *Appeal* provoked the issuance of Charles Chauncy's *The Appeal to the Public Answered* in April 1768, which contended that Chandler and his associates were aiming for a civil bishop in the English pattern. Chandler then produced *The Appeal Defended* (1769) and *The Appeal Farther Defended* (1771). Chauncy released *A Complete View of Episcopacy* (1771) before Chandler's publication of the same year.[21]

As well as contributing to the vast outpouring of printed material on episcopacy, Chandler's *Appeal* served to divide colonial Anglicans. Although he presumed that his appeal would answer all reasonable objections, many fellow clergymen did not share his views. Even among his middle colony brethren and fellow SPG missionaries, Chandler and his associates were criticized for being too forceful in their demands for a resident bishop. William Smith and Richard Peters, both of Philadelphia, complained about their uncompromising approach. Smith disapproved of the popular appeals, as well as the 'great zeal of our late Jersey conventions, for which they thought me too cold.'[22] Richard Peters found the well-meaning New Jersey clergy too resentful about the lack of bishops and unable to 'observe any temper in the affair of Bishops.' Whereas Smith and Peters preferred a plan to reintroduce colonial commissaries in lieu of a colonial episcopate, they found that their pro-episcopal colleagues had 'got[ten] it into their head that the appointment of Commissaries is like throwing cold water on the design of sending us Bishops and will oppose all Commissorial Powers with all their might.'[23] A friend of proprietary interests in Pennsylvania, Smith no doubt recognized that Anglican support of episcopacy would have displeased the Penn family.

In Maryland, neither the proprietary 'court' nor the lower house 'country' factions supported colonial episcopacy, and the minority of the clergymen who favored the plan of their northern colleagues risked the anger of both governor and assembly. Unlike their northern colleagues, Anglican ministers in Maryland had not nourished any longstanding campaign for episcopacy. Instead, a 1768 regulatory bill, which created a lay-clerical council to judge and punish ministers accused of improprieties, provided an impetus for pro-episcopal opinion among a few prominent ministers. Henry Addison, Jonathan Boucher, and Bennet Allen came to favor episcopal regulation of the clergy over the proposed committee.[24] Hugh Neill provided a thorough critique of the presbyterian character of the proposed spiritual court, which was to be composed of the governor, three clergy and three laymen.

> No one disputed the necessity of having some power to call irregular Clergymen to an account; but as this was a presbyterian form of ministers and ruling lay Elders, and laying a foundation for a presbyterian Government in the Church of England in Maryland, as well as subversive of the canons of the Church, which give the Bishop alone power to pronounce sentense [*sic*] in such cases, it alarmed all such of the Clergy as were true of the Church of England.[25]

In August 1768, a convention of Maryland clergy drafted petitions for an American episcopate, an event which Boucher remembered as straining his relationship with the influential Dulany family, but these petitions were not presented before the assembly nor sent to England.[26]

In Virginia, the likelihood of a successful episcopal campaign remained very slim after the tumultuous Parsons' Cause, and the pro-episcopal views of a previously controversial figure, Rev. John Camm, rendered any proposal even more suspicious. In the late contest over ministerial salaries,

Camm had displayed the temerity to appeal to England over the heads of the colonial legislators. In fact, Camm believed that disputes with his vestry, in part, had led to his pro-episcopal opinions.[27] In response to the visitation of two SPG missionaries from New York and New Jersey, the Virginia Commissary, James Horrocks, called for the meeting of Anglican ministers on 4 May 1771 in Williamsburg to discuss plans for a resident bishop. So few attended that another meeting was scheduled, but at the 4 June gathering only 12 Virginia clergy attended and four of these adamantly opposed the proceedings. By resolving to petition the King for a colonial bishop, this small convention unleashed a pamphlet and newspaper battle in Virginia. In *A Letter to the Clergy of New York and New Jersey* (1772), Thomas Gwatkin and Samuel Henley opposed the resolutions of the late Virginia convention and articulated their arguments against episcopacy.[28] When Rind's *Gazette* later published a notice of the House of Burgesses which thanked Reverends Henley and Gwatkin, as well as Richard Hewitt and William Bland, for the 'wise and well timed opposition they have made to the pernicious project of a few mistaken Clergymen, for introducing an American Bishop,' Virginia's political authorities indicated their official disapproval of colonial episcopacy.[29]

While Gwatkin and Henley recognized that Anglican candidates for orders might benefit from the proximity of a resident bishop, they believed that 'the Interest of the Whole, and not the Advantage of a few, ought to be the Object of Attention to Government.'[30] In this manner, these two Virginians accused the northern promoters of episcopacy of advocating a self-serving plan which would deliberately violate the rights of dissenters and contradict the ecclesiastical laws of colonial assemblies. Such an episcopate, if created, would not only renew Anglo-American disturbances, but would also encroach upon the power of Virginia's General Court and 'overturn the Constitution of our Church.'[31] The resulting damage to colonial constitutions and religious liberty would far exceed any benefit to the church or its clergy. In a similar vein, Rev. John Gordon of Maryland wrote in 1770 of his and Rev. David Love's opposition to the recent addresses of their brethren in favor of episcopacy. Gordon also demonstrated a belief that the alleged benefits to the church would not justify the accompanying damage to the social fabric.[32]

Accepting the nature of lay authority as it had evolved in the southern colonies, many clergy opposed episcopal innovations which would have altered the balance of power. Gwatkin and Henley believed that it was inappropriate for a ministerial convention to make an application for an episcopate without the agreement of colonial civil authorities, and most southern laymen of the Church of England did not support the northern campaign for episcopacy. In North Carolina, South Carolina and Georgia, no controversy over episcopacy emerged, implying, in part, general agreement about the inadvisability of such a proposal.[33] In their attempts to regulate the clergy, Maryland and Virginian legislators also preferred a presbyterian method, a lay-clerical tribunal, rather than a hierarchical-episcopal one. In this manner, they demonstrated how southern Anglicanism had formulated a Low Church vision of episcopacy by the middle of the eighteenth century.[34] Northern Anglican ministers who campaigned for episcopacy did not share their southern colleagues' antipathy for hierarchy nor their fervent defense of colonial constitutionalism, and consequently misunderstood the character and prevalence of these anti-episcopal views.

Church of England advocates of episcopacy consistently denied the existence of any widespread opposition among laymen or fellow ministers. Chandler argued that once educated on the terms by which bishops would be appointed, any continuing objections would have no credible foundation. 'Indeed it has been for Want of understanding the true Design, that any American Episcopalians have ever discovered an Aversion to the Residence of Bishops in the Colonies, excepting perhaps a few Clergymen, who dread their Inspection.'[35] By enclosing a letter from a prominent layman, Charles Ridgeley of Dover, Charles Inglis believed that he provided the Secretary of the SPG with proof of lay sentiment. Ridgeley had written to Inglis, 'I sincerely wish we had one or more Bishops in America, with such a limited power as you mention. It would, I believe, remedy or prevent many Evils, & could introduce none.' From this extract, Inglis concluded that 'Lay members of our Church here are not averse to Bishops, as our Enimies [*sic*] would falsely represent; but, on the contrary, are sensible of the necessity of Bishops in America, & desire it.'[36] Inglis did not sufficiently consider that Ridgeley expressed a minority opinion.

Even if episcopal spokesmen recognized the existence of some dissension within their ranks, they did not believe that such opposition should defeat their attempts, or even slow their advance. Instead, efforts should be redoubled, particularly if opponents included corrupt individuals who feared episcopal supervision. As a group of Anglican ministers in Connecticut wrote to Bishop Richard Terrick:

> We are sadly sensible … that some of the principal colonies are not desirous of Bishops … some even of the Clergy of those Colonies, where the Church is established, that (insensible of their miserable Condition,) are rather averse to them; but this is so far from being a reason against it, that it is the strongest reason for Sending them Bishops.[37]

These Connecticut clergymen perceived that religion was declining without ecclesiastical government, and laid particular blame on the unworthy southern clergy, whose very opposition to episcopacy offered additional evidence of their neglect of duty. Specifically, these High Church advocates of episcopacy attributed the anti-episcopate views of their southern colleagues to their dread of inspection. 'Indeed we had always thought it impossible ... that any episcopal Clergymen should be averse to the Presence of Bishops, excepting only such Delinquents as have Reason to dread their Inspection.'[38] Similarly, those southern clergy, such as William Willie of Virginia, who did advocate colonial bishops referred to their opponents as 'some unworthy Sons of the Church.'[39] James Horrocks, Virginia commissary, expressed great surprise in 1771 that so few Virginia clergy supported the application for bishops and so many opposed it 'in the most extraordinary manner, & in their writings set themselves against the very Institution of Episcopacy itself.'[40] Northern clergy shared Horrocks' surprise, but by characterizing opposition to episcopacy as indicative of poor or impious churchmanship, zealous advocates of an American bishop accentuated regional divisions within colonial Anglicanism.

In comparison with their southern counterparts, SPG missionaries of the northern and middle colonies enjoyed more unanimity in their approval of episcopacy. In their own minds, they were simply good churchmen to hold such beliefs, but their High Church attitudes resulted in part from their more intimate connection with English authorities and from their conversion from Congregationalism. Many SPG missionaries, particularly in the northern colonies, were raised as Congregationalists, and some had practiced as dissenting ministers before converting to Anglicanism. The tale of the Yale apostasy of 1722 repeated itself in the lives of many individuals, whose own beliefs had been altered through careful study of the reasons for and against episcopacy.[41] Timothy Cutler, one of the famous Yale converts, provided a model for emulation, since he had presided over Yale College until 'in the course of reading and critical enquiry, he found himself under a necessity of conforming to the church of England.' In preaching Cutler's funeral sermon, Henry Caner stated that since Cutler had a large family, only his conscience could have caused him to abandon his means of support, and 'as he had deliberately entertained a high opinion of the constitution of the church of England, so he was ever zealous in its defence.'[42] The special zeal with which these Anglican converts defended the tenets of their faith and the necessity of a resident colonial bishop revealed itself in several testimonials. Matthew Graves, an SPG missionary in New London, Connecticut, composed a letter of recommendation for Mather Byles, which elaborated on the fact that Byles was formerly a Congregational minister. According to this commentator, a thirst for knowledge had led Byles to the conclusion that 'Episcopacy opens ye regular Door into ye vineyard & Fold of Christ …'[43] If a man's long-acquired and carefully constructed belief in episcopacy had altered his career path in this manner, he would naturally be one of its firmest advocates.

In the 1760s and 1770s, the campaign for an Anglican bishop failed to win the support of its laity and never reconciled the substantial internal divisions within colonial Anglicanism. Northern SPG ministers, who initiated the conventions of the mid-1760s, proved unable to persuade their southern colleagues. Dissenter opposition proved fierce, and some credit, or blame, also belongs to the English church which did not complete the hierarchical structure of its colonial church.

Responding to the persistent question of why the English church never sent a bishop to the colonies, one perspective is to point to the 'fatal alliance' of the Church of England with the state and British ignorance of American affairs. The church appeared consistently unable to make its concerns relevant to the government, and on the eve of the American Revolution, politicians acknowledged that they had very little to gain by involving themselves in the controversy over episcopacy.[44] British officials also recognized the potential volatility and extreme inadvisability of introducing a bishop in the aftermath of the Stamp Act riots, especially given the instability of the government's ministries.[45] The Bishop of London, Richard Terrick, considered one American petition from the clergy of the middle colonies quite untimely and perhaps even impertinent. In his response of July 1766, Chandler urged that they were not trying to dictate to their superiors; he also reminded his lordship that the address had been signed before the outbreak of these late disturbances. Nonetheless, Chandler continued to underestimate the gravity of the situation by suggesting that with the proper campaign, they might even then introduce bishops to America.[46] Perhaps Charles Martyn, SPG missionary to South Carolina, displayed a more realistic understanding in his October 1765 comment that 'it would be as unsafe for an American Bishop (if such should be appointed) to come hither, as it is at present for a distributor of the Stamps.'[47] Martyn's earlier assessment is a more obvious one, but since the repeal of the Stamp Act had temporarily eased tensions by the summer of 1766, Chandler's optimism was not entirely without foundation.

The untimely character of the 1760s and 1770s for the appointment of a bishop does not explain why over a century and a half of Anglican expansion in the colonies had not already resulted in the appointment of a resident bishop, or even the visitation of a single English prelate. Throughout the eighteenth century, significant domestic English political factors mitigated against the appointment of such an official. Although an episcopate was almost created under Queen Anne, subsequently the Hanoverians attempted to maintain the existing order rather than engage in innovations which could render them more unpopular with their English subjects. English politicians, especially Whigs, as well as English and colonial dissenters, adamantly opposed the sending of bishops to the colonies and thwarted the attempts of several English bishops to do so.[48] Congregationalist ministers in the colonies, such as Charles Chauncy and Jonathan Mayhew, also proved formidable opponents, particularly as New England Congregationalism forged cooperative links with English dissenters. Colonial dissenters and English politicians even utilized similar arguments against episcopacy. In 1750, Robert Walpole's influential brother, Horatio Walpole, denied that the American colonists actually desired such an official, an allegation repeated later in dissenting polemics against the colonial church.[49] Ministerial instability from the beginning of George III's reign until the appointment of Lord North in 1770 also encouraged several ministries to avoid any issues which might create controversy, and imperial officials recognized that the settlement of an American episcopate had virtually no chance of a peaceful, uncontested introduction.

The Church of England itself may be indicted for its role in inhibiting the appointment of an episcopate for the colonies. Although the campaign had the support of several English bishops, the middle of the eighteenth century was not an era of English church reform, but rather an era between reform movements. English church leaders found great defects in administrative structure, clerical stipends and church discipline, but fundamental reforms did not immediately occur. The failure of the movement to establish colonial bishops in America provides further evidence of a general situation of failed church reforms.[50] Several English divines in the 1750s and 1760s, especially Secker and Sherlock, favored the appointment of a colonial episcopate, but members of English government opposed such proposals because they wanted to avoid debate about church reform so as not to revive old party conflicts. In particular, Whig ministers feared that debates about the church might revive Toryism and resurrect that rage of parties which had characterized Queen Anne's reign. Many bishops supported church reform, but as members of government English prelates also feared the potential consequences of political controversies centering on the church.[51] Emphatically, the Bishop of London expressed to his colonial clergy his support for a colonial episcopate, but also his opinion that government should be allowed to decide about the timing of such an appointment.[52]

The inflexible character of the Church of England may be considered another reason for the failure of the bishop movement. Conservatism mitigated against the evolution of an officer capable of serving the peculiar needs of the 13 colonies. Bishops with purely spiritual powers were completely foreign to the post-Reformation English experience, with the exception of the disregarded non-juring bishops (those bishops who, after the Glorious Revolution, could not take the oath to William and Mary). These nonjurors did not prove to be a positive model for institutional emulation as long as colonial Anglicanism looked to the English church for guidance.[53] Proposals for colonial bishops without civil powers seemed incongruous with the very definition of an 'episcopate' in the eighteenth century. According to English experience, Georgian prelates wielded considerable influence in advancing the interests of their party in parliamentary elections, a function of their political power in the House of Lords, and suffragan, or purely spiritual, bishops had disappeared since the reign of Elizabeth I.[54] Given the long history of bishops connected to the state, the likelihood of the English church and state abandoning these traditions, to create bishops with truncated powers, seemed remote to all but the most optimistic advocates of episcopacy. Furthermore, the dignified, exalted position of a bishop would not fit comfortably in the social milieu of the colonial backwaters. Dissenters recognized this definition of the esteemed social position of bishops when they feared that a large home in Cambridge, Massachusetts, built in 1761 for Rev. East Apthorp, would become the 'bishop's palace.'[55]

Dissenters' understanding of traditional bishoprics and their subsequent disbelief in the veracity or sincerity of Anglican proposals played a significant role in their opposition to any plans for a colonial episcopate. The call for suffragan bishops indicated that colonial advocates of episcopacy acknowledged certain local realities, but dissenters consistently ignored the distinction and accused pro-episcopate spokesmen of duplicity. In their collective memories of ancestral persecution in England, colonial dissenters conceived of bishops as the 'iron-hand' of both royal and ecclesiastical tyranny.[56] Puritans recalled Laudian persecution, and although English bishops had become more moderate since then, New Englanders continued to think of bishops as intolerant leaders of persecution.[57] Such an observation did not escape the notice of Samuel Johnson of New York, who remarked that Jonathan Mayhew's *Observations* (1763) unfairly attacked the Church of England's intolerance and persecution of nonconformists by using examples from 150 years past. In Johnson's mind, such persecution and tyranny had ceased after the Glorious Revolution, and he insisted that the church had been 'altered much for the better.'[58]

Perhaps Johnson's views had been shaped or reinforced partially through correspondence with Thomas Secker, who earlier urged that colonial dissenters ought to be taught that English bishops, whatever they had been like when Puritan ancestors came to America, now defended toleration.[59] By the middle of the eighteenth century, latitudinarian philosophies within the English church permitted greater toleration of nonconformity.

Dissenter opposition to the institution of episcopacy may also have stemmed from more modern notions of Anglican bishops as tools of political Walpolean–Hanoverian corruption. New Englanders disbelieved Anglican claims that these proposed colonial prelates would be stripped of all civil powers. Bishoprics, as a corrupt and corruptible institution, would naturally acquire additional powers to replicate their English position, erect ecclesiastical courts, and impose colonial taxes for their own support.[60] Furthermore, dissenter-patriots objected to the Parliament's role in appointing such an official. As John Adams recognized, '[t]he objection was not merely to the office of a bishop, though even that was dreaded, but to the authority of parliament, on which it must be founded.'[61] Episcopal advocates in the colonies must have recognized that dissenters' objections to both episcopacy and stamp duties or other taxes shared a common trait of antagonism toward Parliamentary authority. Anglican clergymen knew their opponents alleged that '... our Plan [for episcopacy] is not less subversive of *religious Liberty*, than the late obnoxious *Stamp-Act* was of *civil Liberty*.'[62]

Although it was assumed that an Act of Parliament would be required to settle an episcopate in the plantations, Church of England officials did ponder alternative solutions. In 1764, Archbishop Drummond wrote that four suffragan bishops to the sees of Canterbury or London could be appointed by the king rather than Parliament, in conformity with a statute from King Henry VIII's reign.[63] Unless the suffragan's duties exceeded those exercised by previous commissaries, Drummond's musings would still offer no solution to the absence of episcopal powers in the colonies. Since dissenter opposition to episcopacy derived not only from their objection to Parliamentary power, but also from their abhorrence of the office itself, opponents would have rejected an episcopate appointed by the king as fiercely as one created by Parliament.

The Old World experiences of their Puritan ancestors and eighteenth-century understandings of the role of bishops gave New England dissenters special cause for concern. Additionally, these fears became heightened with the prevailing tone of political 'conspiracy' which surrounded the Revolution itself. Anxiety about the appointment of bishops tapped into a latent fear among nonconformists about the existence of an ecclesiastical conspiracy, precisely at the same time that new British policies appeared to threaten civil liberties.[64] The combination of these religious grievances with socio-economic objections to British taxation only reinforced the explanatory power of the conspiracy thesis. Proto-revolutionaries considered colonial taxation and the appointment of an episcopacy to be 'Parts of one general System; and that the latter is as unfriendly to our religious, as the former is to our political, Privileges.'[65]

A succession of events in the colonies provided dissenters with further evidence of a developing ecclesiastical plot against colonial civil and religious liberties. The King's College controversy, which raged in New York in the 1750s, convinced Presbyterian William Livingston that the establishment of this college was a conspiracy to undermine legislative authority and to extend a program of Anglican establishment throughout New York.[66] Attacks on the charters of dissenting churches created additional fears that the SPG aimed to 'episcopize' America. As a 1768 broadside warned, the rejection of Presbyterian and Lutheran petitions for incorporation in New York proved that dissenters should both expect and guard against the establishment of an American episcopate.[67] Later, colonial interpretations of the Quebec Act of 1774 further suggested the existence of a secret British plot to advance popery.

These conspiratorial explanations of Anglican behavior have represented the Church of England's advocacy of American bishoprics as part of a deliberate policy to extend imperial political control. Instead of depicting a political plot which consisted of Anglican aggression against non-Anglicans, alternative theories may be articulated, particularly those which insist upon religious as well as political considerations. By acknowledging the religious dimensions of this problem, one can interpret the campaign for American bishops as an attempt to deal with shortcomings in church organization.[68] Some clergymen suggested political benefits, but their arguments for episcopacy can best be described as complex and multifaceted.

Anglican attitudes about episcopacy derived from many sources, and episcopal advocates created complex justifications for a colonial bishop. The following analysis considers what historical, theological, political, or religious reasons Anglican clergymen offered as proof of the necessity of colonial bishops. Although exclusively historical and theological justifications characterized the beginnings of the campaign, by the mid-1760s Anglican authors incorporated a discussion of politics with other socio-religious matters, including concerns of church growth and clerical demography.

Among colonial Anglicans, pro-episcopal opinions derived from several sources, including English High Church tradition, which emphasized the importance of bishops. In the eighteenth century, High Churchmanship derived its authority from a theological understanding of apostolic succession in the early church as well as the heritage of the English religious establishment.[69] Inquiring into the historical arguments for episcopacy, Jeremiah Leaming asserted that the reformers in the age of Henry VIII, Edward VI and Elizabeth believed that episcopal (and not presbyterian) government was of divine origin. As he put it, '[t]he *British* Church has from *first* to *last* been *episcopal*.'[70] Samuel Johnson articulated the dual authority of episcopacy by stating that the Church of England's

> Clergy are without all doubt, regularly ordained according to the Establishment of the most pure and primitive Church, by Bishops who have an undoubted Succession from the Apostles.... And that all these are established by the Laws of our Mother Country, not only at Home, but in all the Territories thereunto belonging.[71]

Although Johnson implied that the establishment of the Church of England extended to all British territories, most clergy remained uncertain about the legalities, particularly north of the Chesapeake colonies. John Beach of Connecticut stated, 'as to the Church of England's being strictly and legally established in this Country, it having always appeared to me disputable, I leave it to be disputed by Lawyers ... [but i]f the Church be not established here, besure [*sic*] no other Way is.'[72] Perhaps Beach articulated the uncertainty of many Anglican clergymen (and their denial of the Congregationalist establishment); if their colonial establishment was to be strengthened by the appointment of a resident colonial bishop, the decision would rest with English lawyers, politicians, and church officials. Until that time, the colonial churches would remain under the jurisdiction of the Bishop of London.

Throughout the colonial period, Church of England pamphleteers wrote traditional defenses of episcopacy based on historical and scriptural precedents and directed largely toward their dissenting neighbors. In the 1720s, John Checkley's provocative writings set the tone for future theological debate between dissenters and churchmen on the necessity of episcopal ordination. Subsequently, Anglican clergymen, including John Beach and Jeremiah Leaming, described and defended Anglican doctrines and practices.[73] Collectively they asserted the Anglican belief that episcopal succession in the church had never been broken and that since there could be no true ministers of Christ without such an uninterrupted succession from the Apostles, dissenting ministers in New England had no authority from Christ. As Anglican authors insisted, the Church of England alone could claim the one necessary quality of the true church – episcopal ordination.[74] Countering dissenting arguments that episcopacy constituted a departure from Christ's presbyterian model, Jeremiah Leaming argued that the dissenting practice of ministerial election had no scriptural foundation, but rather depended upon the civil law of the province. As Timothy became the Apostle, or Bishop, of the Church at Ephesus by the authority of St Paul, so bishops succeeded the Apostles in the same order of office.[75]

In the 1760s, dissenters' polemics against the Church of England shifted the terms of the debate. The so-called Mayhew Controversy sparked a long-standing antagonism between dissenters and Anglicans over episcopacy. Jonathan Mayhew's indictment of the SPG and his criticisms of episcopacy encouraged responses from several colonial Anglican ministers, including Henry Caner of Massachusetts and Arthur Browne of New Hampshire.[76] The Archbishop of Canterbury, Thomas Secker, also replied to Mayhew's *Observations* by restating the proposed terms of settling a purely spiritual episcopate without coercive powers over the laity or civil authorities. These exchanges marked a turning point in colonial dissenter–churchman relations as previous liturgical and theological disputes lost prominence, and the political issue of establishing a bishop became the focus of controversy.[77]

A similar incorporation of political issues may be noted in Anglican writings on episcopacy of the 1760s, although the doctrinal disputes between Anglicans and nonconformists did not disappear. Jeremiah Leaming's two defenses of episcopacy, published in 1766 and 1771, presented traditional arguments about the unbroken succession of bishops from the Apostles without arguing about the need for colonial bishops, but Chandler's *Appeal* (1767) reveals a topical shift in the episcopal literature. While the *Appeal* began with a discussion of apostolic succession and primitive church practices, it consisted of much more than a defense of episcopal ordination; it advocated the appointment of a colonial episcopate by explaining the reasonableness of sending bishops and answering the objections of opponents.[78]

Increasingly, political concerns influenced colonial Anglican writings on episcopacy, as pamphlet literature became less a forum for describing the origins of episcopal ordination and more of an avenue for acquiring a colonial bishop. Nonetheless, any evaluation of political goals of ministers must begin with a consideration of how religion and politics merged in their minds. The question (implied by conspiracy theories) of whether Anglican ministers in the colonies conceived of themselves more as political agents of the Crown or religious emissaries of God certainly creates a false dichotomy. In some measure, colonial ministers acted in both capacities as long as the King of England also functioned as the head of the church, although the emphasis each individual placed on his dual role varied.

In letters of recommendation to the Bishop of London or other English ecclesiastical officials, colonial clergymen habitually described specific candidates for orders as loyal to the church and government. In typical fashion, a group of Maryland clergy noted in 1768 that the candidate Daniel McKinnon was a 'sober, orderly, virtuous, and pious Person, and well affected to the Government both in Church and State.'[79] In this manner, the referees affirmed the orthodoxy of the candidate, as required by canon law. As Anglo-American tensions increased, testimonials sometimes included additional details about a candidate's political character. In a recommendation of 1772, the referees described John Hyde Saunders as 'a sensible young Man' who had written in defense of episcopacy and who supported the application for an American bishop.[80] Even if they conceived their primary calling to be of a religious nature, Anglican clergymen collectively recognized certain responsibilities which they owed the Crown and the state.

Appeals for a colonial Anglican bishop also demonstrated a vision of the world in which politics and religion were intimately intertwined. In an address to the SPG in 1751 which advocated a colonial bishop, several Anglican ministers in Connecticut insisted that such an officer would benefit the 'Church & the Interest of Religion in general, as well as the political Interest of the Nation.'[81] This linkage of the Church of England, religion and the nation reveals a holistic yet tripartite vision of nationalism. The denominational partisanship of Anglican ministers frequently revealed itself in comments which implied that the progress of religion in the colonies might be considered synonymous with the church's own advancement. Additionally, establishmentarian philosophies implied not only the joint cooperation of church and government, but also the mutual suitability of episcopacy and monarchy.[82] Consequently, the petitioners asserted that even a periodic episcopal visitation every five or seven years might promote 'the true Interests both of Religion & Government.'[83] In 1771, the Connecticut clergy again asserted that to deny their appeals for an episcopate would prevent the church's growth and 'thereby operate to the Disadvantage of Religion and Loyalty.'[84] In the opinion of George Craig, SPG missionary at Chester, Pennsylvania, a bishop might also promote a unified establishment and 'that unity of an establishment in ye Chh. would naturally (in time) bring about a unity in ye state, and without an establishment of some national Chh. the state will ever be lyable to frequent convulsions & in ye end prove fatal to one party or another.'[85] Many northern clergy believed that a bishop and a national church could secure political stability as well as church growth.

By the late 1760s, many friends of the Church of England proposed that a stronger position on episcopacy in the first half of the eighteenth century might have prevented present riots and turmoil. Henry Barnes of Massachusetts believed that had a bishop been secured a century earlier American opposition in that decade would not have escalated as it did.[86] An influential Maryland layman, Daniel Dulany, considered the establishment of a bishop in America in the same breath as a review of the northern colonies' charters which, in his opinion, conferred too extensive privileges upon the people. In Dulany's mind, Anglican missionaries had attempted to alter the constitutions of northern colonies, but they had failed to reconcile dissenters to the Church of England.[87] Establishmentarian beliefs survived, and in the organization of British North America after 1783 English officials paid particular attention to the role the Church of England could exercise in promoting the stability of government.[88]

As Anglo-American tensions escalated, Anglican advocates of an American bishop employed additional religio-political arguments, changing their tactics to suit the individuals they aimed to convince. In their petitions, Anglican clergymen displayed their debating skills by assembling an arsenal of varied arguments. Addresses to the king or other British politicians did not rely exclusively on spiritual arguments; that strategy had proven insufficient over the course of the eighteenth century. In their letter to the Earl of Hillsborough, Secretary of State for the American Department, New Jersey and New York clergymen speculated that ' "Independency in Religion will naturally produce Republicanism in the State." ' This echo of James I's dictum 'No Bishop, No King' made sense to British ministers worried about a growing revolutionary spirit in the colonies.[89] Likewise, pamphlets and newspaper articles, which hoped to win colonial acceptance of Anglican bishops, sensibly avoided any argument which suggested that bishops could episcopize America and make the colonies more obedient to the designs of the mother country.

While Anglican petitioners became quite adept at supplying their addressees with the arguments most likely to elicit a favorable response to their campaign for bishops, advocates were not equally skilled in convincing skeptics of their truthfulness. After writing his *Appeal*, Thomas Bradbury Chandler confided to the Bishop of London:

There are some other Facts and Reasons, which could not be prudently mentioned in a Work of this Nature, as the least Intimation of them

would be of ill Consequence in this irritable Age and Country: but were
they known, they would have a far greater Tendency to engage such of
our Superiors, if there be any such, as are governed altogether by political Motives, to espouse the Cause of the Church of England in America,
than any contained in the Pamphlet. But I must content myself with
having proposed those only which could be mentioned safely, and leave
the Event to Divine Providence.[90]

Were pro-episcopate spokesmen guilty of duplicity by using these varied
methods? They certainly were 'guilty' of tailoring arguments to convince
different audiences, but such tactics do not necessarily imply malevolence
or 'ulterior political motives' such as subverting colonial liberties.[91]

While High Church philosophies of establishmentarianism could have
been an ingredient in the psyche of a political conspirator, the mere belief
in a religio-political philosophy shared by much of the eighteenth-century
world does not provide even circumstantial proof of an Anglican political
conspiracy. Furthermore, the existence of political arguments for episcopacy is understandable given the intertwined nature of religion and politics
and the fact that the clerics directed these arguments at English officials
motivated, they thought, by political concerns. Proof of a political conspiracy requires not only the existence of political motives, but also a measure
of duplicity. Many opponents of episcopacy, whether dissenters or churchmen, believed that Anglican clergymen who promoted colonial bishops
disguised their real intentions and were insincere in claiming that they
wanted only to administer to their own parishioners, that no episcopate
should be sent to New England, and, most importantly, that they desired
only a purely spiritual bishop. On all of these points, dissenters had some
cause for concern for many northern Anglicans did hope to broaden their
influence through the appointment of a bishop.

The belief that the Church of England intended to episcopize the northern colonies gained attention after the publication of Jonathan Mayhew's
pamphlet in 1763, and in response, many influential Anglicans, including
the Archbishop of Canterbury, defended SPG practices. Samuel Johnson
denied that Anglicans deliberately proselytized among dissenters and
claimed that any converts from dissenting churches to Anglicanism had
been 'accidental.'[92] As John Beach had written in 1751, the SPG 'never
send Missionaries to convert Protestants to the Church of England; but to
minister to Church People; and if Dissenters by that Means are added to the
Church, they are not ashamed to own, they do not think by this any Evil is
done.'[93] As Johnson asked, should not Presbyterians or Congregationalists
in New England have as much right to conform to Anglicanism as Church

of England people to become dissenters?[94] Dissenters who interpreted Anglican advances as part of a deliberate conspiracy also disbelieved the widely publicized view that Anglican clergymen did not desire an episcopate within New England, where dissenters held political power. Such instincts sometimes proved correct. Despite the public claims of Connecticut clergy, Henry Caner privately disapproved of the proposed concession that no bishop be sent to New England or other dissenter-dominated colonies. In his words, 'This I apprehend would rather be like sending a Physician to the whole [rather] than the Sick ...'[95] To Caner, such concessions were illogical.

Advocates of colonial bishops continued to insist that they wanted spiritual bishops, but their claims were considered impossible, impractical or mere subterfuge. Such a conclusion resulted, no doubt, from long-standing antagonisms and mistrust between dissenters and churchmen, but did these suspicions consist of only 'malevolent Conjecture'?[96] Did Anglican promoters of episcopacy really hope that an English-style bishop would eventually be created, even while they consistently stated in public that they proposed only a spiritual bishop, stripped of civil powers? In his *Appeal* Chandler could not have been clearer: in campaigning for bishops, Anglican advocates meant 'suffragan' bishops only.[97] Such officials were to have only spiritual authority, derived from the church and not the state, to ordain and govern the clergy and to administer confirmation, but no authority over dissenters or property. A few years later, Chandler answered continued objections by asserting that '[t]he Advocates for an American Episcopate are sincere and candid in their Proposal ... they aim at no more than they pretend.'[98] In an address to their Virginia brethren, the clergy of New York and New Jersey argued that they had never petitioned for an English-style episcopate. Furthermore, they quoted from SPG abstracts in an attempt to prove that early SPG missionaries had asked only for suffragans.[99] Nonetheless, as early as December 1707 the Bishop of London had composed a paper about the settling of a suffragan bishop in America, in which he stated that an absolute bishop would not be appropriate (for it would alarm the colonists), but one might be appointed in time since every new establishment, he argued, should be developed gradually.[100]

A different answer to the question of Anglican sincerity can be gleaned, particularly before the Stamp Act crisis, by examining unpublished addresses. In 1751 the Connecticut clergy appealed to the SPG for a bishop in a manner which revealed their preference for an English-style official. They stated that they 'would like an episcopate with full power as in England but will accept a limited one as better than none.'[101] The clergy of New Jersey and New York assembled in convention in October 1765 agreed that they were willing to accept a purely spiritual bishop, but the wording of their petition to Bishop Terrick revealed the lukewarmness of this conviction. They would accept a suffragan and hoped it would be sufficient, while they noted it was 'less than could be reasonably expected in a Christian Country' especially given the long history of bishops with civil powers.[102] Clearly some pro-episcopate individuals regarded a suffragan bishop as insufficient in the 1750s and 1760s, but such opinions do not suggest that campaigns for a purely spiritual bishop merely operated as a smokescreen for their real intentions. Even in these earlier petitions, the clergy clearly stated their awareness of the necessity of compromise; a bishop on any terms was preferable to none at all. After the Stamp Act crisis, if not earlier, most clergy recognized that an absolute bishop, however desirable, was a practical impossibility. In public episcopal spokesmen denied that they ever wanted anything other than a bishop with purely spiritual powers.

The arguments for episcopacy which the clerical advocates employed most forcefully may be characterized not as theological or as political, but as ecclesiastical. Ecclesiastical reasons, broadly defined, consisted of various extra-theological arguments related to competition with dissenters, the operation of the colonial church, and matters of professional demography. Anglican ministers naturally desired the growth of the church, and some considered a bishop an effective tool for increasing membership. 'Hard indeed is our case that we cannot have a Bishop sent to America. Should that happy time arrive our Church would then be countenanced & supported, whereas at present she droops her head and languishes.'[103] In demanding a colonial episcopacy, Anglicans utilized the well-seasoned arguments of English and colonial dissenters. The rhetoric of toleration and religious liberty, effective tools for nonchurchmen, became weapons in the hands of Anglican clergymen who used such dissenting arguments for their own purposes. With incredulity, many pamphleteers or petitioners noted that Roman Catholics in Canada and Moravians in Pennsylvania had bishops and that Presbyterians were allowed their synod government, but the Church of England was not permitted to complete its hierarchical church structure. Connecticut petitioners in 1766 characterized this situation as one of 'glaring partiality against the Church of England.'[104] Charles Inglis commented that members of the Church of England 'only claim the like privileges for themselves, and an exemption from their insults.'[105] Responding to allegations of Anglican wrong-doing, Samuel Andrews, SPG missionary in Connecticut, asserted that

> ... our Crime consists only in not being Dissenters from the Church of England, and in wishing to have a Bishop resident among us on such

Terms as cannot be detrimental to the Rights of Anabaptists, Papists, Moravians, and other Dissenters, and which we have candidly laid before the Public; our Religion has taught us to hope for forgiveness in claiming such Liberties as we have freely given to others.[106]

By employing this argument about religious toleration, episcopal promoters did not have to resort to more controversial establishmentarian defenses of episcopacy; instead, they appealed to a denominationalist perspective by claiming that they wished to be put on an 'equal footing' with other North American religions.

Using this seemingly sensible argument that the Church of England should be permitted at least the same privileges as other denominations, colonial Anglican ministers insisted that no one could oppose the scheme, except 'out of Malice, or mere wantonness.'[107] As long as the Anglican episcopate possessed only spiritual powers, Henry Caner argued, no dissenters had any 'reasonable Excuse' for opposing measures which would not interfere with their interests.[108] Perhaps William McGilchrist most clearly stated the pro-episcopate clergy's belief in the hypocrisy of dissenters. 'The Gentlemen in this Province [Massachusetts] are all in a manner professed advocates for universal toleration and liberty of conscience, and yet in direct contradiction to this principle, the Dissenters avowedly oppose with all their interest a Bishop's being sent over to America.' After asking some nonconformists how they reconciled this conduct with their principles, McGilchrist found that their answers revealed 'as strong an instance of prejudice and blind attachment to a Party as ever I met with in my lifetime.'[109]

By attributing dissenter reaction to hypocrisy, Anglican clergymen failed to consider why their arguments were disbelieved. In his *Appeal*, Chandler asserted the natural connection between the Church of England and the civil constitution of England, thereby revealing his belief that Anglicans should possess a privileged position relative to other denominations. Only a few pages later, he argued that if all religions in America 'are to be treated on the Footing of a perfect Equality, for which some have contended; then, the Church of England is as fully intitled to the compleat Enjoyment of its own Discipline and Institutions, as any other Christians.'[110] Given his belief in the perfect suitability of episcopacy and monarchy, did Chandler seek only religious equality? In his *Appeal Defended*, Chandler argued more forcefully in his defense, '[w]e want not an Episcopate on the Footing of a *State-Establishment*; we desire no more than a compleat Toleration, which we have not at present; and thereby to be raised to an Equality with other religious Denominations in the Colonies.'[111] Five years later in print, this same author, obviously frustrated by the continued failure of appeals for a bishop, described the lack of a colonial episcopate as 'the greatest [of] political Absurdities ... such as has never been paralleled in any Age or Nation of the World. One would imagine, that the national Religion in the Colonies would be honoured with some Kind of Distinction: but all the Distinction it has hitherto met with, is ... real Dishonour.'[112] By employing the language of denominational equality almost in the same breath with arguments of religious privilege, Anglican advocates of episcopacy undoubtedly confused their friends and worried their opponents. Colonial Anglicanism rejected religious uniformity, but continued to expect certain privileges.[113]

As well as providing a rhetoric of religious liberty, Anglican experience with dissenters in the colonies led to a perception of the bishop campaign in terms of the intercolonial competition for souls. In arguing about the appointment of a bishop, advocates and opponents recognized each other's institutional progress. Having acknowledged the recent growth of colonial Anglicanism, dissenters feared a bishop could further accelerate the pace of religious anglicization. Likewise, Anglicans also took dissenter strength quite seriously; without a bishop, some feared 'the very appearance of the Church will, in time be lost, and all kinds of Sectaries will soon prevail ...'[114] The headless plight of the American Anglicanism appeared a matter of considerable concern to William Smith and other Pennsylvania clergy who considered the disadvantages under which they labored and the relative advantages of dissenters who already had plans of union, methods of discipline, and the means of supplying ministers for their church.[115] Three years later, Smith further elaborated on the national and possible international consequences of a prolonged deprivation of colonial episcopates. In his partisan view, Quakers and local Germans did not oppose Anglican bishops, but rather understood that Anglicans sought only their 'natural Rights.' Furthermore, they actually hoped colonial Anglicans might receive a bishop, so that the Church of England could grow 'as a Balance to Presbyterians' and thereby prevent Presbyterianism from endangering religious liberty in America and perhaps in England as well.[116] Smith believed that bishops could act as the ultimate trump card in the colonial contest for souls; an episcopate could not only assist in the growth of the Anglican church, but would also curtail the advance of the most undesirable dissenters.

In comparison with dissenting churches, the colonial Church of England operated under considerable institutional restraints and deficiencies. As described in the previous chapter, the lack of bishops and the inadequacy of colonial colleges significantly inhibited the church's ability to develop a self-sustaining ministry which could keep pace with demographic growth.

While Anglican ministers perceived the need for an episcopate in terms of theological, political and religious reasons, they also considered the extreme importance of this church leader to their own professional regulation and demography. Although episcopal advocates occasionally mentioned confirmation as an important rite which bishops could restore, the main ecclesiastical functions of the proposed colonial bishop consisted of government of the clergy and the ordination of ministerial candidates. Among the causes which led to the declining state of the Anglican church by the late 1780s, Rev. John Andrews listed first the lack of bishops. 'Destitute of Bishops, our candidates for the ministry have been forced to seek for ordination in another hemisphere; at a great expence; which many of them were but ill able to bear. From the same defect we were without union, without government.'[117] By imposing regular government upon the colonial clergy, bishops would improve both professional morale and their collective reputation. As northern Anglican ministers reminded their southern colleagues, even among the small number of Apostles chosen by Christ there was one traitor. Therefore, in so large a number of clergymen as existed in the American colonies, occasionally the need for discipline and correction arose.[118] The existence of a resident bishop could deter profligacy and reduce the number of clerical delinquents.

For Thomas Bradbury Chandler, the inability of the church to ordain candidates, without an expensive and dangerous voyage overseas, carried even more serious consequences than the lack of clerical regulation. In his words, 'a greater Disadvantage, if possible, than the Want of a regular Government, attends the Church of England in America in its present State, I mean the Want of Ordination.'[119] Colonial clergy and English prelates both recognized that a resident bishop could strengthen the colonial church by encouraging more American-born men to become candidates for Anglican orders. Laymen also recognized this potential benefit: Graham Frank, a Virginian who described himself as the son-in-law of a Church of England minister, articulated a similar concern in a letter to Thomas Sherlock, Bishop of London. In Frank's mind, many people would take orders if it were not for the dangers and expense of the voyage to England.[120] In their published writings and correspondence with English officials, colonial clergy repeated this layman's concern. By 1795, a Maryland minister also expressed his belief that the aim of the bishop movement had been to secure sufficient numbers of Anglican ministers in the colonies. '[A] natural wish to perpetuate themselves set them about completing their ecclesiastical orders ...'[121]

The eloquence with which Anglican clergymen campaigned for a bishop underscored their sense of desperation about the church's pressing needs and their own sense of grief about fallen colleagues and lost opportunities. On occasion candidates had been lost at sea or captured by enemies and 'confined like Malefactors, in Prisons and Dungeons' in foreign lands.[122] Such tragedies, although infrequent, greatly inconvenienced colonial parishes and threatened the continuance of the local Church of England. The very unlucky parishioners at Hebron, Connecticut, struggled for 20 years to acquire an ordained minister: the first candidate perished at sea in 1745, a second died on his passage from London to New England, a third was traveling to England in 1757 when taken prisoner by the French, and a fourth candidate contracted smallpox in London but recovered and finally returned to Hebron.[123] Such stories proved inconvenience persuasively, but episcopal advocates undoubtedly exaggerated the dangers of an Atlantic crossing and the horrors of a forced sojourn in England.[124] As dissenters noted, a visit to England assisted clerical candidates in forging a personal link to the English church. At least one minister believed that his stay in London, and his exposure to great orators, actually improved his character.[125]

Nonetheless, an extended stay in London could prove very costly, as well as dangerous. Samuel Johnson, who estimated that the journey for orders could not be accomplished 'with Decency' for less than £100 sterling, knew personally of the dangers. In the late fall of 1722, Johnson had traveled with Timothy Cutler and Daniel Brown to England for ordination. Cutler and Brown soon fell ill with smallpox, a disease which took Brown's life by April 1723.[126] In 1755, Johnson wrote to Bishop Sherlock that he hoped to see his son become a minister, but feared his journey to England for orders, since many clergy who had crossed for ordination died before their return either of smallpox or because they were lost at sea.[127] Anxious English bishops also observed that smallpox proved 'peculiarly fatal' to American-born candidates.[128] In the case of his son, Johnson's fears were well-founded: the younger Johnson died of smallpox in 1756 during his trip for orders.[129] Ever mindful of the cause of episcopacy, Johnson lamented the death of his son by writing, 'I should scarce have thought my dear son's life ill bestowed (nor I believe would he) if it could have been a means of awakening this stupid age to a sense of the necessity of sending Bishops.'[130]

In requests for the appointment of bishops to the colonies, Anglican clerics habitually mentioned the advantage these dangers gave to dissenters. Individuals who otherwise would have considered Anglican ordination frequently were deterred by the prospect of this dangerous and expensive voyage.[131] In particularly impassioned prose, Rev. Hugh Neill assessed the disastrous impact of this practice.

Such, alas! are the misfortunes and I may say persecutions, that attend the poor distressed Church of England in America, that whilst the Dissenters can send out an innumerable tribe of Teachers of all sorts, without any expence, we must send three thousand miles, cross the Atlantic Ocean, at an expence of all we are worth sometimes and as much more as we have credit for as well as the risque of our lives before we can have an ordination: this is a difficulty that has and always will prevent the growth of the Church in America. Few Englishmen that can live at home will undertake the Mission. The great expences and dangers of the Seas that the Americans must encounter with before they can obtain an ordination, damps their spirits and forces many of them (who have strong inclinations to the Church) to join the Dissenters and become teachers among them. Thus, when a vacancy happens among them, it can be filled in an instant, while a vacancy among us is some considerable time before they can have a Minister. All this time the Dissenters are making such havock among the Church people, that when a Missionary comes to one of these destitute places he has all the work to begin again and many years before he can collect his scattered Flock.[132]

Rev. Devereux Jarratt noted in his autobiography that when he deliberated about whether he should become a Presbyterian minister or a Church of England clergyman, he considered that all of the disadvantages of 'expence, peril and danger might be avoided, by taking orders among the Presbyterians.'[133] As Thomas Barton aptly described the situation of the colonial Anglican church, '[t]he great danger of the seas ... and the great expence attending a voyage to England must ever be checks to its growth and prosperity.'[134] In discussing this financial burden, Chandler took his cue from patriot objections to the stamp duties and likened the expenses of Anglican ordination to an oppressive tax which unfairly fell only on churchmen, while other churches not only escaped the costs of an expensive voyage but were allowed the means to secure their own ministers more cheaply.[135]

By the 1760s, Anglican missionaries had argued for decades that English ordination caused unbearable danger, hardships and expense. Increasingly, some individuals came to interpret colonial demographic trends as creating a special urgency for their proposal. In 1767 the times appeared briefly to favor episcopacy since strained relations with Britain had subsided temporarily. Chandler urged that 'the Arguments for sending Bishops to America, were never so urgent and forcible as they are at present.' As he reminded his readers, previous efforts had been made when the number of Anglican clergymen and parishioners was much smaller, but tremendous population growth made the appointment even more warranted. 'The amazing natural Increase of the Colonists, and the vast Accession of Europeans to the British America, have, in the Compass of Fifty or Sixty Years, so enlarged the Number of its Inhabitants...' that he estimated that one-third the population of America, or one million people, were Church of England members.[136] Dissenters questioned the veracity of these figures, but also mused that if colonial Anglicanism really flourished so well, perhaps it did not require a bishop. Episcopal advocates considered the absence of episcopacy an even greater crime of negligence given the large number of souls affected.[137] Furthermore, bishops could provide a solution to the demographic challenges which faced the church and its clergy in America. As John Beach wrote, 'the clergy in these parts... in some proportion to the Increase of the Church People... cannot be expected till they are Blessed with a resident Bishop.'[138]

In this manner, many Church of England clergymen campaigned for a resident American bishop by assembling a plethora of arguments in their favor. Theological and historical justifications of episcopacy accompanied but were superseded by High Church views of the positive influence an episcopate could have on political stability. Additionally, episcopal advocates insisted that the church required bishops for internal and institutional reasons, particularly given the demographic trends of the late eighteenth century and continued competition with dissenters. For each decade that the Church of England continued to operate without a bishop, and therefore without American ordination, dissenters gained immeasurably.

That the bishop movement of the 1760s and 1770s failed in its goal of securing an episcopate should not suggest that the controversy was inconsequential to the colonial church. Edward Winslow, SPG missionary at Braintree, Massachusetts, described in 1768 the prevalence of 'too great bitterness of Spirit against the Church on account of the recent addresses on the subject of resident Bishops on this continent.'[139] The bishop controversy increased the antipathy of dissenters towards the colonial Church of England and enlarged rifts between northern and southern Anglican clergymen. While many southern ministers found their New York and New Jersey brethren bothersome, meddlesome, and strong-armed in their campaign for bishops, pro-episcopal advocates in the north considered their southern counterparts recalcitrant for opposing episcopacy. Such internal antagonisms would have to be reconciled after the Revolution in the formation of the new American Protestant Episcopal Church. Although only a few colonial ministers actually launched and promoted vigorously the campaign for bishops, the entire church became tainted by association as pamphleteers labeled them 'Tories.' The vilification of the colonial Anglican church during the bishop campaign served as a poignant reminder for the rest of the Revolution of the church's association with the king and the English state.

The episcopacy controversy also created the fault line along which clerical opinion would divide during the Revolutionary War. One can notice clearly a link between pro-episcopal opinion and later loyalism, as well as between anti-episcopal opinion and patriotism.[140] Although decisions of patriotism or loyalism rested upon many considerations, views on episcopacy served as a successful predictor in many notable cases. The most prominent episcopal spokesmen in each colony, namely Thomas Bradbury Chandler, Henry Caner, Jonathan Boucher, and John Camm, became loyalist exiles. Their episcopal opinions formed part of a larger, more encompassing political philosophy which favored deference to hierarchical authority.

Ministers holding pro-episcopate views also may have expressed a colonial self-image which was falling out of favor among the general population. Whereas the patriot movement harnessed the adolescent energy of colonies seeking independence from Father King and Mother Country, pro-episcopal Anglican ministers may have envisioned their colonial church as infantile and therefore in need of paternal guidance. Conversely, in their respect for colonial civil authority, anti-episcopal clergy of the southern colonies may have projected a view of the self-sufficiency of their church as a result of its older, more developed character. A certain 'missionary' outlook also may have encouraged a conceptualization of the colonial Church of England as incomplete, or child-like, and therefore in need of direction. As an SPG missionary wrote in the mid-1760s, without a bishop for discipline and government, 'the Church of England alone sits like a distressed, mourning child that has lost a tender Parent and will not be comforted.'[141] For those ministers who conceived of their colonial church as underdeveloped, episcopacy provided an avenue for maturation and anglicization as well as opportunities for growth relative to dissenting populations.

4 The Political Philosophies of the Two Extremes

In the eighteenth century, organized religion concerned itself with such worldly issues as man's duty to support government and his right to resist duly constituted authority, although religious denominations differed in their interpretation of the proper balance between these two competing forces. In part, the struggle between patriots and loyalists during the American Revolution involved opposing philosophies about the nature of government and human obligations to support existing political institutions. From the contractualist character of God's covenant with his people, Puritan ministers concluded that if the king violated God's commands in a serious and sustained way, his people had a religious duty to resist the monarch. These principles, when adopted or modified by revolutionaries, provided a religious justification for rebellion.[1]

In contrast to latently revolutionary Calvinism, the Anglican church's traditional doctrine of passive obedience and non-resistance, although modified by the Glorious Revolution, associated its members more closely with loyalism since both shared a conservative faith in the merits of existing political structures. Unlike Quaker pacifism, Church of England views did not entail the conscientious objection to the bearing of arms nor the consistent promotion of non-violent principles. Instead, Anglicans endorsed 'just war' concepts that recognized the occasional need for resistance but typically emphasized obedience to acceptable monarchs. Whereas Quakers refused to take oaths to civil authorities, the Church of England deliberately encouraged obedience to monarch and government, and it required its clergy to take a solemn oath of allegiance to the king. The church proclaimed that subjects ought to obey divinely instituted authority, but obedience had limits. Passive obedience insisted that unjust commands should not be obeyed if doing so violated God's laws (and so the doctrine opposed unlimited obedience), but rather than plunge into war the disgruntled should more quietly accept the civil penalties for non-compliance.[2] For Anglicans, lessons learned in the English Civil Wars of the mid-seventeenth century and the Glorious Revolution of 1688 helped to define the appropriateness of both obedience and resistance, as well as the limits of each.

In late eighteenth-century England, High Churchmanship affirmed the union of church and king, and the church's official message remained one of subordination to divinely constituted authority. Almost unanimously, the clergy of the established church in England supported the Crown during the American Revolution. Their identity established by law, Anglican clergymen, like English justices of the peace, overwhelmingly defended Parliamentary supremacy against the illegal activities of the colonial rebels.[3] From the king's proclamation of rebellion, the clergy in England united in their loyalty; they signed few petitions for conciliation, and only three bishops disagreed with the administration's policy of coercion. Fast sermons preached by these English clergy publicized their loyalism; only a small minority displayed sympathy for the American cause. When Richard Watson, Divinity Professor at Cambridge, declared that the war against the American colonies was unjust, he found himself accused of republicanism and disloyalty.[4] Dissenting ministers and laymen led the protest against government policy, but since dissenters comprised only a fraction of the population, their ability to attract lay Anglicans into the opposition camp was quite important. Dissenter and Low Church Anglican cooperation in some regions broadened the nature of protest.

In the colonies, many prominent loyalists, including five of the best Tory propagandists, were Anglican clergymen.[5] The notoriety of these individuals has served, in part, to characterize all Anglican clergymen as loyalists. One need only think of such colorful examples as Samuel Seabury Jr, Thomas Bradbury Chandler, or Jonathan Boucher. By declaring their political views, these men incurred the wrath of local patriots and gained subsequent historical fame as arch-Tories. In addition to being the first Bishop of Connecticut, Seabury is remembered as the author of the famous 'Letters from a Westchester Farmer.'[6] After penning *An Appeal to the Public* in 1767 which advocated the introduction of colonial bishops, Chandler also wrote several pamphlets against the Continental Congress.[7] Boucher, a Maryland minister, so antagonized his parishioners that, before fleeing to England in September 1775, he found it necessary to preach with a pair of loaded pistols on a nearby pillow.[8]

Despite the fame of several influential loyalists, many colonial Anglican clergymen supported the Revolution, especially in the southern colonies where the Church of England was established.[9] The story of John Peter Gabriel Muhlenburg, an Anglican minister of Lutheran heritage, represents the opposite extreme of political affiliation. Muhlenburg participated in many of the major battles of the Revolutionary War, including Brandywine, Germantown, and Yorktown, and by 1777 was promoted to brigadier-general in the Continental army.[10] Similarly, the military service of other Virginia ministers, including David Griffith and Charles Mynn Thruston, has been accepted as evidence of their extraordinary patriotic fervor.[11]

If political affiliation were plotted on a spectrum, ultra-loyalism on one end and extreme patriotism on the other would bracket a large middle section containing gradations of less fervent zeal and neutrality. The purpose of this chapter is to explore the political views of the most extreme Anglican clergymen at either end of the spectrum, thereby illustrating the poles of political affiliation. At least a few famous colonial Anglican clergymen occupied positions at one or the other pole, as an arch-Tory or a fervent patriot. What accounts for this divergence of opinion? Did patriotic Anglican clergymen have to reject the teachings of the church, specifically non-resistance and passive obedience, to embrace the prevailing patriot civil religion, or was Anglican civil religion sufficiently broad to encompass both points of view? For the purposes of this chapter, civil religion refers to a religious perspective on government which may articulate its divine origin and characteristics or describe the nation's providential destiny.[12] By focusing on select ministers, this chapter describes the political philosophies at each pole and their religious underpinnings to depict how two such divergent paths emerged from Anglican teachings.

The American Revolution itself may be considered a form of religion. Sons of Liberty became missionaries for the new civil religion; the Revolution endowed objects and places such as the Liberty Tree, Bunker Hill, and Valley Forge with religious significance; and George Washington emerged not only as a great revolutionary hero and the new nation's first president, but as the founder of American civil religion. Furthermore, the Declaration of Independence and the Constitution evolved into sacred texts analogous to the Scriptures. Nonetheless, the task of distinguishing between the worship of Washington and what John Adams called 'superstitious veneration' still remains problematic.[13] Instead of seeing these political entities as a distinctive religion, civil religion may be more of an effort to use sacred rhetoric to hallow the secular.

In either case, civil religion did not appeal to all colonists. Rituals performed at the liberty tree aimed to unify the colonists in their support of the Revolution, in part, through the public exclusion of undesirables. Mock trials and ritual hangings provided the local community with the opportunity to label and punish selected scapegoats who represented that tyranny which threatened colonial liberty. From the loyalist point of view, patriot rituals served only as a means of manipulation and intimidation. Loyalists did not conceive of the Revolution as a rite of passage; nor did they embrace the prevailing 'spirit of youth initiation' by which patriots distinguished themselves from others.[14] It appears, therefore, that civil religion provided one fault line along which loyalists and patriots divided.

In addition to religio-political symbolism, providential and millennial understandings of the American Revolution coexisted with natural rights philosophy and other patriot ideologies which justified revolution. The masses of God-fearing patriots demanded a philosophy of revolution which placed God squarely on their side. In millennial thought, participants found a conceptualization of the future which encouraged a decisive break with tradition.[15] Providentialism can be traced to early Puritan notions of their errand, but such a belief that God's hand directs human events transcended any particular denomination. Loyalist groups, who similarly presumed that they had the Lord's support, felt that they understood God's will better than their enemies. In their view, He was a God of Order and not a God of War or Confusion.[16] When patriots presented secular political change as part of divine progress, they redefined and expanded the meaning of the American Revolution by associating it with the redemption of mankind. Consequently the use of the terms 'political millennium' and 'American millennium' became frequent in the early republic. As the Founding Fathers believed throughout the Revolution and the framing of the Constitution of 1787, their efforts would decide not only the fate of republican government, but also the destiny of mankind. America had become the refuge of liberty. Revolutionary millennialism merged the meanings of political liberty and tyranny to pre-existing religious millennial traditions; just as tyranny was closely identified with sin, liberty was laden with religious connotations. Although religious millennialism in America had incorporated political values before the 1770s, during the Revolution it assumed a more radical meaning as themes of a distinctive national mission took shape.[17] Loyalists, however, rejected this notion of America's elect status and affirmed that America's future lay within the British Empire and an emerging British national identity, which (between 1707 and 1815) was based on a shared Protestantism and heightened by recurring wars.[18]

A developing sense of British nationalism undoubtedly influenced Anglican civil theology, but perhaps two expressions best summarize the fundamentals of Anglican political thought as understood by the American colonists. When Rev. Philip Reading found the words 'No More Passive Obedience and Non-Resistance' painted across the doors of his church in the summer of 1775, he may have felt considerable outrage at this expression of patriot antipathy towards his teachings, an action which indicated the erosion of a political middle ground in his community. He must also have realized that the graffiti captured two of the church's central tenets of political conduct.[19] For many colonial Anglican clergy, the church's position on passive obedience, as well as its continued association with England and the British monarch, inhibited their involvement in the Revolution. Despite the 'rebuffs' he received, Reading pledged that he was 'not deterred or discouraged from inculcating the principles of Loyalty to our most gracious Sovereign and a due submission to the powers of Government on all proper occasions.'[20] Those ministers who did embrace patriotism had to reconcile their actions with this religio-political principle, as Rev. David Griffith of Virginia attempted to do in his sermon of 31 December 1775, which he entitled 'Passive Obedience Considered.'[21]

By encouraging deference, passive obedience reinforced the hegemony of existing hierarchical social and political structures. Because the cosmology of the 'great chain of being' affirmed that social distinctions fostered the well-being of the community, political obedience to one's social superiors was a civic duty. The widely disseminated Anglican educational tract, *The Whole Duty of Man*, encouraged respect for one's superiors and affirmed the necessity of class distinctions.[22] That one owed obedience to 'God [who] has assigned each of us our station' was a message frequently repeated to Anglican congregations, and to Revolutionary or British troops.[23] As Charles Inglis of New York preached in 1780:

> Government implies Subordination. Where Government is, there must be some who preside or govern – and others, over whom that presidency is exercised: From the very Nature and Design of Government, it is the Duty of the latter to honour and obey the former. This is also the 'Will of God.'

Even if men failed to regard this precept as God's will, Inglis insisted, 'yet at least for their own Sake they should do so: For on a due Observation of it, the Stability of Government and the Peace of Societies depend.' One person's offense in dishonoring the king threatened the entire community. Seditious language could easily produce disloyal acts.[24]

Passive obedience was more than a civil responsibility. It also was a religious obligation because of specific scriptural injunctions and because God Himself had created government. In the opinion of Isaac Campbell, a Maryland clergyman, legitimate civil government was derived entirely from God and not from any so-called laws of nature or the will of man. Similarly, Jonathan Boucher denied natural rights philosophy and asserted that kings and princes received their commissions from God and not from popular consent or suffrage.[25] In an address to like-minded members of the king's army, Samuel Seabury also insisted that

> [o]ur Duty to obey our Rulers and Governors arises from our Duty to obey God. He has commanded us to obey Magistrates; to honor all Men

according to their Degree in Authority. If we fear God we shall obey his
Command from a Principle of Duty to him. – Civil Government is
the Institution and Ordinance of God: – He hath ordained the Powers
that are …[26]

If God had ordained civil powers, then it naturally followed that 'when
Christians are disobedient to human ordinances, they are also disobedient
to God.'[27] Biblical passages which affirmed these Anglican teachings
included the very simply constructed text 'Fear God. Honour the King' of
I Peter 2: 17, but also the often cited passage in Romans 13: 1–2, 'Let
every soul be subject unto the higher powers. For there is no power but of
God: the powers that be are ordained of God. Whosoever therefore
resisteth the power, resisteth the ordinance of God: and they that resist
shall receive to themselves damnation.' On these two texts, many loyalist
clergy based their political sermons.

    If God had not only created civil government, as Campbell, Boucher,
and Seabury contended, but also continued to sanction the ruling powers,
then disobedience to government would entail a rejection of God's explicit
ordering of the world. Remarking that 'not a sparrow falls to the ground
without his knowledge,' Jacob Duché acknowledged God's providential direction; if God withdrew his influence, then disorder would soon
follow.[28] Similarly Rev. James Madison asserted that God 'still upholds
his works by the same parental voice which spoke them into being.'[29]
As Rev. John Bracken inferred in 1795, God was not merely a watchmaker
who, having made the world, permitted it to operate according to scienti-
fic laws of nature. Rather, Bracken attributed a more active role to the
'great Governor of the universe … who first *formed*, must still continue to
uphold, this great machine of the universe … [All things] are in the *last
result* to be ascribed to the *direction*, or at least the *permission* of
Almighty God.' Writing after the Revolution, Bracken articulated a belief
that God had directed events to ensure the eventual success of patriot
arms. Respect for duly constituted authority survived for this patriot
Anglican, turned Federalist, who instructed his republican listeners
that '[i]n one word, our first duty is to *fear God*, our next, and in subordination thereto, *to honour and obey those who are lawfully invested with
authority.*'[30]

    While post-revolutionary injunctions about the need for civil obedience
utilized a language very similar to earlier loyalist defenses of British policies, the message's meaning altered dramatically once patriot Anglicans
had accepted republican political innovations. Traditionally Anglican
views on passive obedience merged with a long-standing respect for the
institution of monarchy. Opposing Thomas Paine's radical denigration of

monarchy in *Common Sense*, Charles Inglis wrote that '[h]ereditary monarchy is infinitely preferable to elective, and more conducive to the welfare of mankind.'[31] Although the philosophy of divine right of kings had fallen from favor by the eighteenth century, contemporaries still attributed the success of individual monarchs to the hand of Providence. The king, by acting as the head of government and the church, linked the secular and sacred worlds and functioned as God's servant. As Samuel Seabury described the role of the English monarch, '…the sacred Person of our Royal Sovereign, considered in a religious view…is the viceservant of God, to whom He hath committed his sword of justice and His right and power to govern the British Empire.'[32] The king deserved the affection and obedience of his subjects because he acted as a guardian of the laws of the state. The loyalist views of Samuel Seabury resulted not only from his belief in the duty of man to obey the king, but also from his conceptualization of George III as a particularly virtuous monarch.[33] In a respectful tone, Inglis also described King George III as 'a Sovereign whose numerous Virtues add Lustre to his Throne; yet is abjured by those who owe him true Allegiance …'[34]

Oaths to the king and his government fulfilled a particular role in Anglican civil theology by uniting the subject with both government and God. Additionally, oaths protected a sometimes precarious balance between secular and sacred worlds, which ultimately, Anglicans believed, sustained the English constitution. Anglican ministers took oaths to the king twice, before ordination to the diaconate and before ordination to the priesthood. In the Oath of the King's Supremacy, these candidates affirmed their belief that 'no foreign Prince, Person, Prelate, State, or Potentate hath, or ought to have any jurisdiction, power, superiority, preeminence, or authority, Ecclesiastical or Spiritual, within this Realm.'[35] Although the Anglican laity did not subscribe to such explicit promises of political fidelity, colonial ministers of the Church of England believed that the obligation extended to all the church's members. According to Charles Inglis,

> …the Oath of Allegiance…does not increase the Civil Obligation to Loyalty; it only strengthens the social Tie by uniting it with that of Religion. This may serve to expose the Delusion of some, who imagine they are under little or no Obligation to Loyalty, or 'to honour the King,' because they have not taken the Oath of Allegiance.[36]

One's duty to obey civil powers was not created by the oath, but rather oaths affirmed previous obligations.

Given the union of church and state in the English monarch, colonial Anglican clergymen considered their church particularly suited to encourage civil obedience. In conjunction with their sacred oath, ministers also recognized their professional duty to inculcate loyalty to government. Especially in comparison with dissenters, the Church of England's members asserted the church's long-standing fidelity to the Crown and to principles of order. As Thomas Bradbury Chandler wrote,

[t]he principles of submission and obedience to lawful authority are as inseparable from a sound, genuine member of the Church of England, as any religious principle whatsoever. This Church has always been famed and respected for its loyalty, and its regard to order and government. Its annals have been never stained with the history of plots and conspiracies, treasons and rebellions. Its members are instructed in their duty to government by Three Homilies on Obedience, and six against Rebellion, which are so many standing lessons to secure their fidelity.[37]

Charles Inglis agreed emphatically that the church's principles inculcated loyalty to the sovereign. 'How any one therefore who is well grounded in the Principles of this Church, can rebel against his rightful Sovereign ... or attempt to destroy that happy Constitution, whose Ruin would involve that of his Church – is utterly unaccountable.'[38] From these judgments, ministers reasoned that it was their special responsibility to encourage peaceableness and political fidelity. In an address to the governor, the clergy of Pennsylvania promised in 1760 that '... we are heartily disposed and shall at all times esteem it a most essential part of our Duty whilst we are propagating the interest of Religion & Virtue to inculcate obedience to our most Gracious Sovereign and to all who are put in authority under him.'[39] In exchange for their loyalty, a few Anglican ministers even suggested that they should be rewarded with the appointment of a colonial bishop.[40]

During the riots over stamp duties and subsequent disputes about Parliamentary authority, SPG missionaries in New England wrote to British authorities emphasizing their own loyalty, their parishioners' fidelity, and the positive influence of Anglicanism, in contrast to dissenting churches. Jeremiah Leaming of Connecticut reported that '[i]n the northeast part of this Colony there have been most rebellious outrages committed, on account of the Stamp Act, while those towns where the Church has got footing, have calmly submitted to the civil authority. This has been remarked, and by the dissenters themselves, to the honour of the Church.'[41] A letter from the clergy of Massachusetts and Rhode Island dated 15 May 1766 similarly proclaimed their goal of encouraging 'Obedience & Loyalty.'[42] As well as noting their loyal efforts, several individuals also took the opportunity to lay blame for the turmoil upon dissenting clergymen. William Agar from Cambridge, Massachusetts, wrote to the SPG in April 1766 that the 'Harangues' of some Congregationalist and Presbyterian ministers had encouraged riots, insulted government, and threatened those who did preach loyalty.[43] The Bishop of London agreed that the episcopal clergy had demonstrated the 'Temper and Moderation' of their profession.[44] Contrasting themselves with their dissenting neighbors, Anglican ministers considered the inculcation of obedience and loyalty to government as a vital part of their responsibilities as members of the established church.

The Anglican sense of obligation to defend the civil powers may be attributed not only to establishmentarian philosophies, but also to their understanding of English history in the seventeenth century. Differing interpretations of seventeenth-century England encouraged churchmen and nonconformists to view civil authority in an opposing manner. In his sermon of 30 January 1750 at Boston, on the anniversary of the beheading of King Charles I, the Congregationalist minister Jonathan Mayhew derided the Anglican policy of unlimited submission by challenging their interpretation of Romans 13.[45] Anglican ministers also remembered the anniversary of Charles I's death, not to applaud the right of resistance, but rather to lament those dark days of rebellion. Charles Inglis's sermon on the same date in 1780 described the reasons for Anglican celebration of this anniversary. 'To raise a just abhorrence for such atrocious Crimes – to preserve in our Minds a proper Sense of the Honour due to our Sovereign ... For these great Purposes, our Church has wisely and piously set apart this Day, as a Day of public Humiliation and Prayer.'[46] For this Anglican clergyman, 30 January represented an opportunity for reflection and recollection of the chaos which resulted from disobedience to lawful authority. By restoring the British monarchy 11 years after Charles I's execution, the hand of providence had clearly interceded on behalf of monarchy. Noting that 'a Rebellion of the same Kind now afflicts this Country,' Inglis wanted his American listeners to consider the lessons of their English past.[47] Similarly, Jonathan Boucher looked to the English Civil War to explain the events of the American Revolution. Because of the failure of that English 'Grand Rebellion' and the subsequent restoration of the monarchy, Boucher concluded that the American Revolution, as well as the French Revolution, would fail and monarchy be restored.[48] Like Inglis, Boucher believed that the hand of providence would intercede decisively on behalf of monarchy.

For Anglican clergymen, the lessons to be learned from England's Glorious Revolution at the end of the seventeenth century were considerably more ambiguous. This revolution, which resulted in the flight of King James II and his replacement by William III and Mary II, generated controversy concerning the legitimate limits of human obedience to divinely instituted authorities.[49] When the ruling powers change, to whom does one owe obedience – the *de jure* or the *de facto* king? Most of the High Church Party, which emphasized passive obedience and devotion to hereditary monarchy, disapproved of William and tried to maintain their loyalty to the House of Stuart. The Archbishop of Canterbury, some of his colleagues, and three or four hundred inferior clergy, refused to swear allegiance to the new sovereigns since they previously had sworn fidelity to James II. Consequently, these non-jurors were deprived of their offices and many fled to Scotland. Latitudinarians of the church, who benefitted from the defection of non-juring bishops, were able in good conscience to serve William and Mary.[50] Such individuals reconciled their behavior with the church's principle of obedience by suggesting that scriptural injunctions to obey the governing authorities were metaphoric lessons to encourage obedience to authority; when the ruling powers changed, so should one's allegiance.

As inheritors of the Glorious Revolution Settlement, which had included provisions for constitutional monarchy and religious toleration, colonial Anglican clergymen of the late eighteenth century did not wish to dispute or unravel the political changes made since 1688. Even Anglican loyalists, who affirmed the political superiority of British institutions, wanted to separate themselves from non-juring, and therefore disloyal, doctrines of passive obedience and non-resistance. Clearly referring to the Glorious Revolution, William Smith, a Philadelphia minister who inclined toward patriotism before 1776, asserted that '[a] continued submission to violence is no tenet of our church,' and he reminded his listeners that nearly a century ago Englishmen had required their King to govern according to the laws. He further explained that '[t]he doctrine of absolute NON-RESISTANCE has been fully exploded among every virtuous people. The free-born soul revolts against it.'[51] Two loyalists also wanted to disassociate themselves from the doctrine of passive obedience. Charles Inglis asserted emphatically, 'I am none of your passive obedience and non-resistance men,' and similarly Samuel Seabury insisted that 'passive obedience and non-resistance … is too much for *me*. I cannot swallow it; and if I could, I am sure my stomach would never digest it.'[52] By affirming William's revolution and the subsequent political settlement, the Church of England ministers had modified the church's traditional message of passive obedience to English monarchs; colonial ministers during the American Revolution drew upon that legacy.

The Church of England's pursuit of a theological *via media* or 'golden mean' between Puritanism and Roman Catholicism may have served as a model for its political position on civil obedience.[53] After the Glorious Revolution, Anglican civil theology as articulated by Whig clergymen of the Church of England no longer asserted a doctrine of absolute obedience. Nor did it proclaim the right of human resistance with the passion of a Puritan sermon. Preferring a middle path, Anglicanism continued to assert the importance of civil obedience and order, but recognized the necessity and propriety of human resistance to unlawful authority, particularly in the legacy of the Glorious Revolution. The existence of a middle ground does not suggest, however, any unanimity of opinion. Much as High Churchmen and latitudinarians differed about the width of the Anglican middle path, particularly about toleration toward dissenters, so the concept of a middle path also helps to explain differing Anglican political philosophies by the time of the American Revolution. If compared, the opinions of individuals on each outer edge of the path might share so few qualities that they would appear, at first glance, to be following different roads. By examining the views of several of the more partisan Anglican ministers, the diversity of ministerial opinion, or the width of this 'middle path,' becomes apparent.

Jonathan Boucher and George Micklejohn held opinions on passive obedience which approached absolute non-resistance and closely resembled the high-Tory position in the eighteenth century. Basing his text on Romans 13: 1–2, Rev. George Micklejohn of North Carolina delivered a sermon, entitled 'On the Important Duty of Subjection to the Civil Powers,' to Governor William Tryon and the troops raised to quell the Regulator insurrection. Micklejohn, a Scot who had come to North Carolina as an SPG missionary two years earlier, served as a mediator for the Regulators. Speaking on 25 September 1768, he condemned resistance to government as an offense against the Lord and provided the ultimate reason for subjection to government. '... [T]hough they [rebels] may escape from the sword of justice in this life, they cannot escape the DAMNATION of HELL.'[54] Envisioning no justification for resistance, his text employed a language which seemed, with its repetition of the word 'never,' to advocate absolute passive obedience regardless of the circumstances. 'Let it be considered then, that resistance to that lawful power and authority which God hath set over us, can never possibly be productive of any thing but the wildest uproar, and most universal confusion; and, in the end, can never fail of being attended with the most shocking and dismal effects.'[55] Although his comments concerned the Regulator disturbances specifically, Micklejohn appeared to attribute no admirable qualities to resistance – ever.

Jonathan Boucher, who became a most articulate spokesman for passive obedience, made his position clear in four colonial sermons which were later published as *A View of the Causes and Consequences of the American Revolution* (1797).[56] In 1770, he was appointed to St Anne's parish in Annapolis, Maryland, and the following year he acquired another parish in Prince George's County. Boucher's personal relationships influenced his subsequent loyalism; he married into the Dulany family and was a friend of Governor Robert Eden. A prosperous tobacco planter, Boucher earned a handsome annual salary and by 1775 owned property worth over £5000. A political conservative, Boucher's politics and social position dovetailed.[57] He has been described as an advocate of absolute obedience and non-resistance, but when his Maryland contemporaries leveled similar charges, Boucher denied them. '[It] ... is said to have been obtained that I have preached up the doctrine of *unlimited obedience* ... It is surprising that men, who pretend to some accuracy both in speaking and thinking, should thus confound things and words so totally different as *unlimited obedience* and *passive obedience*.'[58] Boucher's sermon 'On Civil Liberty, Passive Obedience, and Non-Resistance' did represent an extreme conservative view which, despite his protests, narrowed the difference between unlimited and passive obedience. He had likely become more conservative and reactionary by 1797 because of his understanding of the French Revolution. Having witnessed the ultimate effects of unbridled rights of resistance, Boucher assumed a defensive posture which affirmed the benefits of order and good government.

Boucher recognized that since the Glorious Revolution, the doctrines of passive obedience and non-resistance had been denounced by virtually everyone who wrote upon the subject, thereby acknowledging that his own contrary views were a minority position.

It really is a striking feature in our national history, that, ever since the Revolution, hardly any person of any note has preached or published a sermon, into which it was possible to drag this topic, [passive obedience and non-resistance] without declaring against this doctrine. It seems to have been made a kind of criterion or test of principle, and the watchword of a party ... whilst the right of resistance has thus incessantly been delivered from the pulpit, insisted on by orators, and inculcated by statesmen, the contrary position is still (I believe) the dictate of religion, and certainly the doctrine of the established Church, and still also the law of the land.[59]

Boucher refused to believe that non-resistance involved a continued submission to violence since, in his mind, violence could never exist within a lawful government but rather consisted of man's rejection of the authority of government. To him the doctrine of non-resistance was not a 'degrading and servile principle' but rather a philosophy of 'superior dignity.' Wise men, Boucher reasoned, will endure some inconvenience rather than 'self-opinionatedly disturb the quiet of the public.'[60] Furthermore, human rights of resistance did not depend upon the character of the government. Humans owed obedience to a mild and free government, but '[i]f it be less indulgent and less liberal than in reason it ought to be, still it is our duty not to disturb and destroy the peace of our community, by becoming refractory and rebellious subjects, and *resisting the ordinances of God.*' Boucher stopped just short of declaring absolute or unlimited obedience by distinguishing between active and passive behavior. No government can rightfully compel its subjects into 'an active compliance' with anything inconsistent with God's laws since men had a prior and superior obligation to obey God. Therefore one could not perform any act which would violate God's laws, but neither could men rebel against the civil authority; in such cases, passive obedience consisted of non-compliance with civil law, but an acceptance of the worldly penalties attached to such disobedience.[61]

Although Boucher's own words and subsequent historical analysis stamped a reactionary political doctrine on colonial Anglicanism, undoubtedly many ministers adopted a more moderate position. Another loyalist, Samuel Seabury, did not deny the right of active resistance as categorically as Boucher, but rather he contextualized the problem with more direct references to the Anglo-American disputes. Born in Connecticut and educated at Yale, by the late 1760s Seabury was serving as rector of St Peter's Anglican church in Westchester, New York, where he penned a pro-British series 'Letters from a Westchester Farmer.' During the war he served as a British chaplain, but despite his loyalism he later became the first bishop of the American Protestant Episcopal Church. Both an American and a defender of the empire, Seabury recognized a legitimate role for human resistance to authority, but he very carefully qualified and contextualized the principle. St Peter and St Paul had lived under the government of heathen emperors who persecuted Christians, he noted. 'And yet it was to these Emperors and Magistrates, – even to Nero and Caligula – that the Apostles commanded Honor and Respect, at all Times; and whenever it could be done consistently with Obedience to God, Duty and Submission.'[62] Buried within this injunction of obedience, Seabury included the principle of resistance: one need not submit to a ruler if that would be inconsistent with obedience to God. Nonetheless, the failure of rulers and governors to perform their duty should not necessarily encourage a disobedient reaction from their subjects. Men sometimes misjudged those in public positions. As Seabury asked:

> Shall we give the Reigns to Passion and Whim and Caprice, and break through all the Bonds of Society, because they whom God's Providence hath placed over us have failed in their Duty? To act thus would be to endeavour to remedy an Evil by doing a greater. It would be to dissolve all the Ties of Government, and introduce Anarchy, and Oppression, and Confusion, because some of the Officers of Government had behaved amiss.[63]

Seabury wanted his readers to weigh the unlikely benefits of justified opposition against the probable disastrous consequences, namely the destruction of law and order.

In Seabury's mind, the level of public resistance against authority needed to match the severity of the crimes, and he simply did not believe that the patriots' cause was justifiable. 'The operation of the laws certainly ought not to cease any farther than the necessary struggles for liberty require. A small struggle will not justify a total subversion of law and good government.' Resistance to authority sometimes could be justified, as in the Glorious Revolution, but Seabury distrusted those who generalized about men's rights of resistance from that example. He defended the principle of resistance as it applied to the Glorious Revolution, but emphatically denied that the American revolutionaries possessed any such justification.

> Some ... plead the necessity of the times, and pronounce boldly, that when any people are struggling for liberty, the operation of the laws must, of course, cease, and the authority of government subside: And in support of this position, they alledge the instance of that memorable revolution in England, which placed the great King William on the throne. However necessary that revolution may have been to secure the rights and liberties of the English nation, no man, I am persuaded, who really loves his country, would wish to see it again torn by such violent convulsions as it then endured. People who talk so very feelingly, and with so much pleasure about revolutions, and who are ever ready to justify the most violent, and the most needless opposition to government, by the example of the great revolution in England, seem to me to be too fond of revolutions to be good subjects of any government on earth.[64]

As Seabury also argued elsewhere, the pretenses for the American Revolution were 'frivolous and groundless ... [and] founded in Impiety, Ingratitude and Falshood.'[65] Given the impropriety of the colonial rebellion and the greatness of William's revolution, any comparison with the Glorious Revolution would be, at best, inappropriate and, at worst, sacrilegious. Patriot ministers often tried to prove the righteousness of the rebel cause by describing the extent and severity of British oppression. Put in these terms, the difference between loyalist and patriot political philosophies did not center so much on the actual right of resistance, but rather on the necessity of resistance in a given set of circumstances. From the pages of the Old Testament, patriot Anglicans cited examples of corrupt kings and oppressed subjects as evidence for the propriety of their own resistance. From I Kings 21: 3, Rev. John Lewis of South Carolina employed the lesson of Naboth and Ahab to denounce George III and his ministers. Ahab, the King of Israel, had demanded the small, fertile vineyard of his subject Naboth, which the monarch intended to convert into a herb garden. When Naboth refused to give away the vineyard, his only inheritance, Ahab's wife, Jezebel, told her husband that Naboth's refusal of this property was 'highly derogatory of the kingly dignity and the power of the crown ...'[66] Jezebel then arranged for two men to bear false witness against Naboth by claiming that he had blasphemed God and the king, after which Naboth was removed from the city and stoned to death. As the patriot minister Lewis interpreted this lesson, Naboth died 'for asserting the just rights of man ... against the designed encroachments of an insolent and capricious tyrant. Thus proceeded Ahab, King of Israel, by the assistance of mean and wicked agents.' Passing beyond the scriptural lesson, Lewis provided an explanation of the text. Not only did Lewis create an analogy between Ahab and George III, but he also sought to prove that the crimes of the British monarch were more severe. Ahab had offered Naboth compensation for the vineyard, but Britain sought not only the vineyard but also colonial liberty without offering anything in return. Describing the British monarch as a 'modern Nero' and worse than Ahab, Lewis contended that Ahab had destroyed one man, but George III 'is not contented with the death of thousands ... In malignity and barbarity, he has far transcended all former history; and by a most happy effort, at length he has raised himself to such a glorious pitch of infamy, that he will never be excelled, or even equalled, by any tyrant of a future age.'[67]

Liberty, an important concept in Lewis's sermon on Naboth's vineyard, enjoyed a similarly exalted position in many patriot sermons. The very articulation of the word aimed to encourage support for the patriot cause by drawing upon both sacred and secular traditions: English political messages of liberty and the privileges of Englishmen, Enlightenment philosophies about the natural rights of man, and age-old religious injunctions against sin. In his depiction of liberty, Jacob Duché of Pennsylvania concerned himself with both civil and religious liberties. Although he later became a loyalist and tried to convince General George Washington of the errors of his ways, Duché's views on liberty in 1775 encouraged a patriotic outlook on the Anglo-American disputes. That year Duché, a native of the city and graduate of the College of Philadelphia, had become rector of Christ Church, Philadelphia. His sermon of 7 July 1775, based on Galatians 5: 1, argued that civil liberty was as much the gift of God as spiritual liberty '… and consequently, that we are bound to stand fast in our CIVIL as well as our SPIRITUAL FREEDOM.'[68] In his answer to Duché's patriotic sermon, Jonathan Boucher refuted his colleague's interpretation of civil liberty from this text. Boucher further contended that '[t]he word *liberty*, as meaning civil liberty, does not, I believe, occur in all the Scriptures.'[69] From his dual construction of liberty, Duché argued that the Apostles' injunctions to submit to human ordinances for the Lord's sake could not entail a submission to the unrighteous ordinances of unrighteous men.[70]

In replying to Duché's sermon, Jonathan Boucher deliberately began with the same scriptural text, Galatians 5: 1. Likewise, patriot ministers sometimes chose popular loyalist texts since their justifications of rebellion appeared stronger if argued from texts usually employed to defend the principles of passive obedience. In composing his patriot sermon of 31 December 1775, David Griffith of Virginia began with the same scriptural passage as George Micklejohn's speech of 1768. In fact, Griffith noted that advocates of an 'implicit obedience' often used this particular text, Romans 13: 1–2, 'which, they say, amount[s] to a full proof, that God commands and expects us to follow, implicitly and blindly, every dictate of our superiours.'[71] From this common starting point, the two ministers took diametrically opposite paths. Whereas Micklejohn's use of the text may be described as conventional, Griffith aimed to turn this classic text of passive obedience on its head. He defended resistance by describing the lives of the Apostles Peter and Paul, whose injunctions on behalf of obedience to civil authority were well known. When punished wrongfully, Paul did not submit quietly to injustice, but complained loudly and at Philippi refused to obey the commands of the magistrates.[72] Griffith reasoned that since the Apostle would never have behaved contrary to his preachings, Paul must not have advocated absolute obedience.

While recognizing the need for subordination in society, Griffith believed that mankind ought not to obey 'every dictate of their superiours, without doubting or murmuring.' Earlier in his career, Griffith had been accused of disobeying the SPG, but between 1771 and May 1776 he served Loudoun County parish in Virginia, which he left to become surgeon and chaplain of the Third Virginia Regiment. A distinguished patriot and later the first bishop-elect of Virginia, in 1775 Griffith affirmed the right of resistance. He declared that '[w]as infallibility conveyed to man with the powers of government, I would instantly subscribe to the doctrine.'[73] Seabury's recognition of human fallibility had led him to an entirely different conclusion; instead of justifying rebellion against authority, he urged hesitation since those who disobeyed government might themselves be wrong.[74] Fundamentally, Griffith's argument depended upon his notion that God consistently aimed for the happiness of mankind; human submission to tyrannical governments would thwart that goal. On another level, Griffith argued that the rebelling colonists were not 'resisting a power ordained of God, a power to whom they owe[d] obedience.' Colonists did not owe obedience to Parliament since 'the doctrine of transubstantiation is not a greater absurdity than the notion of America's being represented in the British parliament.'[75] In Griffith's analysis, the rebelling colonists aimed only for their rights as Englishmen.

In their assessment of England's crimes, patriot Anglicans found a justification for rebellion which relied on contractual principles or asserted the defensive nature of their struggle. In these responses, patriot Anglican ministers borrowed the arguments of dissenters or drew upon general justifications employed by patriots. Given the Church of England's traditional defense of the king and the English government, the decision of these patriot ministers to support the rebellion is fascinating. Unlike their loyalist brethren, patriot ministers had to modify their outlook, and active patriots concerned with matters of conscience had to rationalize their break with church leaders. In the Glorious Revolution, some found a precedent for opposing the king. Of course, George III was not James II, but the events of 1688 proved that even Anglicans could support the overthrow of a tyrannical monarch.

Northern missionaries, who wrote about their continued devotion to the king and the English government, sent letters to the SPG or the Bishop of London. In such documents, Anglican clergy usually insisted upon their loyalty or neutrality. Comparable pools of evidence about the rationalizations of patriot ministers do not exist. These clergymen demonstrated their patriotism more by their actions than by their introspective prose. Some of the most committed patriots resided in the southern colonies, but southern Anglican clergymen did not match their northern colleagues in the publication of books or pamphlets. In comparison with the voluminous private correspondence of SPG missionaries, the surviving literary material of patriot ministers is slim, and while behavioral evidence clearly demonstrates different levels of commitment, it rarely explains individual decisions or actions. John Bracken preached sermons requested by the revolutionaries on fast days and following the American victory at Saratoga. John Braidfoot refused to read Governor Dunmore's royal proclamation, and later served as chaplain to the Second Virginia Regiment from 1778 to 1781.[76] In these cases, the historical record demonstrates the patriotism of these ministers, but their reasons for joining the rebels remains a mystery. Only in a few rare instances did patriot clergymen, such as David Griffith or John Hurt, share the political philosophy which permitted them to support the rebel cause.

Although subject to individual interpretation, Anglican views on passive obedience and human resistance steered a middle path. This moderation as well as the conviction, shared by most clergymen, that the level of protest needed to match the degree of oppression, encouraged a kind of political casuistry to measure the justness of resistance in particular circumstances. As men of the gospel, Church of England ministers promoted peaceableness and social harmony, but they recognized the occasional need for armed confrontation, particularly in the defense of religious and civil liberties. As William Smith wrote of the Seven Years' War, '... if human Societies are instituted for any end at all, independent States may not only *defend* their Rights when invaded; but if they are already deprived or defrauded of them, they may demand restitution in the loudest and most importunate manner ...'[77] For many colonists, the circumstances of the 1760s and 1770s warranted a defensive posture. The dynamism of the revolutionary period, which found everything in flux, also challenged the very concept of obedience and facilitated stronger expressions of the right of resistance, even among Anglicans.

Revolutionaries, who did not feel any pressing need to justify warfare, carefully defended the justice of the American Revolution by interpreting the intentions of its participants and the defensive nature of the struggle.[78] Frequently motives were described in terms of the opposing concepts of tyranny or slavery and liberty. As John Hurt wrote in 1777, '... it was not through licentious opposition, or for conquest, we drew the sword, but for justice; not to introduce, but to prevent slavery ... in defence of the plainest rights.'[79] According to Rev. Thomas Coombe of Pennsylvania, in his patriot fast-day sermon of 20 July 1775, '[w]hatever measures have been entered into on our part, we can, with conscious sincerity, appeal to heaven, were purely *defensive*; and such as we were compelled to take, by the precipitancy ... and violence with which we have been proceeded against.'[80] Rev. Robert Cooper of South Carolina similarly defended the cases in which warfare was lawful: when one state is invaded and liberty or property threatened, or when one part of the nation or the governing party violates the country's original compact and threatens the constitution. In such cases, warfare is 'not only lawful but duty.' As long as the contest was not motivated by ambition or avarice, God would side with that injured party.[81] Rev. Daniel Batwell also reflected on the sincerity of patriot motives; he stated that if the Continental Congress aimed solely for the preservation of colonial rights and 'if no sparks of disloyalty ... lie concealed beneath the fair outside of public good ... then we have a good cause' and could expect divine aid.[82]

Loyalist clergymen who denied the propriety of resistance insisted on the necessity of order and, unlike patriots, attributed no such purity of motives to colonial rebels. Jonathan Boucher postulated that indebtedness had been 'an essential ingredient in the character of a conspirator' and perhaps a number of colonists had considered a political rupture with Britain as a means of escaping from their British debts.[83] According to Henry Caner, riots and mobs were '... the Effects of popular Govrmt, Sedition, Anarchy, & Violence, & all this flame kindled & kept alive by about 1/2 doz. men of bad principles & morals.'[84] Charles Inglis concluded that 'Republicans, smugglers, debtors and men of desperate fortunes, were the principal promoters of this unnatural rebellion.'[85] Instead of justifying warfare, loyalists attributed the spirit of rebellion to delusion, madness or infatuation.[86] In a language reminiscent of Anglican denunciations of evangelicalism, Rev. Ebenezer Thompson referred disapprovingly to patriotism as 'that Spirit of political enthusiasm ...'[87] Loyalists believed that these rebels may have employed techniques of deception as well as delusion. As Samuel Andrews of Connecticut warned, considerable ambiguity surrounded patriot evocations of 'liberty,' a word which could be used as a 'Cloak of Maliciousness.'[88] Rev. William Clark of Dedham, Massachusetts identified the liberty which infected people's minds as, in fact, an infatuated licentiousness, and Samuel Seabury also sounded the alarm by suggesting in 1774 that patriots who claimed only to desire redress of grievances secretly sought independence.[89]

Whereas patriots emphasized the justice of resistance, loyalists gave priority to the maintenance of constitutional law and public order, or 'legal liberty.'[90] They counseled that opposition should be directed through legitimate channels of authority, petitions, and remonstrances, even after patriots had lost patience with these tactics. Rather than locate oppression in the actions of British authorities, loyalists warned of enslavement through the activities of revolutionaries and their illegal committees. Insisting that revolutionary committees would bring about 'the most abject slavery,'

Samuel Seabury declared his preference for royal absolutism. 'No, if I must be enslaved, let it be by a KING at least, and not by a parcel of upstart lawless Committee-men. If I must be devoured, let me be devoured by the jaws of a lion, and not *gnawed* to death by rats and vermin.'[91] After likening the revolutionary committees of public safety to a 'papish Inquisition,' Seabury argued that the rebels had violently infringed upon the laws of society. 'But the congress are a body unknown to the government. In a *legal* sense, they are no *body at all*.'[92] Similarly, Samuel Andrews hoped that those who had 'assumed a self-constituted Power of nullifying Acts of Parliament ... will not legalize Resistance against the Supreme Power of the Nation.'[93] As the poet Jonathan Odell expressed, tyranny had passed to the hands of the multitude, as embodied in the Congress.[94] Rather than restoring peace and harmony between Britain and her colonies, Thomas Bradbury Chandler argued that the Continental Congress had 'inflame[d] their minds with resentment against their lawful superiors, and animate[d] them to rebellion.'[95]

In the tumult, freedom of speech had been curtailed, and at least one Maryland minister claimed that the right of *habeas corpus* had been suspended.[96] From jail in Baltimore, Rev. John Patterson demanded repeatedly that he be provided with a copy of the charges brought against him, but to no avail. He wrote to the Governor and Council of Maryland that he had been deprived of his freedom for more than six months not by any lawful authority, but by arbitrary power.[97] Rev. William Clark similarly likened his court experiences to a 'Romish Inquisition,' since he did not know the charges alleged against him, he was denied legal counsel, and he could not hear the proceedings due to his deafness. With equal indignation, Clark also noted that he had been shut in a room for almost an hour to stare at a picture of Oliver Cromwell.[98] From the perspective of constitutional conservatives or imprisoned loyalists, rebel committees had appropriated power in an illegal manner until they themselves became the voice of tyranny.

In addition to considering the legality of the Revolution, many loyalist Anglican ministers displayed a calculated pragmatism as they considered the possible outcome of a violent contest with England. As Chandler remarked, 'Even a final victory would effectually ruin us; as it would necessarily introduce civil wars among ourselves, and leave us open and exposed to the avarice and ambition of every maritime power in Europe or America.'[99] If victory would ruin America, so too would defeat, and without military stores, discipline or money the rebel colonies had little chance of success against Britain's accomplished army and navy.[100] Seabury also reasoned that if the Anglo-American disputes escalated to the point of war, in all probability 'the power of the British arms would prevail: And then, after the most dreadful scenes of violence and slaughter – CONFISCA-TIONS and EXECUTIONS must close the HORRID TRAGEDY.'[101]

On the subject of non-importation and non-exportation, several ministers assumed the pragmatic position that the proposed activities would not yield the desired effects. The tax on tea was but a 'trifling' issue according to Chandler, an issue which could easily have been avoided by not purchasing the controversial commodity or by sending it back undamaged.[102] Because the Sons of Liberty at the Boston Tea Party had acted in a manner inconsistent with the law, Chandler considered that the punishment of 'merely shutting the port until satisfaction made for injury' was merited.[103] Jonathan Boucher and Samuel Seabury both opposed non-importation schemes in which, they believed, colonial advocates had overestimated their importance to Britain's economy. As Boucher asked:

> Can we seriously believe, that this wealth, and power is derived almost entirely, from her North American Colonies? ... Shall we punish ourselves, like froward children, who refuse to eat, when they are hungry, that they may vex their indulgent mothers? ... Let us beware how we engage in such an unequal contest, lest while we are giving her a slight wound, we receive a mortal one.[104]

Seabury considered that non-importation might be effective, but 'to our own hurt.' He likened the scheme to the act of firing a pistol; it shoots vigorously no matter where it is pointed, but the consequence of aiming at oneself greatly changes the outcome. Britain would soon find new sources of trade and '[o]ur malice would hurt ourselves only.'[105] Instead, like other opponents of non-importation, he advocated the use of petitions and remonstrances which were consistent with the law. They had worked previously to repeal the Stamp Act and the Townshend duties on glass, lead, and paint, he argued. Asserting an imperial vision of economics, Seabury contended that the earlier repeal of these measures proved that duties injurious to trade, once felt in England, would be amended.[106]

Privileging order and the imperial connection, loyalist Anglican clergymen frequently described the Revolution as an 'unnatural' conflict. The dispute was unnatural, since it arose within a single family and escalated to the point where it could not be resolved by rekindling traditional affections.[107] Charles Inglis declared in 1776 that '[t]he present Rebellion is certainly one of the most causeless, unprovoked & unnatural that ever disgraced any Country – a Rebellion marked with peculiarly aggravated Circumstances of Guilt and Ingratitude.'[108] Most often, loyalists and not patriots described the war as unnatural, although a patriot could cite the irregularity of a parent invading the rights of a child.[109] In particular, the rising level of disaffection toward the king appeared quite unnatural to colonial Anglicans. Although loyalists described their allegiance to the king in the most glowing terms, even Anglican patriots appeared reluctant to denounce the monarch in the abusive manner of their non-Anglican colleagues.

A carefully cultivated belief in the justice of their cause and the sincerity of their intentions inclined patriots and loyalists each to believe that God was on their side. In turn, that understanding encouraged opposition to the machinations of their enemies and a fervent denial that one's opponents enjoyed God's favor. The patriot minister John Hurt warned his listeners that they should not 'shut God out of our councils and designs … [o]ur unnatural enemies have their earthly king, their lords spiritual & temporal to apply to on this occasion; let us chuse on our part the Lord of lords for our God and for our king.'[110] In his mind, loyalists merely had the support of earthly ecclesiastical authorities. Similarly the loyalist Charles Inglis denied his opponents' claims of divine assistance:

> Let enthusiastic Republicans belie Heaven, if they will, by claiming its Sanction to Schemes which have Falshood, Rebellion and Usurpation, for their Basis – turning Faith into Faction, and the Gospel of Peace, into an Engine of War and Sedition. We dare not thus prevaricate, or trifle with the living God; or handle his Word deceitfully.[111]

Inglis believed that patriot claims of providential guidance involved both duplicity and self-deception.

Each side urged its followers to sustain this divine support through prayer and the avoidance of all sinful behavior. As Rev. William Currie of Pennsylvania explained in the middle of the eighteenth century, national judgments resulted from national crimes, which proceeded not from ignorance of God's commands but rather from deliberate defiance of His laws.[112] During the revolutionary contest, community repentance formed an integral part of patriot activities, in part due to the belief that God had unleashed civil war as a punishment for community sinfulness. As Jacob Duché understood, 'the dark cloud of judgment, which now hangs over our heads, hath risen from our unnumbered sins and rebellions' against God. Only repentance and reformation could reinstate or ensure the continuation of God's blessings.[113] A program for the reformation of manners could lead, in turn, to the political salvation of the nation. 'Being *united*, in what we believe is a righteous cause … we should be *sure* that the cement of our union be VIRTUE – *Political* salvation, as well as *spiritual*, *depends* on virtue.'[114] As they argued, both political and spiritual salvation depended upon the unanimous expression of a spirit of virtue.

Despite this belief in divine punishment for community sinfulness, patriots continued to perceive the American colonies as peculiarly favored with God's blessings. Like Old Testament Israelites, colonial Puritans had conceived of themselves as a 'chosen people,' but throughout the eighteenth century this divine mission had been transferred to the American landscape itself. From the first settlement, the American colonies had been distinguished by providential blessings: '[t]hey have indeed been a VINE-YARD PLANTED BY THE LORD'S RIGHT HAND.' Consequently, opposition to Britain could be justified because the mother country threatened to 'cut down and destroy this branch of thine own vine, the very branch, which Providence hath made strong.'[115] Similarly, Rev. Thomas Coombe considered that America was peculiarly blessed since the country had arisen 'beneath the smile of heaven.'[116] In a sermon in November 1775 the South Carolina minister Paul Turquand articulated similar sentiments by describing America's holy demeanor and its first settlers as 'chosen seed.'[117] In a manner sympathetic to both Puritanism and patriot civil religion, Rev. Robert Cooper attributed the founding of New England to divine providence.

> In respect of that colony which is at present the seat of war, it may be also said, that God did great things for their ancestors, which I cannot but think affords encouragement to hope, that he will not now forsake that people. They were brought from a land, then groaning under oppression in regard of religious liberty, and stained with the blood of persecution, not through the Red-sea, but across the Atlantic; and preserved through all the difficulties and dangers attending a settlement among wild beasts and savages. Al[l] who read the history of the planting and progress of the colony of Massachusetts-Bay, may find great instances of God's goodness ...[118]

Such an account may reveal great tolerance for dissenters in its depiction of providence's role in the settling of Massachusetts, but also Cooper may have been affected by a political unity of purpose with dissenting patriots which was more significant to him than religious divisions. On American soil, even where the first colonists had rejected the Church of England, God's providence could be found. In very persuasive prose, Rev. James Madison similarly proclaimed, 'America has become the theatre, whereon the providence of God is now manifested.'[119]

By affirming England's role as the source of colonial destiny, loyalist civil theology articulated a very different idea from the prevailing patriot interpretation of America's favored status. Although Boucher considered the period of colonial infancy to be past, he believed that colonial destiny did not lie outside the British empire.

From the infancy of our Colonies, to this very hour, we have grown up and flourished under the mildness and wisdom of her excellent laws ... We have been very lately rescued by her from enemies ... Let us then no longer disgrace ourselves by illiberal, ungrateful reproaches, by meanly ascribing the most generous conduct to the most sordid motives.

In Boucher's view, American colonists owed their birth and progress to Britain. By pleading with Congress to open the eyes of 'our infatuated countrymen' and show them 'their happy situation, [when compared] with the wretchedness of nine tenths of the globe,' Boucher asserted his belief that the providential destiny of the colonies depended upon their continued relationship with the mother country.[120]

Whereas Anglican political thought by the eighteenth century included both principles of resistance and obedience, the American Revolution caused a dichotomization of that aspect of civil religion which involved ideas of national destiny. In the aftermath of the Declaration of Independence, patriots sought their political destiny independent from Britain, whereas loyalists continued to believe that American prosperity depended upon the imperial relationship. Independence, by rupturing the empire, mitigated against the adoption of any middle path between conflicting beliefs about the colonies' providential destiny. A patriot philosophy which drew upon dissenting traditions to assert the favored status of American soil conflicted directly with earlier notions of an imperial and transatlantic British community. Whereas Anglican theology since the Glorious Revolution had accepted and operated within a delicate balance between resistance and obedience, the diametrically opposite views of national destiny that emerged in the Revolution could not be reconciled. The casuistical balancing of commitments to obedience and resistance could no longer serve as a guide for Anglican civil theology, which in the Revolutionary environment broke into patriot and loyalist portions.

5 The Depoliticization of the Colonial Anglican Clergy

The American Revolution transformed and popularized politics, which expanded beyond the traditional assemblies to revolutionary committees and the community at large, but the Anglican clerical community experienced an opposite but parallel process of depoliticization. One result of the political mobilization of the people consisted of a corresponding decline in the relative socio-political influence of traditional community leaders, including the clergymen of many denominations. The Revolution also witnessed a broadening of the republican aversion to artificial social distinctions into a denunciation of all differences. Among a growing segment of the voting public, experience, education, and wealth became liabilities rather than assets in attaining public office. This collapse of traditional deference affected religious leaders as well as politicians since the American Revolution, like the Great Awakening, involved a reordering of ecclesiastical power relationships. Revivalism emphasized a more direct relationship between God and man, thereby limiting the influence of clerical mediators, and the American Revolution also involved a restraining and reordering of clerical political roles.

Ministers of established Protestant denominations found their status in society had eroded as a consequence of the Revolution and the empowerment, or growing presumptuousness, of their congregations. The public demanded that ministers be more responsive to their particular religious opinions, and ministers found themselves far more vulnerable to dismissal.[1] Disestablishment and the burgeoning trend of separating church and state also affected ministerial influence. By examining the Anglican clergymen's activities and political involvement during the turbulent war years, this chapter demonstrates how the majority altered their political conduct. While many clergy continued to perform baptisms, weddings, and funerals, circumstances forced them to consider discontinuing other public services of worship and even shutting their church doors. As tensions escalated, most ministers of the Church of England withdrew from the public domain, even as they made choices of loyalism or patriotism.

The proportion of loyalists and patriots among the Anglican clergy varied regionally. In the middle colonies and New England, the vast majority of Anglican ministers were loyalists, but in the southern colonies most were patriots. The proportion of Anglicans who were loyalists in each colony was in inverse ratio to their numbers, as conscious religious minorities tended to be loyalist.[2] In Virginia, where Anglicanism had a long history as the established church, the Anglican clergy clearly favored patriotism, although individual levels of participation varied. One might estimate that one-third of the clergy were patriots in Maryland, three-quarters in South Carolina, five out of 11 in North Carolina, two out of four in Georgia, and almost 80 per cent in Virginia.[3] Table 5.1 presents slightly differently results by including neutrality. In New York and New Jersey only one minister in each colony was a patriot, and in Pennsylvania the rural clergy displayed their loyalty to Britain and the five ministers of Philadelphia were divided in opinion.[4] In Connecticut, the 23 ministers were loyalists, and the vast majority remained at their posts through the Revolution. In New England, outside of Connecticut, only a few ministers can be considered patriots, or more suitably, lukewarm Tories. In fact, many of the clergy became loyalist exiles, and at the end of the Revolution, there were only four in Massachusetts, one in New Hampshire, and none in Rhode Island or Maine.[5]

Table 5.1   Political orientation of Anglican clergy, 1775–83

	Loyalists	*Patriots*	*Neutrals*	*Total**
Virginia	28	58	44	130
Maryland	17	11	30	58
North Carolina	3	6	2	11
South Carolina	5	6	11	22
Georgia	2	2	0	4
Pennsylvania**	6	1	9	16
New Jersey	7	1	3	11
New York	16	1	2	19
Connecticut	23	0	0	23
Massachusetts	11	2	3	16
Maine	2	0	0	2
New Hampshire	2	0	0	2
Rhode Island	1	0	3	4
Total	123	88	107	318

*Total number of Anglican clergy in each colony, 1775–83.
**Pennsylvania category includes Delaware.
Note: Table 5.1 provides only a general guide since it does not measure time-specific elements of political affiliation or account for the changing position of ministers. Each minister has been assigned to one particular category based on his entire revolutionary career.

Although studies on Anglicanism in the Revolution have noted different degrees of political commitment as they have separated loyalists from patriots, this structural dichotomization gives little attention to issues of neutrality or the changing process of depoliticization. For the purposes of this chapter, depoliticization refers to the voluntary or involuntary behavior of withdrawing from discussions or actions of political import. The revolutionaries deliberately attempted to quiet those who opposed them or were lukewarm in their affection for the patriot cause. Such behavior on the part of Anglican clergymen sometimes resulted from an acquiescence to rebel demands, but neutrality, they thought, or at least a convincing outward appearance of silence, might also offer protection against individual persecution and serve as a strategy for the survival of the colonial church. Neutrality, or depoliticization, could be achieved in several different ways. One might draw upon an accepted trait of Anglican peaceableness to promote an Anglo-American reconciliation since a speedy resolution of the conflict would end all personal and professional danger. When reconciliation became unlikely, individuals could refrain from making public commentaries on the Revolution or cease to perform actions associated with the advance of any particular political position.

Depoliticization does not describe every individual, since some followed the Revolution's process of radicalization or were eliminated from the debate. While living in Scotland in the 1760s, Alexander Balmaine sympathized with American resistance, and his patriot inclinations did not wane with his arrival in Virginia. In 1777 he became a chaplain of the Thirteenth Virginia Regiment.[6] Alternatively, loyalists like Charles Inglis, Jonathan Boucher, or Thomas Bradbury Chandler were vocal opponents of the Revolution; their exile to England clearly diminished their colonial political influence, but they were not depoliticized so much as forced out of the American political discussion. Nonetheless, as a general concept, depoliticization still helps to explain the experiences of the majority of colonial Anglican ministers.

Because the concept of depoliticization presumes a level of political activity and community involvement from which historical characters withdrew, an evaluation of the public roles of pre-Revolutionary Anglican clergymen serves as a necessary point of contrast. From the pulpit, colonial ministers of all denominations provided their parishioners with a regular medium of public communication. The churched population certainly exceeded the unchurched, and colonial ministers did not look down from their pulpits upon empty pews.[7] Despite reduced attendance during wartime, clergymen still had opportunities to influence their parishioners. As educators and authors, Anglican ministers often acquired respect and social standing.[8] Many enjoyed friendships with powerful local elites or royal governors, and others had married into prominent colonial families. Although the eighteenth-century world determined social standing from a combination of traits, the office of clergyman did confer a degree of respectability.

The themes of colonial Anglican sermons do not indicate any great propensity for political discussions before the Revolution, as sermon literature focused on salvation and spirituality. The message from New England dissenting pulpits also remained other-worldly. Occasional sermons provided ministers with the opportunity for political commentary, but regular preaching centered on salvation.[9] Like their dissenting counterparts, Anglican ministers delivered political sermons at particular moments throughout the eighteenth century. Unique events such as the coronation of George III or the Seven Years' War inspired sermons on colonial allegiance to the king, the empire and Protestantism. At the local level, elections or internal conflict provided occasions for political discussion. Thomas Barton's *The Conduct of the Paxton-Men* was a response to a popular uprising in Pennsylvania.[10] Such opportunities existed after the Revolution as well, at the death of George Washington or at the anniversary of patriot victories. Nonetheless, these post-Revolutionary moments were also occasions for the expression of Federalist sentiment, or political conformity. Later, the War of 1812 found the bishops and ministers of the Episcopal Church more united in their support for the American cause than in 1776.[11]

Although moments for political commentary existed in postwar America, ministers did not enjoy the same stature in the community. Deference to ministerial opinion had declined, and consequently the collective impact of their political messages subsided. Clergymen of many denominations noted their loss of prestige in the last half of the eighteenth century, and they did not find in revolutionary politics a certain avenue for recovering their already declining intellectual leadership.[12] The patriotism of New England dissenting ministers temporarily helped them to weather the political storms of revolution, at least longer than colonial Anglicanism, but the disestablishment of Congregationalism soon followed in the nineteenth century. Consequently, the depoliticization of the Anglican clergy was not an entirely unique phenomenon, but rather a trend which the Revolution enhanced or even accelerated. The colonial Church of England's association with the king and the English government meant that its ministers would experience this trend decisively during the Revolutionary War, but in many ways the SPG missionaries of New England or the middle colonies had regularly distanced themselves from local politics. The minority status of their church in these regions had long prevented any close association with provincial government.

In the early years of the Revolution, many Anglican clergymen took an active role indicative of their status as community leaders. Ministers who owed their positions to the local establishment, Anglicans in the southern colonies or Congregationalists in New England, performed a number of official duties. Particularly in Maryland, Virginia, and the Carolinas, Anglican ministers served as chaplains to provincial governments. SPG missionaries in New England or the middle colonies usually did not share in these public duties. Jacob Duché delivered the opening prayers at the convening of the First Continental Congress, but many other clergy performed similar functions in provincial governments.[13] The chaplaincy of the Maryland House of Delegates was an official duty of the rector of St Anne's, but Jonathan Boucher claimed with little humility that he also had considerable influence in shaping legislation.[14] In Virginia, Thomas Gwatkin served in 1775 as chaplain to John Murray, Lord Dunmore, Governor of Virginia, and for many years William Hubbard acted as justice of the peace in his community. The South Carolina minister, Henry Purcell, was named in 1778 Deputy Judge Advocate-General of South Carolina and Georgia. James Reed of North Carolina also served as chaplain to the provincial assembly, which met in Newbern.[15]

Before independence, several ministers of the established Church of England served as chairmen or members of their local committees of safety or promoted non-importation agreements. As many as 23 Virginian ministers served on such committees, and on 27 May 1774 13 joined members of the House of Burgesses in signing an Association, which protested against the closing of the port of Boston.[16] SPG missionaries in the north were divided on the issue of taxation protests; William Clark of Massachusetts believed that Boston's Solemn League and Covenant would only herald civil war, but several New York missionaries supported non-importation.[17] In August 1774 the SPG missionary, Daniel Earl, served as the chairman of the freeholders meeting of Chowan County, North Carolina, which protested taxation measures, opposed the closing of Boston harbor, and determined to use only American manufactures. This meeting professed continued allegiance to the king.[18] Such participation was not necessarily indicative of a nascent American patriotism, since even the loyalist George Micklejohn performed services in 1775 at the Provincial Congress in Hillsboro, North Carolina, a body which also declared its allegiance to the king. In New York, the Reverends Auchmuty, Inglis, Moore, and Bowden all offered opening prayers at the meetings of the Provincial

Congress in 1775. Such government service only rarely extended beyond 1776. Thomas Price of Virginia had served as chaplain to the House of Burgesses since 1766, and continued in that capacity in 1775 and 1776, but not afterwards.[19] Samuel Provoost declined to preach before the New York Provincial Congress in 1776, and explained that because he held opinions which differed from his brethren, he had 'formed a resolution never to accept of any preferment during the present contest.'[20] Indicative of their committed patriotism, Reverends Madison and Cupples continued in government service. James Madison served as chaplain of the House of Delegates in Virginia for several sessions during the Revolution, and Charles Cupples was appointed chaplain of the North Carolina General Assembly in 1779, 1780, and 1781.[21]

During the Revolutionary War, Anglican ministers generally withdrew from positions in government which they held before the Declaration of Independence. In the period before 1775–76, Anglican clergy had more opportunities for political involvement since the possibility still existed for a settlement of the Anglo-American disputes within the framework of the empire. Like other moderates, several Anglican clergy advocated reconciliation or emphasized traits of peaceableness. Later, when forced to choose between America and Britain, political involvement became problematic, and incentives increased for the clergy to remain quiet.

Virtually all men of the Gospel could advocate peace as part of their Christian calling, and not surprisingly, sermons of every political inclination included such prayers. For loyalists, patriots and neutrals, the horrors of civil war and 'fraternal slaughter' especially encouraged a fervent desire for peace. In fact, the majority of ministers of all denominations between 1774 and 1776 hoped that a peaceful reconciliation could be achieved.[22] Among Anglicans, such prayers for peace did not necessarily assume a neutral tone. Patriot injunctions frequently included a supplication that George III be inspired with wisdom 'to discern and pursue the true interest of all his subjects' and that America obtain a redress of grievances and the restoration of 'her invaded rights.' Conversely, loyalist prayers hoped that the Americans could be brought 'to their Allegiance.'[23] The underlying desire for reconciliation sometimes encouraged a more neutral and forgiving tone. In a moment of magnanimity, loyalist Charles Inglis wrote 'I would most gladly, were it in my power, draw a veil of eternal oblivion over any errors which Great Britain or the colonies may have fallen into.'[24] At this juncture after the publication of *Common Sense*, Inglis wished for a peaceful resolution which would forgive all sins. The pragmatism of such prayers for peace resonate in the writings of Anglican clergymen. If all disputes could be resolved quickly, almost magically

by the hand of God, without the further escalation of disputes, the ministers' precarious personal and professional situations also would be solved.
As tensions escalated into civil war, such hopes faded.

Validating a quality they labeled 'peaceableness,' Anglican clergymen
could justify political inactivity when hope of a peaceful reconciliation
failed. In describing the characteristics of the Church of England, clergymen focused frequently on passive obedience and respect for government,
as well as an associated trait of peaceableness. Ebenezer Thompson, a
New England missionary, considered it his duty to inculcate religion in
such a way 'that we should always be possessed with an easy, peaceable
disposition, and that we study to be quiet and mind our own business, and
as much as lies in us to live peaceable with all men, and pay a ready and
dutiful obedience to the lawful commands of our superiors.'[25] Richard
Mansfield similarly acknowledged that patriots vilified Anglican ministers
for merely 'inculcating upon their Hearers the Duties of Peaceableness and
quiet Subjection to the Parent State.'[26] In stating this dual goal of living
quietly and yet simultaneously obeying authority, Reverends Thompson
and Mansfield did not consider how, in the context of revolution, these
goals became mutually contradictory.

While peaceableness was a prerequisite for a loyal submission to British
authority, its quietness could communicate a stance of neutrality. A clergyman of quiet demeanor, who chose not to participate actively in the Anglo-
American disputes, wished to offend neither side. Thomas Barton and
other Pennsylvanian clergy believed themselves to be 'under moral obligations ... to give no offence to either of the contending parties.'[27] As Rev.
James Reed of North Carolina reasoned, 'all America is in a most violent
Flame and every good man wou'd forbear as much as possible adding the
least Fuel to the Fire.'[28] Such behavior could easily be interpreted as disguised loyalism. William Smith acknowledged that his exhortations for a
peaceful reconciliation had been so frequent that he had been considered
'an advocate for the measures of administration against the Colonies.'[29]
The patriot view that loyalists included everyone who did not actively support revolutionary measures encouraged such conflations of peaceableness
with loyalism.

Although peaceableness could encourage a quiet inactivity, at least a
few ministers explored their potential role as mediators for peace. In his
diagnosis of Anglo-American disagreements, William Smith commented
in 1774 that the situation had resulted from a lack of 'mutual Good Will.'[30]
By inculcating Christian benevolence, ministers might provide an antidote
to the imperial disaffection, but their underlying desire not to offend mitigated against the adoption of any active or militant role as peacemakers.

In a letter to the Bishop of London in June 1775, the clergymen of Philadelphia expressed a wish that they might help to end the dispute. 'Would to God that we could become mediators for the Settlement of the unnatural Controversy that now distracts a once happy Empire.'[31] Like a wish made upon a star, these men had no intention of actively or publicly pursuing its achievement. They claimed to have missed no private opportunity to encourage peace

> [b]ut as to public advice we have hitherto thought it our Duty to keep our Pulpits wholly clear from every thing bordering on this contest, and to pursue that line of Reason and Moderation which became our Characters; equally avoiding whatever might irritate the Tempers of the people, or create a suspicion that we were opposed to the Interest of the Country in which we live.[32]

In his sermon of 20 July 1775 Rev. Daniel Batwell related the biblical story of King Rehoboam who assembled the house of Judah with the tribe of Benjamin to fight against the house of Israel, only to have war averted when a prophet convinced them to disarm. Batwell suggested that the parties of the present Anglo-American disputes needed a similar prophet to speak to them saying 'ye shall not go up, nor fight … return ye every man to his house.'[33] How attractive such a mythical character must have seemed to those clergy who wanted to avoid the appearance of supporting either side!

When reconciliation became unlikely after 1775, many Anglican ministers attempted to portray themselves as neutral participants by omitting political information or by refraining from commenting about public events. Thomas Jefferson himself recognized that some Virginian clergymen, at the beginning of the Anglo-American disputes, attempted to remain neutral, or in his words, 'aloof.'[34] Such silences present certain interpretative challenges. The omission of detail may have been inadvertent, deliberately intended to disguise virulent opinion, or conversely could reveal personal disinterestedness. When writing to friends or professional colleagues in England, ministers recognized that their position as eyewitnesses conveyed a certain responsibility to communicate the latest news about the war. How much detail they recorded depended upon their particular circumstances, their level of interest in politics, and their fear of discovery. Because a letter might be intercepted, ministers frequently communicated through a third party, especially the bearer of the letter, who could answer questions in person.[35]

Rev. Robert Andrews of Virginia began a letter in 1769 by declaring that if his reader expected political news, he was mistaken. Although the times warranted such discussions, Andrews suggested that his addressee probably would appreciate a relief from repetitive discussions of politics. Andrews wrote about astronomy.[36] Of course Andrews' professed boredom may disguise his apprehensions about a candid account of politics. Several Anglican ministers stated their anxieties in a manner which left less doubt. Ephraim Avery of New York attributed the lack of detail in his letter of 1776 to illness and the 'troublesome Times.' Similarly Rev. Christopher Newton in 1766 referred to 'the commotion in the country.'[37] Such vague references masked personal opinions and served to explain the infrequency of clerical correspondence. Other ministers attributed their negligence in writing to other difficulties of conveyance.[38]

The many extant vestry records and few ministerial notebooks or memoranda written during the Revolution rarely made reference to the war, except in the most general terms. Typically, William Selden of Virginia recorded payments received from his students and for baptisms, marriages, and funerals, but omitted other details.[39] Fearful of the potential repercussions, most churchwardens and vestrymen omitted all details about the war, and in many cases no vestry meetings are recorded after 1776 or 1777 until after the peace. St Paul's parish of Chowan County, North Carolina, which in April 1776 declared its firm support of the Continental Congress, represents a noteworthy exception. After a profession of allegiance to the king, this rare political statement affirmed that neither Parliament nor any other branch of the British government had the right to impose taxes on the colonies or to regulate internal matters.[40] Occasionally annual ledgers or other brief notations demonstrate continued clerical incumbency, but they rarely offer evidence about clerical political activities or the opinions of the vestry.[41] Prudence dictated the omission of such details.

Patriots closely observed the behavior of Anglican ministers who were assumed to be loyalists because of their personal and professional ties to England and due to the fame and vocality of a few loyalist clergy. Several Anglican ministers assembled in New York in 1777 reported that their 'Foes [were] ever watchful to turn every inadvertent Word, or Action, into [a] Matter of Accusation.'[42] Perhaps Abraham Beach of New Jersey best described the situation which he and his colleagues faced. 'To enter into Particulars would perhaps expose me to the Resentment of my Neighbours, which I would wish to avoid for the sake of the Church, as well as for my own. Every Letter is in danger of being exposed to public View, & Exceptions are taken at the most innocent Expressions.'[43] Charles Woodmason knew personally those dangers; Maryland authorities had intercepted his correspondence, thereby discovering him to be the author of several essays which defended episcopacy. With some confidence, Philip Reading sent his letter dated 18 March 1776 to the SPG; it had previously been seized from a ship bound for London and returned to Philadelphia. Since it subsequently passed the examination of a committee of inspection, Reading felt assured that it could now be safely sent again to London. While many loyalists or suspected loyalists omitted details in their correspondence, at least one patriot considered the posthumous ramifications of leaving a record of his opinions. Adam Smith of Virginia requested in his last will and testament that all his sermons, except two, be burned.[44]

Clerical reticence to discuss politics resulted undoubtedly from their fear of detection, but the SPG injunction against interfering in the internal affairs of the colonies also supported non-involvement. During the Seven Years' War the SPG had warned its missionaries to observe carefully the 11th Instruction to 'give no Offence to the Civil Government by intermedling in Affairs not relating to Your own calling & Function.'[45] By including the comment, 'I meddle but little with political Matters,' Roger Viets undoubtedly told the SPG what they wanted to hear.[46] During the Revolution, missionaries used this same injunction to assure state governments that they had been ordered not to interfere in civil affairs and that, consequently, they had done nothing inimical to the American cause. In an attempt to convince the Pennsylvania assembly in 1778 of their innocuous character, several clergy quoted from the text of the SPG instructions and claimed that they had adhered to their instructions and had 'not *intermeddled* directly or indirectly in the present melancholy contest nor done any act or thing inimical to the liberty or welfare of America.'[47] These petitioners did not choose to debate the mutual incompatibility of several injunctions. To revolutionaries the inculcation of obedience to traditional British authorities was itself an offensive form of interference.

The legacy of the Seven Years' War for SPG missionaries did not consist of a simple lesson on their duties to avoid all civil disputes. In fact, the entire text of the SPG instructions contained various internal inconsistencies, since it ordered missionaries to avoid 'intermeddling' in civil affairs, but simultaneously to encourage intercolonial cooperation and defense efforts. Philip Reading's *The Protestant's Danger, and the Protestant's Duty* (1755) defined American blessings, described the tyrannical practices of the French and Spanish, and proposed a program to avert the impending danger.[48] Reading's fervent call to action indicates his belief that he had a role to play as a motivator in the French–English contest. His geographic location in Pennsylvania, where pacifist Quakers were reluctant to engage in battle, may have occasioned such a succinct articulation of these beliefs in print. Also in 1755, Thomas Barton published a text, *Unanimity and Public Spirit*, intended to animate his parishioners into an active and unified effort to defeat the combined forces of tyranny and popery.[49] In the preface to Barton's essay, Rev. William Smith defended what he considered likely objections to this publication. '[Y]ou will hear it said – "A Minister professing the doctrine of the meek and blessed Jesus, should confine himself to Subjects spiritual and eternal. What have the clergy to do with civil and temporal Concerns?" Instead, Smith argued that Protestant ministers should not be apolitical. Rather they should endeavor 'in all their public Addresses, to inspire every Bosom with a rational Zeal for our holy Protestant Faith, and an utter Aversion to all Sorts of Slavery, especially in the present Emergency.'[50] In the spirit of this holy war, Smith and Barton both considered that the defense of the empire and the Protestant faith warranted the public and political involvement of ministers.

Other ministers also chafed at the suggestion that the clergy should not become involved in political issues. Jonathan Boucher of Maryland proclaimed that '[t]he peremptory tone with which we of the clergy are so often interdicted from meddling with politics in our pulpits, has long appeared to me ... dictatorial.'[51] While Boucher reasoned that the Church of England clergy should possess a political voice since, in his opinion, they preached a brand of politics consistent with good government, he also noted that opponents of his political sermons took offence '... not so much because some of us preach on politics, as because we preach what are called unpopular politics.'[52] The denunciation of Samuel Auchmuty of New York in a published letter signed 'C.J.' reveals a similar objection to clerical meddling in politics which only disguised the author's real disapprobation of specific loyalist pronouncements. After the discovery of a letter which Auchmuty had written to Captain John Montresor, 'C.J.' wrote

> [m]any of your Parishioners formerly considered you as a peaceably [*sic*] Man, heartily attached to the Church, and one who did not meddle with Politicks; they attended your Preaching with Pleasure ... but since your Letter ... they consider you as holding Sentiments unfriendly to American Freedom, and yet as being of so mean and dastardly a spirit as not to dare avow them openly.

In criticizing Auchmuty for his involvement in political issues, 'C.J.' actually denounced his particular brand of politics. He articulated a community expectation that clergy should be 'Examples of Meekness, Charity, Good-Breeding, and Liberality of Sentiment' and that they should aim both 'to avoid Party Spirit and Party Prejudices, and to join heartily in support of ... the last Congress.'[53]

To Anglican ministers, many of the attacks on loyalism which began with an interdiction on political participation seemed intimately intermingled with pre-existing dissenter attacks on the church or its theology. Anglicans denouncing the Revolution sometimes utilized an anti-evangelical language which pointed to enthusiasm as the cause of both religious and political turmoil.[54] In the northern colonies dissenters, who many churchmen believed had been imbued since birth with hatred for the Church of England, led the Revolution. Quite colorfully, Rev. Weeks described that among dissenters 'groundless prejudice and unreasonable rancour against the Church of England have been sucked in the Mother's Milk and carefully cherished by a false & narrow Education.'[55] By assuming a public role as advocates for the Revolution, dissenters provided themselves with a forum for criticizing England and loyalist Anglicanism. Samuel Johnson believed that almost all the church people were called 'Tories' as well as 'every other person who is against the most violent measures.'[56] 'Papist' was another frequent epithet. Later remembering the Stamp Act riots, Rev. Samuel Peters described mobs breaking 'Churchmen's windows, and cry[ing] out, "No bishops! no popery! no kings, lords, and tyrants!"'[57] Commenting upon a local occurrence, William McGilchrist of Salem, Massachusetts, described the declarations of a revolutionary 'Demagogue' who 'declaimed vehemently in the general Court against the oppressive impositions, as he term'd them, of the English ... [and] inveigh'd bitterly against his Grace of Canterbury and the Bishop of London, and pursued a parallel between the former and Archbishop Laud.'[58] Samuel Seabury also believed that his rebel persecutors took particular pleasure in insulting him 'by reviling the King, the Parliament, Lord North, the Church, the Bishops, the Clergy & the Society ...'[59]

SPG missionaries denounced the overt political behavior of dissenting ministers because of specific attacks on churchmen and Anglicanism, but these Anglicans also charged dissenters with fomenting rebellion for the express purpose of destroying the Church of England. While civil liberty was 'the Bait that was flung out' to attract popular support, Charles Inglis claimed the dissenting leaders aimed deliberately and unanimously for the 'Abolition of the Church of England.'[60] By uncovering this hidden agenda, Inglis thought he had explained the vocality and unanimity of dissenters in support of the Revolution. Similarly Richard Mansfield asserted that, in fomenting rebellion, the dissenting teachers of New England proceeded from 'a Lust of Power.'[61] Samuel Seabury also insisted that the conspiracy theory which dissenters articulated against the Anglican ministry was itself a deception. While dissenters accused Church of England ministers of conspiring with the British government, Seabury believed that 'those people who raised this Calumny [did not] believe one syllable of it.' Rather they intended it only as 'an Engine to turn the popular fury upon the Church; which ... will probably fall sacrifice to the persecuting Spirit of Independency.'[62]

Not all colonial Anglican ministers interpreted the Revolution as an attack on their church; in southern colonies where Anglicans largely favored patriotism, its ministers did not make such bold pronouncements. Patriot Anglicans tended to define the Revolution as a response to constitutional, not religious, challenges by Parliament, but Anglicans of different political stripes deplored the dissenters' use of the pulpit as a patriot propaganda tool. In Rev. McGilchrist's opinion, the character of peaceableness and moderation distinguished Anglicans from dissenting clergy, whom he described as 'a Regiment of Black Coats' who fomented rebellion and thereby greatly assisted the rebels.[63] William White stated that, despite his patriotism, he 'never beat the ecclesiastical drum ... Being invited to preach before a battalion, I declined and mentioned to the colonel ... my objections to the making of the ministry instrumental to the war.'[64] In this manner, patriot White and loyalist McGilchrist both found the boisterousness of dissenters who participated in the Revolution inconsistent with the Anglican ideal of rationality and peaceableness.

Anglican ministers could avoid controversial public issues by insisting that political duties were inappropriate to their calling. The most partial clergymen, including patriots J. P. G. Muhlenberg and Jacob Duché, disagreed. In defence of his military activities, Muhlenberg replied 'I am a clergyman, it is true, but I am a member of society as well as the poorest layman, and my liberty is as dear to me as to any man.'[65] Similarly, in 1775, Jacob Duché believed himself 'under the twofold character of a minister of Jesus Christ, and a Fellow-Citizen of the same state, and involved in the same public calamity with yourselves.'[66] More often, reticent ministers expressed modesty about their political acumen or the inappropriateness of their political commentary. Following the Seven Years' War, Henry Caner wrote to Francis Bernard, Governor of Massachusetts, that '[n]either my station nor abilities, permit me to enter into the policy's of state,' but he concluded with the astute political observation that the peace had increased Britain's commercial interests as well as her territory.[67] In a 1764 pamphlet, Thomas Barton toyed with the question of whether clergymen should comment on politics. His defense of the Paxton men indicated his willingness to announce publicly his position on a local issue, but a certain language of humility about his own political savvy permeates the text. 'For my part, I am no[t] Adept in Politicks ... By my Principles as well as Situation in Life, you know, my dear Sir, that I have no political Ends to serve ...'[68] Ultimately Barton twisted his language of humility into a defense of his own objectivity. In answering why he had refused to sign the Association of 1774 which pledged adherents to support non-importation and the authority of the Continental Congress, Rev. John Sayre argued that ministers of the Gospel should not be involved in political matters. He urged that '[i]t can be [a] matter of very little importance to the community, whether I subscribe the association or not; for I am no politician; am not connected with politicians as such, and never will be either. Those things belong not to my profession. ...'[69] Sayre defended non-involvement in his clear dichotomization of the worlds of religion and politics. To avoid further personal examination, Sayre claimed that politics clearly lay beyond his calling. Ebenezer Dibblee similarly stated that one of the clergy's duties, particularly during the Revolution, consisted of the avoidance of politics.[70]

If politics could be avoided even partially, several clergymen noted the potential benefits for the church. Thomas Barton claimed that he had avoided entangling civil issues which would 'injure the Cause ... of Religion' and similarly Rev. Matthew Graves considered it his duty to avoid politics, especially in prayer, since political discussions detracted from the lessons of Christ.[71] A Mohawk sachem, in defense of John Stuart, paid the cleric the highest compliment by insisting that '[h]e does not meddle in civil affairs, but instructs us in the way to Heaven. He absolutely refuses to attend to any political matters and says they do not belong to him.'[72] Political non-involvement allowed ministers to focus on matters of salvation and possibly even allowed them to extend their spiritual influence. By '[p]reaching the Gospel unadulterated with Politics,' Charles Inglis and several of his colleagues urged that Anglican clergymen had improved the church's public reputation and had even attracted 'serious Dissenters' who disagreed with the political messages of rebellion emanating from dissenting pulpits. A similar claim, that Anglican rationality possessed its own appeal, had been made about the religious enthusiasm of the First Great Awakening.[73] As Ebenezer Dibblee prayed that he and his colleagues 'be inspired with a spirit of primitive Christianity, patiently to suffer,' he noted that revolutionary turmoil might produce an era of spiritual renewal.[74]

As a general concept, depoliticization helps to explain some of the personal and professional changes which many colonial Church of England ministers experienced, especially after 1775–76. For those ministers who were not committed patriots, depoliticization became a strategy for resolving the tensions between traditional clerical dependence on the Church of England

and growing American resistance to British imperial authority. For some, this behavior exhibited itself in voluntary actions such as exile, retirement, or the closing of churches, but several involuntary circumstances also contributed to the larger pattern. Forced exile, imprisonment, and death removed individuals from the public spotlight or limited their sphere of influence. In their letters to the SPG, northern clergymen indicated how their colleagues had been scattered or silenced. In colonies where the Church of England was established, the process of depoliticization did not remove Anglican ministers so completely from the public sphere, partly because their pre-revolutionary duties suggest that they initially functioned at a higher plateau of political activity. Depoliticization reduced the political involvement of both northern and southern Anglican ministers, but it did not eliminate the difference between their respective levels of public participation.

Exile and death both contributed to the declining public role of the colonial clergy. By fleeing to England or other British possessions, Anglican exiles removed themselves from the tempest of colonial politics. Although some clergymen, including Thomas Bradbury Chandler, attempted to effect political change in London, they did not form an effective counter-revolutionary force. The early refugee Samuel Peters, who had arrived in England in late 1774, acted as a liaison for his colonial colleagues who desired an appointment elsewhere, but could not seriously shape British policies.[75] Since these exiled clergymen often possessed strong loyalist views, their removal from the colonies early in the war, in 1775 or 1776, decreased the general tenor of loyalism among their remaining colleagues. At the same time, the notoriety of those loyalist exiles caused popular colonial opinion to link the Anglican clergy as a class to loyalism. The magnitude of the exodus in some areas proved substantial, ranging from 13 per cent in Virginia to 100 per cent in Maine (both clergymen); in total, 25 per cent of the ministers in the colonies at the start of 1775 left for England or other British possessions, or relocated in another American colony or county, often behind British lines. The years 1775 and 1776 together account for almost 42 per cent of all clerical exiles (see Table 5.2). Death, by removing individuals from their worldly situation, contributed to this phenomenon of depoliticization on an individual level. More significantly, the death of Anglican clergymen throughout the Revolution substantially reduced their numbers and weakened their political voice. Because no newly ordained recruits for the Anglican ministry arrived in the colonies during the war, these losses could not be replaced. Of the approximately three hundred Anglican ministers who resided in the American colonies at some point between 1775 and 1783, one in five died during those years (see Table 5.3).

Table 5.2   Clerical exiles,* 1775–83

	1775	1776	1777	1778	1779	1780	1781	1782	1783	Total
VA	4	1	1	5	2	0	2	1	1	17 (13%)
MD	9	4	1	2	0	1	0	0	0	17 (29%)
NC	0	1	2	0	0	0	0	0	0	3 (27%)
SC	2	1	2	0	1	1	3	0	0	10 (45%)
GA	1	0	0	0	0	0	0	0	0	1 (25%)
PA	0	0	1	4	0	0	0	0	0	5 (31%)
NJ	1	1	2	0	0	0	0	0	0	4 (36%)
NY	1	0	1	1	0	0	1	0	1	5 (26%)
CT	2	0	0	0	3	0	0	0	1	6 (26%)
MA	1	3	0	2	2	0	0	0	0	8 (50%)
ME	1	0	0	0	1	0	0	0	0	2 (100%)
NH	0	0	0	0	1	0	0	0	0	1 (50%)
RI	0	0	0	0	0	0	0	0	0	0
Total	22	11	10	14	10	2	6	1	3	79 (25%)

*Exiled ministers include individuals forced (permanently or temporarily) into exile in England or other British possessions or those forced to relocate in another colony or county (often behind British lines). Note that two ministers died at sea before reaching their intended destinations (Daniel McKinnon on route to England and Epenetus Townshend on route to Nova Scotia).

Table 5.3   Clerical deaths in America, 1775–83

	1775	1776	1777	1778	1779	1780	1781	1782	1783	Total
VA	3	5	4	6	1	1	1	5	2	28 (21%)
MD	0	1	0	1	2	1	1	1	3	10 (17%)
NC	0	0	1	0	1	0	0	0	0	2 (18%)
SC	1	0	0	0	1	0	0	1	2	5 (23%)
GA	0	0	0	0	0	0	0	0	0	0
PA	0	1	1	1	2	1	0	1	0	7 (44%)
NJ	0	0	0	0	0	0	1	0	0	1 (9%)
NY	0	1	3	0	0	0	0	0	0	4 (21%)
CT	0	0	1	0	0	1	0	1	0	3 (13%)
MA	1	0	0	0	0	2	0	0	0	3 (19%)
ME	0	0	0	0	0	0	0	0	0	0
NH	0	0	0	0	0	0	0	0	0	0
RI	1	0	0	0	0	0	1	0	0	2 (50%)
Total	6	8	10	8	7	6	4	9	7	65 (20%)

Violence or imprisonment also proved excellent incentives for a quiet demeanor. Rev. Thomas Barton reported to the SPG in 1776 that '[e]very clergyman of the Church of England, who dared to act upon proper principles was marked out for infamy and insult ... Some of them have been dragged from their horses, assaulted with stones and dirt, ducked in water, obliged to flee for their lives, driven from their habitations and families, laid under arrest and imprisoned.'[76] Even the strongest spirit might be convinced to acquiesce to rebel demands under such pressure. Imprisonment by revolutionaries had a similar effect; institutional incarceration or house arrest limited the clergyman's sphere of influence, which in many respects was already diminished as a result of the exile of many parishioners. Prohibitions on traveling outside their town or county further limited the clergymen's range of influence. John Stuart reported that for three years he was confined to live within the town limits of Schenectady, New York, while Alexander Murray of Pennsylvania, who refused to take the required oath of allegiance to the revolutionary government in his colony, was arrested for traveling from his residence.[77]

Of those clergy who continued to minister in the colonies during the Revolution, the vast majority did not maintain a highly visible and public profile after 1775 and 1776. As patriots and loyalists both noted, the beginning of armed confrontation and the subsequent Declaration of Independence rendered any quick and peaceful reconciliation unlikely.[78] Faced with civil war, many Anglican ministers tried to refrain from making public pronouncements, but the Continental Congress, which established days of fasting and humiliation, prohibited prayers for the king and royal family, and required oaths of loyalty to Congress, aimed to separate loyalists from patriots in a clear and decisive manner. Revolutionary powers placed these difficult obstacles before the clergy precisely to force them into an open and declared political allegiance.

As many Anglican clergymen attempted to walk a tightrope between patriotism and loyalism, they came to privilege neutrality as a solution, albeit not always an entirely successful one. As Samuel Magaw explained, 'I have thought it my duty ... to walk, at the present critical juncture, with peculiar caution and circumspection.'[79] As early as 1768 the clergy of Boston in convention wrote that '[w]e are neither allowed to speak nor scarcely to be silent unless we join with those who we believe to be labouring the destruction of our constitution, civil & religious.'[80] Philip Reading's admission in 1776 that '[i]t is hardly possible especially since the commencement of the late hostilities to avoid taking a part on one side or other of the dispute' acknowledged his own difficulties in conveying an appearance of neutrality. The widow of Rev. Thomas Field of Virginia similarly reported that her husband ' "wished to have been quiet." '[81] In 1775, Matthew Graves of Connecticut demonstrated a certain naiveté in his belief that silence could be an effective manner of avoiding all political turmoil. He asserted, 'as I have always been strictly silent about Politics, [I] resolve to continue so: & tho' my Patrons might demand Obedience to their Commands, yet I'm persuaded they will excuse my involuntary Neglect.'[82] Most revolutionaries did not make such allowances for objections of conscience. William Clark undoubtedly spoke too soon when he reported in 1775 that '... as I have little converse or concern with the sons of sedition, I have been preserved.' He was later imprisoned for ten weeks on board a rebel ship in Boston harbor.[83] Jonathan Odell also found that revolutionaries would not tolerate even a private neutrality. After one of his letters to the SPG had been intercepted, Odell expressed his belief that 'Private Sentiments ought not to be made matter of public Notice, much less of public Censure.'[84] Odell utilized a language of pacifism or non-involvement to disguise his private loyalist sentiments, a tactic which he felt had the approbation of the Society. Revolutionaries, however, were less inclined to engage in the deception.

Instead of permitting quietness, revolutionaries attempted to harness clerical support from all denominations by creating provincial or intercolonial days of fasting and humiliation. Throughout the colonial era, ministers influenced their congregations regularly in weekly sermons, but New England election and fast-day sermons especially provided the ministers with the opportunity of speaking directly about public events.[85] By forcing loyalists and lukewarm patriots either to support the Revolution or withdraw from their pulpits, Congressionally approved fast days also served to designate individual ministers as friends or foes of the American cause. As Rev. Luke Babcock lamented, 'the continental Fast ... may be considered as a Tryal by Ordeal, of the Ministers of the Church of England in America.'[86] Although provincial legislatures occasionally appointed particular days of community prayer, the intercolonial fasts, including 1 June 1774 and 20 July 1775 were of particular importance.[87] In the northern colonies, many Anglican ministers did not participate on 1 June 1774, the effective date of the Boston Port Act. As William Clark explained, the fast was kept by the dissenters, '[b]ut as the Governor did not think proper to Issue his proclamation, Episcopalians did not think themselves obliged to keep it.'[88]

Participation in Congressional fast days carried dramatic consequences, as the clergy of Philadelphia recognized before the public fast of 20 July 1775. Previously they had tried to keep politics out of their pulpit, but if they continued to do so they would be labeled loyalists. The Continental

Congress, in ordering this public fast day, forced them to assume a public role which they had been trying to avoid.

... [T]he Time is now come ... when even our silence would be misconstrued, and when we are called upon to take a more public part. The Continental Congress have recommended the 20th of next month as a day of Fasting, Prayer & Humiliation thro' all the Colonies ... Under these Circumstances our People call upon us, and think they have a right to our advice in the most public manner from the Pulpit. Should we refuse, our Principles would be misrepresented, and even our religious usefulness destroyed among our People. And our complying may perhaps be interpreted to our disadvantage in the Parent Country.[89]

Just ten days before the fast day, William Smith described to the SPG the difficult position of the Anglican clergymen. 'To comply may offend their protectors and those that support them in the Parent Country. To refuse would leave them without Congregations every where.'[90] Angering the revolutionaries would be detrimental to the church and its parishioners, but neither did the missionaries wish to offend the SPG or other English ecclesiastical authorities. In these troubled times, ministers argued that the colonies could benefit from a day of prayer and community repentance, and so they often deliberated with their parishioners or felt justified in opening the church at their request.

In writing their fast-day sermons, ministers who decided to preach faced another thorny dilemma. How much, or how little, should they say about politics? Would not the act of merely appearing before a congregation on that day offer support to the Congress which proclaimed the day of fasting? Answering in the affirmative, Luke Babcock of New York refused to 'bow down before an Altar' which Congress had raised.[91] Before Independence, 17 May had also been appointed by Congress as a day of fasting. Charles Inglis agreed to preach at the request of his parishioners on that day, and as he later explained, '[i]t was exceedingly difficult for a loyal Clergyman to preach on such an Occasion & not incur Danger, on the one Hand, or not depart from his Duty, on the other. I endeavoured to avoid both – making Peace & Repentance my Subject, & explicitly disclaimed having any Thing to do with politics.'[92] By preaching on repentance without making too many allusions to present-day concerns, ministers thought they might avoid controversy. Samuel Andrews claimed that his sermon of 20 July 1775 instructed simply that the observance of fast days would be of no benefit without internal repentance, but his selected text (Amos 5: 21 'I hate, I despise your feast-days ...') created considerable controversy, and Andrews' name appeared in the local newspaper. Although the sermon did focus on spiritual matters of repentance, it included a few underlying loyalist arguments about man's duty to higher powers and the patriots' lack of respect for the civil liberties of those who differed in opinion. In an effort to vindicate himself, Andrews published the sermon.[93]

By dissolving colonial political connections with Britain and its monarch, the Declaration of Independence carried tremendous consequences for the clergy of the king's church. At ordination to the diaconate and again to the priesthood, candidates took the Oath of the King's Supremacy. Additionally, by swearing the Oath of Uniformity, they promised to adhere strictly to the liturgy of the Church of England.[94] In the English Prayer Book of 1662, which remained the standard text of the eighteenth century, the services of Morning and Evening Prayer as well as the Eucharist contained mandatory prayers for the king and the royal family. As Philip Reading also noted, the canons of the church did not permit ministers to alter public services or omit any parts. To do so, he believed, would risk excommunication.[95] Independence rendered such oaths and prayers completely antithetical to the American cause, and those ministers who conducted services as usual risked charges of treason or fines. In Massachusetts, the General Court passed a law, with a £50 penalty, which forbade any preaching that might dissuade colonists from supporting independence. Since an annual SPG stipend at this time usually did not exceed that amount, such a fine would have been a substantial incentive to omit prayers or discontinue services.[96] Although quite effective in Massachusetts, threats did not always convince ministers to abandon their previous obligations. The tenacious Rev. John Beach of Connecticut swore that he would continue to pray for the king until the rebels cut out his tongue. Rev. William Clark of Massachusetts testified to the seriousness with which he understood his ordination vows.

> But by vows, oaths, and subscriptions which have been made on Earth and recorded in heaven I am obliged to act as a dutiful subject of His most Gracious Majesty, King George the Third, and to the constant use of the Liturgy of that Church of which under God he is the head ... Both my oath of allegiance ... and my solemnly subscribing to use the Liturgy strongly unite to oblige me to pray for the King's majesty till such time as he shall be pleased to relinquish his right of Government or jurisdiction over these Colonies.[97]

While the eighteenth-century world generally demonstrated a high regard for oaths, these Anglican ministers interpreted their oaths as cornerstones of their faith.

Samuel Tingley of Delaware arrived at an inventive solution which permitted him to keep his church open with only a minimal alteration of the liturgy. To liturgical purists, his actions technically broke canon law and his ordination oaths, but his decision revealed great pragmatism. Tingley decided to adopt certain words in prayer to prevent the scattering of his congregation.

> Instead, therefore, of saying, as we are directed, O Lord, save the King, I said, O Lord, save those whom thou hast made it our especial Duty to pray for.... In the Litany, instead of these words, 'Thy Servant, George, our most Gracious King & Governor,' I said, 'those whom *Thou* has set in authority over us.'

In his report to the SPG in 1782, Tingley insisted that this alteration of required prayers allowed him to continue praying for the king without offending the revolutionaries. Safety precluded explicit prayers for the British monarch and his family, but Tingley explained, 'the Great Searcher of hearts' could determine the 'integrity of our meaning.'[98] In this manner, Tingley asserted that God knew the underlying message of his words, but one wonders what alternative interpretation he might have offered the patriot members of his congregation.

Because Anglican clergymen took their oath to the king very seriously, rebel demands that they pledge allegiance to the Continental Congress posed tremendous, and often irreconcilable, difficulties. While ministers could participate in Congressionally approved fast days without violating previous obligations, to alter the liturgy or subscribe to rebel oaths required a more committed level of patriotism. The Virginia Convention in May 1776 replaced prayers for the king and royal family with those for Congress, an act which Lord Dunmore believed so shocking that the majority of people would resume their loyalty to the king, but in fact little protest occurred. Every free, adult male was also required to swear an oath to the Commonwealth of Virginia before 10 October 1777, and those who refused could not hold office, including appointments as Anglican rectors or curates.[99] The Pennsylvania assembly also required an oath of allegiance to the new revolutionary powers and its state constitution of 1776. Its 1777 test act was repassed in the spring of 1778, and those who declined submission, but were not guilty of treason, could sell their estates and leave the state within 90 days from 1 June 1778.[100] In this manner, provincial governments created litmus tests of loyalism and patriotism which did not permit neutrality.

In deciding their personal course of action, ministers looked to the church's hierarchy or historical precedent for answers, but neither source provided any definitive solutions. Typical of a world turned upside down, the chain of command faltered as colonial ministers and missionaries found themselves unable to secure advice from the SPG or the Bishop of London. While difficult decisions were made by individual, and often isolated, ministers, who sometimes consulted their parishioners, Henry Caner, an experienced minister in Boston, offered advice to local country clergy.[101] Novice ministers frequently directed their questions about the omission of prayers or the closing of churches to their more experienced colleagues, but Samuel Tingley of Delaware was unable to consult his 'Elder Bretheren.' In retrospect, Tingley considered this lack of guidance a blessing since he thought the Philadelphia clergy were 'too Zealous' in promoting the revolution.[102] In a deferential or even supercilious tone, many SPG clergy hoped that their conduct met with the approbation of the Society. After suspending public preaching, Thomas Barton expressed many missionaries' anxieties. 'If I have acted wrong ... I hope the Society will attribute my Faults to the Strictness of my Attachment to what I thought my Duty, and so forgive me. I should have been ver[y] happy to have had their Advice and Direction on so critical an Occasion – [But] that was impossible to be obtain'd.'[103] In southern colonies, the absence of direction from English officials posed fewer problems since vestries and government agencies filled the void. From its inception, southern Anglicanism had nurtured a Low Church inclusion of the laity in church affairs, a situation which encouraged ministerial patriotism.

The English Civil War offered a historical precedent, but the interpretation of its applicability to the colonial situation varied widely. In deciding to keep his church open and omit prayers for the king, Edward Bass supposedly observed that 'the episcopal Clergy, in the time of the grand Rebellion in England, did the same.'[104] In the absence of instructions, Bass looked to this precedent as a behavioral guide, but William Clark opposed Bass's interpretation because in the English Civil War the ministers had been instructed by their bishops. In the present crisis, Clark did not believe that 'we had a right to make any, the least alteration or omission in the Liturgy, without the Direction of our Diocesan.'[105] Similarly, Edward Winslow alluded to the precedent for omitting prayers for the King 'under Cromwell's usurpation when the public use of the Liturgy was wholly interdicted,' but unlike Bass, Winslow did not apply that historical decision to the present circumstances.[106] The existence of a known precedent in English church history did not simplify matters for the colonial SPG missionaries. Some thought the omissions advisable for the sake of keeping the congregations together, but others did not feel personally empowered to make such decisions. Abraham Beach described the confusion of his New York brethren who were divided on the issue: some cited the examples of Bishop Saunderson and Dr Hammond of the English Civil

War, and others could not give any advice.[107] Ultimately, each minister had to decide for himself.

Although precise figures are difficult to determine, most Anglican ministers in the northern colonies shut their churches, at least temporarily. At a convention in New Haven on 23 July 1776, the clergy of Connecticut resolved to suspend public services, and for a time all churches in Connecticut were closed, except those under the direction of Rev. Beach. In New England, few ministers maintained services after the British evacuation of Boston in the spring of 1776, and a Massachusetts decree of 1777 discouraged others.[108] In view of the unanimity of most SPG missionaries in closing their New England churches, ministers who chose an alternative course of action became suspect. In disgust, William Clark reported that Rev. Edward Bass had complied with his people in all liturgical omissions 'to keep up publick worship, using the vulgar Proverb, that half a Loaf was better than no bread.'[109] The SPG must not have agreed with that analogy, for they removed Bass from their list of active missionaries. Samuel Parker, who was not an SPG missionary, continued services in his Boston church; even before the Revolution, this parish had sufficient wealth to pay Parker independently from English sources. After the Revolution, Parker admitted that he had not prayed for the king during the rebellion, but he argued that he had not broken his ordination oath because he neither prayed for Congress nor read their proclamations. As he argued, his was merely a 'sin' of omission rather than commission.[110]

In the middle colonies, as elsewhere, public worship depended upon local circumstances and the presence of troops. In New York City, British occupation and the city's subsequent attraction for loyalist refugees facilitated the continuation of services. The two Anglican chapels in New York City could not accommodate so many additional parishioners, and in 1782 refugee Anglican clergymen began to hold services on Sundays in the city hall.[111] Outside British lines, many clergymen could not conduct services as usual. In New Jersey, the clergy suspended public ministrations in 1776, except for Abraham Beach and Robert Blackwell.[112] Samuel Johnston, a parishioner of Rev. Daniel Batwell, informed the SPG in November 1776 that since the Declaration of Independence, no church services had been performed in Pennsylvania, except in Philadelphia where some clergy had altered that part of the service pertaining to the king. By October 1778, 30-year-old William White was the only Anglican clergyman left in Philadelphia.[113] White, who had been ordained only in 1770, had agreed to alter services.

South of Pennsylvania, more of the Anglican churches remained open. In most cases, the continuation of services required that clergymen subscribe to an oath of allegiance to the revolutionary government, and with few exceptions, ministers who did not comply were removed from their pulpit and often forced to vacate their glebe. Continued incumbency after 1776 may be considered evidence of patriotism and vice versa. Christopher MacRae of Virginia, an exceptional case, was permitted to continue as rector with the support of his parishioners, although he refused to swear the oath. In Maryland, fewer than half the Anglican clergymen took the oath of fidelity to the state.[114] Further south, more ministers were patriots, but in addition to matters of conscience, many were dissuaded from continuing public services by the disestablishment of the Church of England and the subsequent discontinuation of their salaries. Although payments in Virginia had not been made since 1776, salaries ended officially in 1779. In 1776, the new state constitutions of Maryland, North Carolina, and South Carolina provided that there should be no establishment of any particular church, and in 1777 Georgia and New York followed suit.[115] Voluntary subscriptions proved precarious for many clergymen during wartime, and in combination with other factors of conscience, fiscal pressures encouraged many to retire to their farms or to teach school. In Virginia, less than half of the clergymen relinquished their official posts, most of their own volition. Maryland and South Carolina figures approach 40 per cent, and North Carolina one-third.[116]

In shutting the church doors rather than alter the liturgy or disavow previous oaths, many ministers attempted to steer a middle path commensurate with a neutral, or at least politically inoffensive, position. Philip Reading explained: 'I had no design to resist the authority of the New Government on one hand and as I was determined on the other not to incur the heavy guilt of perjury by a breach of the most solemn promises I should decline attending on the public worship.'[117] To omit prayers to the king and royal family would entail a breaking of ordination oaths, but to use such prayers 'would have drawn inevitable Destruction on them. The only Course which they could pursue to avoid both Evils, was to suspend the public Exercise of their Function, & shut up their Churches.'[118] Samuel Seabury insisted that an omission of prayers to the king 'would not only be a Breach of my Duty, but in some Degree countenancing their Rebellion, & supporting that Independency which they had declared. As the least culpable Course, I determined not to go to Church ...'[119] By withdrawing from the public arena, ministers attempted to avoid a direct confrontation with revolutionary authorities on one hand, and a breach of their consciences on the other.

To guard against the utter destruction of colonial Anglicanism, many clergymen, who no longer conducted public worship, visited from house to house to instruct families, marry local couples, baptize and catechize children, and attend the sick and the dying. Philip Reading reported that, having closed his church, his 'sphere of action is now confined to the Catechical and what are strictly termed, the parochial offices of my Mission.'[120] In this manner, ministers communicated to their superiors in London that they continued to be useful. They also articulated a somewhat forced distinction between private and public preaching. In January 1779 Thomas Barton noted that

> [u]pon the Declaration of Independency, when I saw myself excluded from the publick Duties of my Office, I visited my People, from House to House, by & private Instruction, Exhortation &c. endeavoured to render myself as useful as possible. I had the pleasure to find that this method of meeting in secret, & as it were, by stealth, having some-what the appearance of the persecution of the Primitive Christians, it had these good Effects – it Kindled & encreased their Zeal, & united them the closer together.[121]

William Clark had used the full liturgy until approximately Easter 1777, at which time the law forbade prayers for the king in public or private. He then delivered as 'much of the Liturgy as the times will bear, in Private, (where I suppose my self to have that Liberty in Modelling the Prayers, that I have not in Publick).'[122] Individuals committed to maintaining some public interaction with their parishioners found such a dichotomization of public and private duties too limiting. John Sayre of New York preferred to describe two goals of public worship, one of which could still be accomplished even in 1779. He met with his parishioners at Flushing, Long Island, at the usual hour on Sunday morning at which time he read parts of the Old and New Testaments and psalms. In the morning he read homilies, and Sunday afternoon he taught the catechism or discussed some scriptural text. 'By this method we enjoyed one of the two general designs of public religious meetings. I mean public instruction: the other, to wit, public worship, it is easy to believe was inadmissible in our circumstances.'[123]

The decision to close churches must have had a particular resonance for colonial Anglicanism, which had long emphasized to its parishioners the importance of regular public worship. Miles Selden, a Virginia clergyman, delivered a compelling sermon in 1758 to indicate the necessity of public services. Selden warned that neglect of public worship would be fatal to religion; primitive Christians would not have gathered for public worship, at the peril of their lives, if they had believed their God required only private petitions.[124] In farewell addresses, ministers also beseeched their former charges, above all, to be constant in the public worship of God.

Because of the importance of public worship and the sanctity of the church, many clergy and laity must have viewed with grief the wartime use of Anglican churches as barracks, hospitals, or stables.[125] A conviction about the necessity of public worship must also have tugged at the resolve of many ministers, and perhaps convinced Edward Bass or Abraham Beach to keep their churches open. As William Smith reasoned in July 1775, '[i]f our Clergy were generally to quit their people at this time I say we should not have the appearance of a Church or people left.'[126]

Despite their private ministrations, many clergymen noted that religion had declined in their communities after churches closed. The future patriot chaplain, Robert Blackwell, assessed wartime spirituality in 1775, by noting '[t]here is very little hope of inculcating divine truths on the hearts of men, when they are eagerly engaged in worldly matters, that appear to them of the greatest moment.'[127] Such realizations, when combined with tacit approval of English authorities, must have contributed to later decisions to reopen closed churches and resume services. Reversing their decision of 1776, many Connecticut clergy opened their church doors later in the war. In this action, the clergy took their cue from John Tyler, who explained why he and his parishioners had decided to conduct services again in November 1778, with the omission of prayers for the king and Parliament. '[M]y reasons were to this effect: That the cause of religion ought not to be annihilated on a civil account; that public worship was of too much consequence to be totally omitted on account of a few words in a liturgy …'[128]

From England, Thomas Bradbury Chandler offered advice about the propriety of reopening the churches with some liturgical omissions. Chandler had waited on the Archbishop of Canterbury and the Bishop of London, who instructed him that if the Connecticut clergy agreed unanimously that it was necessary to omit the collects of the king and royal family, they could do so. In writing to Samuel Seabury in 1779, Chandler shared their leaders' message that the omission of prayers might be necessary given the circumstances, but that praying for Congress would be joining in the rebellion. News that the SPG would not punish those who made omissions in public services spread slowly to all of its clergy. Not until January 1782 did William Ayers of New Jersey decide to resume public services of worship. He arrived at that decision after learning that a letter from Chandler to Abraham Beach intimated SPG approbation.[129] Another New Jersey missionary, Samuel Cooke, described his meeting with Abraham Beach, who advised him to open his church, as the Reverends Frazer and Ogden had done. Since both his parishioners and the SPG approved (or so he had heard from Charles Inglis), Cooke found himself 'under an indispensable obligation to comply.'[130] After communicating himself with Inglis, William Frazer explained the necessity of reopening the churches. Because of the degeneracy of the times, the 'rising Generation' especially suffered from the want of organized religion. Abraham Beach concurred in 1782; he found religion, particularly among youth, on the decline, a situation which he attributed to the discontinuance of public worship for such a long time. Loyalist clergy gradually resumed services, and by 1783 most northern Anglican churches, which still had resident clergy, had reopened.[131]

Throughout the colonies, the closing of many Anglican parishes raised concerns about ecclesiastical authority and the necessity of public worship to the survival of the colonial church. Lay demands for the alteration of the liturgy undoubtedly alarmed those ministers who assumed an authoritative and patriarchal role over their flock. For both southern Anglicans who had long accepted lay involvement in church affairs as well as British-sponsored missionaries, the war caused them to examine the meaning of their allegiance to the king, the church, and its liturgy, and weigh those considerations against their pastoral duties. In a world turned upside down by revolution, deference could no longer be guaranteed. In fact, clerical pretensions to authority had been met with increasing suspicion in the late colonial period. In 1771 Thomas Bradbury Chandler had declared that the clergy were not free to speak about the appropriate levels of their own remuneration, and four years later Samuel Auchmuty was criticized in print for not displaying a suitable deference to his patriotic parishioners.[132] By insisting that Anglican ministers alter the liturgy of the Church of England and adopt oaths to Congress, revolutionary laity demanded that their civil concerns take precedence over Anglican liturgical tradition.

The depoliticization of the clergy resulted from the strengthening position of revolutionary lay authorities who constructed a mechanism, in proclaiming fast days and requiring oaths, to separate loyalists from patriots. At each step, clerical desires for neutrality increased, but their ability to achieve their goals declined dramatically. Anglican ministers found themselves pushed from the public spotlight, but many also believed that by withdrawing from matters of politics they could preserve their life and their work. By cultivating an image of themselves as neutral observers whose spiritual duties precluded any involvement in political disputes, many chose the path of least resistance. The practical choice of shutting the churches was a natural corollary of such a philosophy. By harnessing traditional values about the ideal character of an Anglican minister, one who is peaceable, quiet, and moderate, they had constructed an implicit plan of action, or rather inaction. Their dichotomization of the worlds of religion and politics and their conscious attempts to separate two inter-twined ministerial spheres, private and public, served as techniques to disguise loyalism in some cases, but above all to claim neutrality. By separating themselves from political issues, Anglican clergymen took a step away from the establishmentarian model of church–state relations. Although they may have considered their actions as temporary, wartime measures, with the subsequent disestablishment of the colonial Church of England and the creation of the American Protestant Episcopal Church, post-revolutionary Anglicanism required such a non-political foundation.

6 Divided Allegiances and Disestablishment

Patriotism and loyalism, in the context of the American Revolution, defined two distinct and opposite political affiliations, one in support of and one in opposition to the colonists' rebellion. According to the rebel maxim, 'those who were not for them, were against them.'[1] For some Anglican clergymen the choice was that clear, but for others this bifurcation of labels disguised a multiplicity of divided allegiances. A variety of factors influenced decisions to side with the colonial revolutionaries or Britain, including matters of conscience and oath-taking, regional and national affiliations, and a sense of duty to family and parish. These last two obligations came to the forefront particularly with the alteration of the church's relationship to the state as a result of both independence and disestablishment. The Revolution also forced individuals to re-examine their personal identification with particular polities, including their local community and the British empire, but especially their relationship with the Church of England.

In divorcing themselves from king and Parliament, the American revolutionaries succeeded in establishing a new political order with revolutionary shifts in the nature of authority. New egalitarian principles also encouraged such developments as disestablishment, the separation of church and state, and the rise of religious voluntarism. While the Revolution forced residents of America to identify with the republic and a new political order, the disestablishment of the church and the subsequent creation of the American Protestant Episcopal Church heralded a new religious world. State salaries for the Anglican clergy ended, and those who chose to remain in the United States had to adapt not only to a new church structure, but also to what was, in most states, a new religious paradigm, that of religious denominationalism, or religious pluralism within a broader matrix of a national Protestant culture.[2]

This chapter examines the divided allegiances which tugged at the consciences of colonial Anglican ministers during the Revolution and its immediate aftermath. The tale of the formation of the American Protestant Episcopal Church forms an integral part of the clergy's adjustment to their new status as republican citizens, but that narrative has been thoroughly treated elsewhere.[3] Instead of depicting the institutional changes, this chapter centers predominantly on the ministers' reactions to their new political

and religious situations. How did Anglican ministers respond to the abolition of establishmentarian legislation during the war? How did these individuals adjust not only to the political realities of independence, but also
to the process of altering personal loyalties to England and its national
church? To what extent did these ministers embrace revolutionary ideals
of egalitarianism and popular sovereignty as these beliefs transcended politics and engulfed religion?

Before examining the range of clerical reactions, a sketch of the process
of disestablishment demonstrates how institutional changes of the late
1770s and the 1780s dramatically altered the nature of church government
and clerical support. In every colony where the Church of England had
been established before 1776, revolutionary governments and new state
constitutions decisively eliminated this privileged position. New York's
constitution of 1777 forbade the holding of any civil or military office by a
clergyman of any denomination and provided for free religious worship
without preference. In Maryland, the Declaration of Rights in November
1776 ended taxation for church support, and the property of the Church of
England was later reserved to its successor, the state Episcopal Church.
The official establishment ended in North Carolina with the adoption of
the state constitution of 1776, and South Carolina's constitution of 1778
established all forms of orthodox Protestantism until that experiment
ended in 1790. In 1777, Georgia's constitution also specified that no one
could be forced to support a minister who was not of one's own religious
persuasion, although theoretically tax-support for one's own church
remained possible until 1798. The Declaration of Rights in 1776 unleashed
dissenter petitions for the disestablishment of the Church of England in
Virginia, and in the same year the assembly exempted dissenters from paying church taxes. Between 1776 and 1780, the legislative committee on
religion in Virginia received 16 petitions favoring disestablishment, while
only three of the 95 parishes requested the retention of the establishment.
By 1779 the state officially terminated financial support for the clergy,
although no payments had actually been made after 1776.[4] Alternative
efforts to secure a general assessment failed to win the support of dissenters,
who considered any such scheme an attempt to renew the old establishment.

Revolutionary ideals encouraged the disestablishment of the Church of
England, but other churches did not entirely escape these currents of change.
Eventually the northern Congregationalist establishments ended: in 1818
in Connecticut, 1819 in New Hampshire, 1820 in Maine, and finally 1833
in Massachusetts. Demands for change in New England did not have the
same sense of urgency which elsewhere disestablished the king's church
during the Revolutionary War, but the separation of church and state proved

an irresistible trend, which eventually affected even those churches known for their wartime patriotism. During the American Revolution and beyond, colonists debated the proper role of the state in religion, and most came to agree that freedom of religion required not only free expression, but also voluntary financial support. To contemporaries, the disestablishment of the Church of England may have been interpreted as a punishment for the church's association with England and traditional dedication to the Crown. Disestablishment, however, resulted from several causes, which included antagonism toward the king's church, but also Enlightenment or deist philosophies of religious toleration and burgeoning trends toward the separation of church and state.[5]

Another related issue of church finance in the post-revolutionary period involved the discontinuation of SPG support in America. According to the terms of the Society's charter, it could not assist Anglican missions outside the British empire, and with American independence achieved in 1783, the Society's missionaries reluctantly faced economic independence. In 1786 Bishop Samuel Seabury recognized that the SPG had to follow its charter, but lamented that '[i]ts old patrons, who, under God, were its great support, have withdrawn their countenance and left it to stand by its own strength. The time, and sudden manner of doing this, are attended with such circumstances as really double the inconveniences.'[6] After enduring civil war, loyalist ministers felt that the elimination of SPG salaries would jeopardize the future of their parishes and punish wartime loyalty. They argued that being cut off from the Society felt like they were being 'forsaken of all our Friends.'[7] Rev. Richard Clarke understood that the continuance of SPG support would be a breach of the Society's charter, but he hoped that salaries might be continued during the lives of the present missionaries, especially given the distress they had recently suffered for conscience's sake.[8] Such appeals to the sympathy of the Society did not alter the policy.

Disestablishment and the withdrawal of SPG support occasioned considerable hardship, but they also freed American Anglicanism to alter its practices and to direct its own church affairs. To cope with their new status, concerned clergymen and laymen reorganized their churches into state conventions and eventually a national one, but the future of the Episcopal Church appeared quite uncertain in the early 1780s. Would the liturgy and church government of the American Episcopal Church bear a close resemblance to the Church of England? How much innovation was necessary, or desirable? Could a national church organization be achieved? These issues proved contentious, as did the consecration of the first bishop for the American Episcopal Church, the former loyalist Samuel Seabury, by the non-juring bishops in Scotland, after English prelates refused.[9] Upon his return to America, Seabury became the bishop of the Connecticut Episcopal Church. Elsewhere his consecration met with opposition, but the inclusion of Connecticut Anglicans into a national church would eventually require a general acceptance of Seabury's consecration.

Other issues which divided American Anglicanism concerned the role of the laity in the new church and the necessity of liturgical revisions. The General Convention of 1785 held in Philadelphia addressed the English bishops and asked them to consecrate those candidates selected by the state conventions and chosen with the agreement of the laity and civil authorities. Connecticut delegates did not attend this convention, which had failed to appoint a bishop as president, and Bishop Seabury denied that the convention possessed any authority to formulate a constitution or alter the liturgy. The constitution, which was adopted officially in 1789, provided for a triennial General Convention (beginning in June 1786) which was to be composed of clergy and lay delegates chosen in state conventions and selected as representatives of their parishes. Each state was to elect a bishop, whose jurisdiction would be limited to his state, and clergymen were responsible to their state convention. The Proposed Prayer Book, which William White, William Smith, and other committee members began during the 1785 convention, proclaimed an adherence to the beliefs of the Church of England, but to conciliate extremists, the Proposed Book excised the Athanasian and the Nicene Creeds, the expression 'descent into hell' from the Apostles' Creed, and all references to baptismal regeneration. Conservative Episcopalians, especially those in the northern and middle colonies, opposed such changes which deviated from the English church.[10]

In 1789, the General Convention of the Protestant Episcopal Church of the United States, composed of two bishops, 20 clergymen and 16 laymen, officially adopted the constitution, a set of canons, and a newly revised prayer book. No New England delegates attended the first session in the summer, but the unanimous resolution asserting the validity of Seabury's orders encouraged their attendance at the second session in September. Although the American Episcopal Church retained most of the beliefs of its ecclesiastical parent, the Church of England, the American offspring internalized several republican principles. The resulting constitution regulated the functions of laymen, priests, and bishops in a manner which created a limited constitutional episcopate divorced from the English monarchy and Parliament. Liturgical changes to the Church of England's 1662 Book of Common Prayer consisted of a series of revisions made necessary by the fact the English monarch no longer ruled the American colonies, as well as two hundred minor changes, most of which modernized the language.

In comparison with the Proposed Book of 1785, the adopted book of 1789 was characterized by its moderation and conservatism. This prayer book remained in use, with very few alterations, until the major revision of 1892.[11]

The 1789 settlement provided a foundation for the American Episcopal Church which reconciled divergent ecclesiastical opinions about church government and forms of worship. Ultimately, regional lines of tension did not prevent the formation of a national church, although underlying antagonisms continued for decades. From the perspective of the 1770s and early 1780s, all of these issues remained unsettled and highly contentious. For each Anglican clergyman, disestablishment, political independence, and the reformulation of American Anglicanism also involved complicated issues of self-identity.

Faced with dramatic changes in the relationship of church and state, Anglican clergymen during the Revolutionary War and its immediate aftermath had to consider carefully matters of financial support. Pre-Revolutionary publications of the Corporation for the Relief of Widows and Children had emphasized that ministers should not engage in most secular employments, but disestablishment meant that ministers with large families had to consider the alternatives.[12] Thomas Barton, who fled to New York in the autumn of 1778, left his eight children and his 'much beloved people' on the Pennsylvania frontier. Although he did not wish to be permanently separated from his parishioners, Barton feared that if legislative obstacles were not removed he would have to ask for an English post.[13] In trying to decide whether he should leave for England in 1782 with the British brigade he served as chaplain, Samuel Cooke acknowledged he would leave behind seven children, but thought it prudent to retain his chaplaincy, which provided support for his family. Lacking a secure salary, many ministers found employment as teachers, farmers, physicians, or chaplains. Many of Abraham Beach's parishioners had moved to New York by 1782, while those who remained had been unable to support him; consequently his support depended 'entirely on the Produce of a little Farm, & the Society's Bounty.'[14] To provide for his family of 12, John Sayre practiced medicine behind the king's lines in New York City. For others, army chaplaincies offered badly needed remuneration. Loyalist ministers who assumed chaplaincies were not always career soldiers, but men trying to make a living. Mather Byles acted as a garrison chaplain in Halifax, but also served a large hospital and a school.[15]

Financial woes, including wartime inflation and taxes, also inhibited the ability of laymen to contribute to the salary of their clergyman. John Rutgers

Marshall in 1782 reported that the Connecticut clergy officiated as formerly, but received only 'a mere trifle' from their parishioners due to 'the very heavy load of taxes they *groan* under.'[16] In the spring of 1785, James Scovil, who then had nine children, described that he had served his Connecticut parishioners for 26 years. They were unable to pay him much, but he feared they would fall victim to vice and error if he left.[17] In such dire situations, deserting a congregation because of its wartime poverty seemed unchristian, particularly when the minister and parishioners had enjoyed an amiable relationship. In his farewell sermon Roger Viets proclaimed his great respect and affection for his parishioners, thanking them for their kindness and friendship. 'Never, perhaps, was a minister and people separated with more reluctance on both sides; never, perhaps, was their mutual regret more equally balanced.'[18] On leaving his flock at Schenectady, New York, Rev. John Doty claimed

it was not my intention to desert them wholly, but only for a season: that, escaping the present storm, I might be of use to them in future ... And indeed the great affection of my people (most of whom surrounded me at my departure and with weeping eyes took their leave of me) is of itself a great inducement to my return.[19]

Under such circumstances of mutual affection, a decision to leave the community must have been especially difficult. When the relationship lacked such amiability, the departure could be accomplished with more ease. Samuel Tingley criticized his former Delaware mission's 'ingratitude, nay their injustice' at failing to pay the arrears they owed him. He moved to Maryland.[20]

During the war, the minister's relationship with his parishioners not only affected decisions of incumbency, but also the general community perception of his political inclinations. Amiable relations with parishioners could encourage local rebels to overlook a minister's lukewarm affections for the Revolution, while a more tempestuous association could prove damaging. Philip Reading noted in 1776 that his lay friends shielded him from potential abuses. 'As to my own immediate Flock I have the comfort to say that in general I live with them on the best terms and it is probably owing to some Gentlemen of influence and authority among them that notwithstanding the danger of the times I continue on a respectable and useful footing in this place.'[21] Edward Winslow of Braintree, Massachusetts, also attributed his family's escape from the general rebel rage to the influence of 'some leading persons' and later 'the rapid progress' of the king's forces.[22] In January 1777 he had long expected to be summoned before the Assembly for continuing to officiate in public without any alteration of the

Anglican service. Christopher MacRae's parishioners in Virginia shielded their beloved pastor from the demands of the revolutionary state and explained his refusal to take the oath of allegiance to the commonwealth as a 'Scruple of Conscience' for he was a 'Strict Churchman.' They even petitioned the General Assembly that MacRae be allowed to remain on the glebe and continue his duties.[23] In contrast, Alexander Cruden's Virginian parishioners were less understanding; when he announced publicly that he could not stop praying for the king nor substitute prayers for Congress in good conscience, his vestry advertised in the *Gazette* for his replacement and stated that the incumbent had abdicated.[24]

Poor relations with parishioners decreased the minister's chances of weathering the storms of the Revolution. Earlier in his career, the unpopular Bennet Allen had failed to endear himself to two Maryland congregations when he insisted on holding both posts in plurality, contrary to the establishment law of 1702. His participation in clerical salary disputes in the 1760s and his criticism of the colonists' behavior toward the British government only further alienated him from his parish, and he sailed to England in 1775.[25] William Douglas of Louisa County, Virginia, believed he had served his parish faithfully, but was dismayed and bitter as a result of his termination. The day before the vestry voted him out, he had traveled fifty miles, married several couples, visited three sick families and baptized seven children. He had returned home 'only about Cock-Crow' the morning of the vestry meeting, at which time he was delivered to the meeting and reprimanded before the vestry for having spoken disrespectfully.[26] Douglas did not choose to comment upon the justice of the charge, but noted rather the irony of his termination after such dedicated and fatiguing service. He felt that influential parishioners had betrayed him through their lack of affection. In July 1776 Rev. J. Graves of Providence, Rhode Island, resigned his post and declined subsequent requests to preach by explaining that his ministerial authority derived not from civil powers but from the ecclesiastical realm, namely bishops and archbishops. Later, in April 1781, Graves denied that he had ever resigned, and appeared quite indignant at the demand that he remove himself from the glebe house after 25 years of service. At the war's end, Graves asked his congregation to overlook the past and rehire him, but they refused, having already made arrangements with another minister. The churchwardens were both surprised that Graves offered to resume his ministry and bitter that he had left them for so long destitute of religious services.[27] Peace in 1783 could not restore that relationship.

While harmonious relations with the laity generally pleased both the ministers and their superiors, the relationship sometimes came under question in the context of the Revolution. In rebel strongholds, ministers such as Edward Bass of Newburyport, Massachusetts, who appeared to be allied too closely with their parishioners, risked incurring the wrath of British officials. Bass's amiable relations with his parishioners caused SPG members to question how he was able to remain quietly after 1776 in such a rebellious province, from which most of the Massachusetts missionaries had fled. Did not his residency in the land of rebels suggest he must have made compromises with the patriots? Several of Bass's colleagues and parishioners testified about his loyalty to Britain, but the SPG dismissed Bass from their service in 1779. Bass did not receive official notification of the charges alleged against him, and lamented 'the singularity of my Fate in being a Sufferer on both Sides, here for my Loyalty, with you [the SPG] for the contrary.' He felt that he was being punished for remaining in New England, since he asserted that many Anglican exiles 'were extremely prejudiced against us who staid behind and kept our churches open.'[28] Aware of the cloud of suspicion hanging over Bass's head, other ministers opposed any mention of their names in the same breath with his. In a letter to J. W. Weeks, Jacob Bailey insisted that Bass, 'without encountering any persecution or difficulty, complied with the first motion of his congregation, (mostly high sons of liberty,) wholly to drop all prayers for the King.'[29] Bass found himself in the most difficult position of being considered an enemy to both sides. As Daniel Fogg explained, Bass's 'situation is very disagreeable. Here he is looked upon as an Enemy to his Country, & by the venerable Society as unfriendly to the British Government.'[30]

The interplay of ministerial duty to family and local parishes coexisted and intertwined with broader personal affiliations. Colonial ministers perceived themselves as members of the Church of England, as part of an informal network of colonial Anglican ministers, or as missionaries of specific organizations, particularly the SPG. Furthermore, their self-identities as Americans or Englishmen had to confront the realities of an altered imperial situation. Ultimately, these issues of personal identification influenced clerical reactions to the creation and structure of the American Protestant Episcopal Church.

Throughout the colonial period, acceptance of England as a cultural center and admiration for her constitution evoked among many colonists a personal attachment to the mother country. During the Revolution and the subsequent creation of state and national constitutions, a distinctive American identity emerged which separated itself from this imperial identity.[31]

As members of the empire, Anglican ministers experienced the cultural and psychological transitions which accompanied the fragmentation of the empire and the creation of a new republic. Because their relationship with England was crystallized in a formal manner, these developments proved particularly critical, but like the colonial population generally, Anglican ministers' attachment to England varied. Some were born in the mother country, others in America, and many had been educated in British universities. All, however, had visited London at least once for Anglican orders. These experiences proved dazzling for some colonial clergymen who personally witnessed the pageantry of the English church and court. In 1771 Rev. James Ogilvie of Virginia described immodestly his attendance at an elite London gathering and his impressions of the Archbishop of York, and the Bishops of Durham and Lincoln, who 'took such notice and showed me several other marks of favour.'[32] As he wrote to his father, Thomas Coombe of Philadelphia believed that living in England improved his character as well as his professional connections.[33]

Early in the war, Anglican ministers, especially suspected loyalists, frequently affirmed that they wished no harm to befall either America or Britain, but rather depicted themselves as a 'sincere friend' to both causes, a position which became increasingly difficult to maintain convincingly. In 1775 Rev. William Smith asserted that 'God knows my love is strong & my zeal ardent for the prosperity of both Countries.'[34] Thomas Bradbury Chandler wrote, 'I consider Great-Britain and her colonies, with her other dependencies, as but one body.'[35] By asserting the unity of American and English interests in a publication which criticized the activities of the Continental Congress, Chandler aimed to prove that he intended no harm to America. In a defensive manner, he proclaimed the unity of the empire, and yet emphasized his own American attachments so as not to anger the revolutionaries. Although colonial rebels had many better reasons for their dislike of Rev. Jonathan Boucher, he thought that at least some of his enemies had labeled him a loyalist due to his English birth, even though he had married in America and owned property there.

> I am ashamed to reply to many strange and random surmises which have been busily propagated as to my supposed inimicality to America, merely because I am not a native of America. It is folly to imagine, that, as an Englishman, interested in the welfare of England, I am not equally interested in the welfare of America. I cannot dissociate the idea of a perfect sameness of interest between the two countries, as much as between a parent and a child.[36]

Boucher thought that such an affirmation of his respect for both America and England would win the approval of his opponents, but rebels remained unconvinced.

Acceptance of England as a cultural center also encouraged a personal identification with England as a parent or a cultural 'home.' British sermons delivered during the Revolutionary War noted American ingratitude by referring specifically to Isaiah 1: 2, 'I have nourished and brought up children and they have rebelled against me.'[37] Rev. George Bisset expected the revolutionaries to come to their senses eventually, and like the prodigal son, return to their father, but he wrote to assure the loyalists of the righteousness of their position. He urged that revolutionary villains had 'torn the ungrateful offspring of Britain, from the embraces of a fond and indulgent parent.'[38] Using the same analogy, Chandler noted that by 1785 many of his parishioners in Elizabeth Town were 'disposed to adopt the language of the repenting Prodigal in the Parable, towards the *Parent* country.'[39] For those ministers who identified with England as a spiritual or national home, independence and the peace of 1783 occasioned great turmoil. Ebenezer Dibblee, in a letter to Samuel Peters, demonstrated the psychological confusion and bitterness which accompanied this process of redefining what constituted 'home.' After inquiring of Peters how English officials 'at Home' viewed Samuel Seabury's consecration, Dibblee continued, '[w]hy did I say at Home, Governt hath disinherited us.'[40]

Conversely, patriot Anglican clergymen came to redefine their national home and even their parent as America. Such revisionism reinforced revolutionary patterns of civil religion since the redefinition of America as not only a home, but also a parent, looked toward the future and conformed to the conceptualization of America as an elect nation. Patriot chaplain of a Virginia regiment, David Griffith frequently reminded his wife, Hannah, of his devotion to her and their 'flock' of children, but also his patriotic duty to his 'Country.' By 'Country,' Griffith undoubtedly meant America, or more probably Virginia, but certainly he no longer referred to any imperial connections.[41] In his address before patriot troops from Virginia, John Hurt declared, 'we are all children of one common mother, AMERICA, our country.'[42] Hurt's definition of America as the cultural parent emphasized what he perceived to be the united interests of the colonies to defend themselves against British encroachments.

Opinions which favored disestablishment also contained distinct themes of civil religion and emphasized the importance of new beginnings. Rev. James Madison of Virginia, a firm patriot during the Revolution, acknowledged in 1786 that ' "the hour cometh and now is when the true worshippers [sh]all worship the father in spirit and in truth." America, presents

the first glorious [in]stance, wherein religion and policy are no longer connected, by an union as oppressive to men as it has been disgraceful to
Christianity.'[43] In addition to heralding a new political era, the American
Revolution was a 'precursor to a general revolution in human affairs.'
Providence intended America to become 'the asylum of mankind.' This
asylum, in turn, created a new foundation for political and religious happiness by separating the realm of politics from that of religion. '[U]nre-
strained by the schemes of political ambition,' the church would blossom.[44]
By 1800, the Connecticut minister John Tyler shared Madison's view of
the new republic. '[T]his extensive, and newly erected Empire [is to be] an
Asylum for the Oppressed and Afflicted of Europe.' Tyler indicated his
adoption of American civil religion in his recognition of America as a
particularly blessed country and Washington as its revered father. He also
rejected Britain's pre-revolutionary maternal image by characterizing the
Revolution as 'our Separation from a great and warlike Nation.'[45]

    At war's end, issues of national identity affected ministers' perceived
roles in the new Episcopal church. Samuel Seabury made the transition to
become the first bishop of the American Episcopal Church in Connecticut,
although his former loyalism concerned many members of the new
Protestant Episcopal Church.[46] Although invited to attend church conventions, William Currie of Pennsylvania declined to participate in the postwar formation of the American church since he had not taken the revolutionary oath to the state. He described himself 'as not being a Citizen' of
the new republic.[47] While the peace of 1783 and the king's acknowledge-
ment of American independence had resolved the Anglo-American disputes of the preceding decades, on a personal level peace created a gulf for
those who continued to conceive of themselves as Englishmen. To what
country did Anglican clergymen owe their allegiance at the war's end? Of
course, ministers had struggled with this question throughout the war, but
in 1783 Rev. Abraham Jarvis believed that since providence had ended the
dispute with the victory of the rebels, American colonists residing in the
United States should consider themselves subjects of the new government.
'We are bound in Duty to acquiesce in the Allotment of Divine Providence;
and it will be our Care to approve ourselves wholsom members, and
peaceable Subjects of that Government under which we are now placed.'[48]
Roger Viets held a contrary opinion; since he had not renounced his
British citizenship, he continued to conceive of himself as an Englishman.
Viets claimed English citizenship was a form of personal property and
self-identity which could not be obviated by a political treaty. His commitment to England and her established church also prohibited him from taking any oaths to the new government.[49] Significantly, Jarvis' and Viets'

self-identification with America or England became apparent in their post-revolutionary careers. Jarvis was later consecrated as a bishop of the Protestant Episcopal Church, and Viets became an SPG missionary in Nova Scotia.

The turmoil of the Revolution and the persecutions endured by loyalists sometimes alienated ministers' affection for America, their native country or adopted home. In the fall of 1775 Rev. John Wiswall, a New England native, declared how popular rebelliousness and his personal sufferings had 'weaned' his affections for his country, America. He concluded, 'the further I go from it the better.'[50] If he had any prospects for a living in England, Mather Byles, another New Englander, explained that he would gladly 'bid a final Adieu to my native Country.'[51] Because many individuals felt they had been compelled to leave, the experience of exile produced a combination of regret, bitterness, and anger. As Jacob Bailey recorded in his journal during his voyage from Pownalboro to Halifax, 'Men can readily quit the land which gave them birth and education when interest, pleasure, or curiosity entice them; but when they are expelled by faction, or legal authority, the case is extremely different.'[52] In Bailey's opinion, the situation was even more distressing because the exiles could not know if they would ever be permitted to return.

For ministers who had spent their entire career in the service of the SPG and the Church of England, a considerable incentive existed to relocate to a mission within the British empire. Ranna Cossit of New Hampshire considered his missionary status part of his self-identity, since he had entered the SPG at a young age. In considering a move to Canada, Daniel Fogg concluded that he preferred to live in a region under the jurisdiction of King George III, rather than 'any of the united States' but he admitted little inclination to move to Nova Scotia. Obviously concerned about the climate, Fogg asked the SPG if there were any vacant missions further south.[53] In most cases, the factors of remuneration and obligation cannot be separated, and only rarely did a minister, such as Roger Viets, offer his reasons for leaving. Before moving to Digby, Nova Scotia, Viets mentioned the issue of remuneration and then declared that

> [a] weighty inducement to my removal arose from gratitude to the pious and venerable society for the propagation of the gospel in foreign parts, who have been my principal and most constant supporters. Reason and gratitude bound me to pay an high regard to their commands. They directed me to remove myself to Digby in Nova-Scotia.[54]

Viets' implication that the SPG had insisted upon his removal may have been exaggerated, since the Society had little reason to oppose a ministerial decision to remain in the former American colonies. He may have supplied an answer to please his friends and parishioners, while offering a clue about additional motives. Viets remarked vaguely that he could not properly comment on whether his decision had been affected by the constitutional differences between Connecticut and Nova Scotia. Significantly, Viets had disapproved of some liturgical innovations in the American Protestant Episcopal Church. A post in Nova Scotia provided him with a secure salary and an opportunity to remain in the service of the SPG and continue his lifelong affiliation with the Church of England.

In the late eighteenth century, the Anglican churches of British North America and the new American republic each took a different path in church–state relations. While the American Episcopal Church integrated republican values, Canada emerged as a new Canaan in the wilderness for those who continued to hold establishmentarian notions of the mutual reinforcing roles of church and state. In fact, one minister suggested that the northerly latitude could not support liberty-poles.[55] The Constitutional Act of 1791, by providing the Anglican church with a landed endowment in Upper Canada in the form of clergy reserves, affirmed a role for the Church of England as a national church. William Knox, Under-Secretary for the colonies between 1770 and 1782, concluded that a general plan to establish the Church of England in British North America could combat and repress colonial republicanism and encourage respect for monarchy.[56] Furthermore, Anglican ministers believed that the loyalists who settled in the Canadian frontier shared their establishmentarian vision. As J. Wiswall explained, 'For what they [loyalists] have suffered from their fanatical brethren in N[ew] England has convinced them of the necessity of standing by the Chh of England as the only way to support the British constitution for whose defence they have cheerfully sacrificed their all.'[57] The inhabitants of Digby expressed a similar sentiment by describing themselves as voluntary exiles who preferred Nova Scotia to the tyranny of republican government.[58] The Canadian wilderness provided a new opportunity for the propagation of the gospel, but also a chance to recover former patterns of an established church supported by royal government. Aboard ship approaching this destination, Jacob Bailey remarked, 'it gave us immense pleasure to behold a country under the dominion of our lawful Prince, and where the tyranny of republican villains had not yet extended.'[59]

The rupture of the civil bond between England and the American colonies forced those Anglican clergymen who continued to reside in America to consider on what foundation the new church could be built. Early in the conflict, beginning in 1776, the ministers first had to assess what role, if any, the English monarch should possess. Could he remain the spiritual head of the colonial church after a political declaration of independence? For fervent supporters of the monarchy, no compromise was possible. During the war, Rev. Matthew Graves reported that he was often asked to officiate, but he 'abhorred the idea of an Independent Church.'[60] Philip Reading announced succinctly in August 1776 that since the Declaration of Independence 'the Church of England has now no longer an existence in the united Colonies of America.' This conclusion he derived from his understanding of the intimate relationship between the constitutions of church and state. 'I look upon the King's Supremacy and the Constitution of the Church to be so intimately blended together, that whenever the Supremacy is either suspended or abrogated, the fences of the Church are then broken down, and its visibility is destroyed.'[61] As a crisis of conscience and behavior, Independence had contributed to the polarization of Anglican clergy into loyalist or patriot camps. As the patriot William White later wrote, he had prayed for the king until the Sunday before 4 July 1776, but shortly thereafter took an oath of allegiance to the United States. As he later explained, he had 'since remained faithful to it. My intentions were upright, & most seriously weighed. I hope they were not in contrariety to my Duty.'[62] Writing in 1819 to Bishop John Henry Hobart, White could be confident that he had taken the right path.

   With the peace treaty in 1783, loyalist Anglican clergymen could no longer hope that everything would be resolved with a British victory. Ministers of every political inclination who remained in the colonies had to decide whether they could participate in the foundation of a church which operated independently from the king and the English church. If a minister's dedication to the Church of England disallowed any compromise, he would have to retire from the ministry or relocate within the British empire. For individuals who had consistently looked to the English ecclesiastical hierarchy for direction and self-definition, the ability of an independent American church to succeed appeared doubtful. Pessimistic laments about the church's chances for long-term survival included Edward Winslow's depiction of the colonial church in 1779 as teetering 'almost on the Brink of Extinction.'[63] Once 'so glorious a Luminary in the Christian World,' John Sayre of New York mourned that the church was 'apparently expiring.'[64] Similarly, Uzal Ogden recalled the church's situation at the end of the war: 'dissevered from that Church from which we descended ... we were in a state of disorganization; cut off, as a stream from its fountain, and, as a religious body, ready to perish!'[65] Certainly many Anglican ministers and laity shared Bela Hubbard's 'gloomy fears

arising from the dismemberment of the Empire that this event may prove
fatal to the poor American Church of England.'[66]

Such doomsday predictions must be understood in the context of the
dramatic changes in the church's identity and socio-political role. Not only
did Anglican ministers have to adjust to a new form of remuneration
which also meant increasing the powers of their vestries, but disestablishment heralded a new religious sensibility which might best be described as
denominationalism. Many ministers had promoted religious toleration in
the past, but to embrace denominationalism, individuals had to accept the
positive attributes of religious competition and simultaneously recognize
the disadvantages of its antithesis, establishmentarianism. Rev. William
Duke of Maryland, who obtained Anglican orders after the Revolution,
represented a new generation of American Episcopalians in his embrace of
a denominational approach to religion. He argued that the post-Revolution
church would enjoy greater success than it had ever derived from civil
power. He prophesied that

> [t]hen it will appear that we are not destitute of religion, though we have
> no legal establishment … For although the partial attention of the civil
> power, in the maintenance of one certain society, would seem to interest
> it more in religious affairs, I believe it will always be found, that the
> less its purposes towards religion are affected, by the peculiarities of
> any one party, the more essentially it will promote the common cause.[67]

From the perspective of the 1790s, the Church of England's history in
colonial Maryland depicted the many pitfalls of establishmentarianism.
Reflecting upon these years, Duke noted that the church derived many
advantages from its connection with government, but that the church grew
in 'bulk if not in virtue' since regardless of whether the clergymen were
'pious or profane, the per poll was the same.' In Duke's interpretation, the
colonial Church of England had grown careless and lost its higher purpose
because its Maryland ministers 'did not seem to interest themselves in
matters of religion, any further than their livings were concerned.'[68]

Duke's acceptance of denominationalism and its corollary, an abhorrence for establishmentarianism, proved a difficult leap for those who, in
the colonial period, had benefitted from their connection to the established
church and for those who held an ideological commitment to the idea of a
national church. In 1770 Bennet Allen of Maryland wrote a treatise which
denounced the principle of voluntary subscription and advocated the continuation of state support for Anglican clergymen. Answering the publication of a Church of England planter, Allen wrote that colonies without

a religious establishment were

thereby deprived of the inestimable Benefit of religious Union, and for Want of a national Church, are by the Equality of all Sectaries, torn and convulsed by continual Struggles, between them for Superiority and Pre-eminence, whilst their Ministers feel all the Miseries of a precarious Dependance often on *in*voluntary Contributions, and are exposed to Contempt, the never failing Attendant on Poverty.[69]

To the suggestion that Anglican ministers' salaries be fixed by the parish vestry, Allen replied, 'What, by voluntary Contribution? Precarious Dependance!'[70] Although Allen wrote before the actual disestablishment of the Maryland church, his opinions were echoed later by other supporters of establishmentarianism.

In the 1770s and 1780s several Anglican ministers shared Allen's abhorrence of disestablishment and utilized a two-pronged defense of traditional practices which emphasized both the inadequacies of voluntary subscription and the admirable principles of establishmentarianism. Most clergymen did not record their opinions. Once disestablishment had passed their state legislature, opposition would have been imprudent, particularly since their association with the English church already rendered them suspect of loyalism. But for the vocal and the quiet both, the separation of church and state affected matters of personal and financial security. Consequently, ministers tended to personalize their accounts of disestablishment. Joshua Bloomer of Long Island wrote that '[b]y the Constitution of the state of New York all Denominations of Protestants are placed on a Level ... by which I suffer the loss of £60 per annum.'[71] In a petition to the General Assembly of Virginia in 1776, several Anglican clergy argued that the abolition of the established church would deprive them of their private property. These unnamed petitioners also argued that a religious establishment promoted civil peace and happiness, and they claimed that in Virginia the mild and tolerant establishment had not restricted the religious liberty of dissenters, who aimed to ruin the Anglican church.[72] In such a manner, materialist arguments of clerical remuneration could be combined with more principled defenses. Rev. Samuel Shield of Virginia asserted in 1784 his continued belief in the principles of establishmentarianism, namely its encouragement of uniformity in worship and discipline. Innovations in politics or religion terrified him, particularly because he feared that change, once initiated, could not be easily contained.[73]

Opponents of religious voluntarism also based their opinions on a certain pessimism about human nature and popular willingness to maintain religion. Abraham Beach of New Jersey opposed voluntary subscriptions since he contended that without civil backing people would not support religion. He claimed that voluntary subscriptions could only be 'trifling & precarious' given the existence of heavy taxes and 'the Cold Indifference with Respect to Religion' which he believed prevailed among 'the greater Part of Mankind when *left to themselves.*'[74] Beach acknowledged that wartime financial difficulties precluded much generosity towards the clergy, but he believed that ultimately religious voluntarism could not be reconciled with human nature.

The efficacy of voluntary subscription depended upon parishioners' affections for individual ministers, and therefore, even after the peace of 1783, financial security depended, in some measure, upon the clergymen's political views during the Revolution. The colonial Church of England's association with loyalism during the Revolutionary War did not generally encourage great generosity on the part of the revolutionary laity toward its ministers. In 1784 Daniel Earl of North Carolina claimed that after disestablishment, only those Anglican clergy who had supported the Revolution received contributions by subscription and even that provision did not last. Instead, dissenters who were thought to have been 'very Instrumental' in the Revolution received the most public favor. Although patriot clergy fared better than loyalists, Earl held little hope that voluntary subscriptions would provide any certain financial security. Since dissenters now had the right to solemnize marriages, the Anglican clergy were deprived of those exclusive rights to perquisites which they had possessed in an established church.[75]

For clergymen who held High Church notions of the superior role of the clergy over the laity, disestablishment, as well as civil revolution, turned the world upside down and reversed the traditional direction of authority. Significantly, it empowered the laity with the tremendously important responsibility of sustaining the church's government and finances. The godly state of the church itself would come to depend upon the laity's 'punctuality, also, in the discharge of their pecuniary obligations to the Clergy.'[76] Rev. Charles Edward Taylor of North Carolina decided to resign his parish in Bertie County after the Declaration of Independence at which time, he noted, 'all Establishment then ceased.' As Taylor explained, he did not want to raise contributions 'by so mean a Method as then was left, a Collection with a Hat being mean indeed.'[77] Taylor did not dispute the effectiveness of voluntary subscription in providing ministers with an adequate salary, but he did emphasize its impropriety. In his opinion, such a system was incommensurate with the dignity of the ministry. Since the tipping of a man's hat traditionally indicated his place in the community's social hierarchy, the idea of a minister having to remove his hat and use it for begging must have been disturbing. In Taylor's imagery, religious voluntarism reduced ministers to objects of parochial charity.

Although the benefits of disestablishment could not be adopted easily or quickly by members of the church which had the most to lose by the elimination of state support, American Anglicanism came to accept the new religious order. This transition can be attributed to several factors, including the substantial wartime exile of loyalists, many of whom affirmed traditional establishmentarian views. Many SPG ministers also decided to leave their American congregations after the war; between 1783 and 1789, Connecticut lost one-third of its ministers.[78] Conservatives who opposed innovations in the foundation of the American Episcopal Church, including Roger Viets, numbered among these post-revolutionary exiles. Less committed conservatives may have been persuaded to embrace denominationalism as a result of the American Revolution and the internalization of republican principles of religious liberty and voluntarism.

The American Revolution had indicated to many Anglican ministers the potentially disastrous religious ramifications of their association with the British state, a connection which brought them to the brink of destruction. During the war itself, many commentators interested in the future of colonial Anglicanism became aware that distance from the British Crown improved their chances of weathering the storm, and, with independence achieved, the church was left 'unfettered by the secular arm.'[79] In 1784, David Griffith noted that the church in Virginia, still legally fettered, had to proceed cautiously. To alter church government, introduce ordination and revise the liturgy, the clergy first had to petition for a repeal of the relevant colonial legislation. In Griffith's analysis, the continued civil connection inhibited the pace of essential ecclesiastical change in postrevolutionary Virginia. Once the church could be separated from the state, Anglicanism then might remodel itself after primitive Christianity.[80]

Former loyalists, as well as patriots, could recognize the advantages of such a separation. From exile in England, Jacob Duché warned against innovations in apostolical succession, but optimistically thought that the new American Episcopal Church might be created closer to primitive practices than any other throughout Christendom. The patriot minister Samuel Parker of Boston, who had continued services at Trinity Church during the war, later expressed a similar belief by arguing that bishops should never have had any civil powers. Before Constantine, they had not possessed worldly powers, and Parker believed that the church would have been better off if that situation had persisted to the present.[81] Even postwar poverty might offer an advantage since a church separated from worldly power would offer little temptation for politically ambitious but spiritually unworthy candidates.[82] Ultimately, the separation of church and state could benefit the new Episcopal Church. While William White of Philadelphia did not wish 'a departure from the properties of the venerable stock from which we spring,' he did perceive the necessity of protecting the church 'from being shocked by any future changes in political interests and opinions.'[83] An apolitical foundation would provide greater security for the church's future development.

Given the possible advantages of separating from government, Anglican ministers debated what role American state or federal governments might assume in the church's reorganization. Samuel Parker recognized by the 1780s a prevailing American opinion that all power, spiritual as well as temporal, originated with the people. Perhaps he learned this lesson when other Anglican ministers and British troops had fled Boston and his vestry voted that he continue services with the omission of those parts of the liturgy related to the king. At war's end, Parker wondered whether Congress would support a request to England for a bishop, but denied that Parliament should have to validate the creation of a purely spiritual office.[84] Other ministers showed less inclination to defer to American governments. John Tyler believed that his Connecticut brethren should not petition the state for permission to settle a bishop. He argued that the principle of religious liberty granted them such a right, and if they were to ask for permission, they would appear to be acknowledging their subordination to civil authorities. Most Connecticut ministers recognized that the General Assembly of their state after the Revolution extended religious toleration and therefore would not oppose a bishop.[85]

A few patriot ministers believed that the virtue of republican citizens would provide a surer foundation for the church than previous civil ties. Despite his great optimism concerning the new republic, Rev. James Madison warned that to survive the republic required virtue, and that without religion virtue would certainly perish.[86] Disestablishment had rendered virtue even more significant. 'Destitute of that coercive power, which compels obedience to civil laws, the enforcement of those which you have adopted, as a christian society, depends entirely upon your virtue ... [and] a high and elevated sense of duty.'[87] Samuel Parker also affirmed that religion and virtue provided the most certain means of obtaining national prosperity, and that if Americans did not remain a virtuous and religious people, God would withdraw his blessings.[88] Ultimately a loss of virtue would result in the general neglect of divine worship and the sacraments, which in turn, 'will be attended with the loss of arts and sciences, good government, liberty, commerce, power and influence.'[89] In the 1790s when many congregations neglected to send lay deputies to the annual church conventions, thereby threatening the viability of the church's government, officials of the church then wondered whether such a strong dependence upon the people's virtue had been a prudent decision.[90]

In the post-revolutionary period, most of the American Anglican ministry gradually accepted denominationalism, a religious value supported by revolutionary ideals of liberty and egalitarianism and reinforced by pre-existing latitudinarian practices of religious toleration. The Church of England's previous colonial status as an established church in six colonies had offered stability and secure clerical remuneration, but in the aftermath of the American Revolution many wondered if the cost had not been too high. By embracing the positive attributes of denominationalism, the new religious paradigm of the post-revolutionary republic, Anglican clergymen provided an ideological foundation for their church which was compatible with the new civil structure. William Smith revealed a denominationalist's perspective on religion in his suggestion that compulsion cannot be effective in winning souls, and every man must answer for himself. He contended that in his enlightened day, 'all churches ... are approaching nearer to each other in christian charity; and those garments which were once rolled in blood are undergoing a daily and silent ablution!'[91] Similarly, William Duke argued, '... as the Church of Christ is digested into a variety of associations, conformably to the unavoidable diversity of sentiment that marks the fallibility of the human understanding, it were much better to attach ourselves to a society of our own sentiments, than make disturbance amongst those whom we suppose to be mistaken.'[92]

An acceptance of religious pluralism and a rejection of establishmentarian definitions of church and state did not necessarily eliminate contention. Instead, the principle erected a new framework of interdenominational competition. Samuel Magaw acknowledged that several denominations of Christians were divided in their interpretation of the practices of the primitive church, and asserted that while Anglican ideas were well-known and convincing, Anglicans did not refuse 'to others that privilege of examining and judging for themselves.'[93] Nonetheless, he opposed the most flagrant forms of contention. Samuel Seabury did not think that the church's new identity in the American republic entailed any acknowledgment of its equality with other religions. Instead, Seabury argued that Anglican ministers needed to understand their religion, 'and be able to give a good account of it, or we shall not be able to defend it, or to convince gainsayers.'[94] Although Seabury believed that religious disputes usually should be avoided, he contended that duty sometimes necessitated involvement in controversy. To be victorious, ministers required a thorough knowledge of doctrines, and the ultimate goal, the winning of souls, remained the same.

In New England, where the Congregational establishment continued, post-revolutionary changes in the relationship of church and state tended to favor dissenters, including Anglicans. As several SPG missionaries noted with pleasure, the elimination of ties to England provided opportunities to ameliorate Anglican–dissenter relations and finally introduce the episcopal structure. Samuel Magaw considered episcopal succession one of the most important benefits of the separation from England. 'In one matter, of very great importance, the having *among ourselves*, the ministerial *Succession* in its respective *Orders*, – we are on a much better footing, than, probably, we should *ever* have been, if our former *political* connexion had continued.'[95] John Tyler also recognized that the Episcopal Church by 1784 was treated with more civility, for dissenters no longer had reason to be jealous of Anglicans' connection to 'the civil Arm' or fearful that the British court's promotion of the Church of England would harm dissenters.[96] In the campaign for an Anglican episcopate at the war's end, the absence of dissenter opposition also testified to a new relationship between Congregationalism and Anglicanism. As Bela Hubbard acknowledged with pleasure in March 1784, the General Assembly of Connecticut had no objection to the plan of the Episcopal clergy to acquire a bishop.[97]

Despite optimism that denominationalism would secure a strong foundation, including episcopal succession, the creation of a new church necessarily involved great controversy. Most importantly, the founders had to decide what ties, if any, should be maintained with England and also to what extent the new church should conform to the principles of American politics. These two issues became inextricably intertwined with disagreements over High Church and Low Church practices, as well as latent antagonisms between northern and southern Anglicans. The ability to accept and embrace change resulted from personal dispositions, or temperaments, but conservatism also tended to be most marked among older individuals.[98] Contemporaries recognized this reality by noting how they had grown grey-headed in the service of the church and consequently abhorred change. Ebenezer Dibblee mentioned that by 1793 the new services, as written in the Prayer Book of 1789, had been widely adopted, 'altho the omissions & verbal alterations, will never be agreeable to the old Tory Church men.'[99] As Dibblee suggested, patriot or loyalist inclinations also influenced personal dispositions towards ecclesiastical change. Loyalists who interpreted the Revolution as an unnatural and unnecessary dispute were predisposed to consider ecclesiastical alterations in a similar light.

Many Anglican ministers, particularly SPG members who resided in the middle or northern colonies, had not desired an entire separation from England. Politically, that issue had been resolved by the king's acknowledgment of the independence of the United States in a speech before Parliament in December 1782, as well as the formal peace of 1783. For clergymen like Thomas Coombe who could not ally themselves with the colonies as long as the sovereign kept 'up his claim of right upon this country,' peace must have been liberating.[100] As William White succinctly observed, 'the Episcopal Church in the United States had been severed, by a civil revolution, from the jurisdiction of the parent Church in England.'[101] Despite this tone of political finality, future cultural and religious relations with England remained uncertain.

Samuel Parker, a Boston patriot, expressed relief at the return of peace in 1783, but also regret over the separation of two countries with such similar interests, customs and religion as might otherwise have suggested the need for 'a perpetual Union.'[102] Many Anglican ministers shared Parker's sentiments and tried to maintain some ties with England, their cultural and ecclesiastical parent. In April 1783 the clergy of Connecticut composed a letter to the Archbishop of York which declared their desire to maintain ecclesiastical ties with England. 'This part of America is at length dismembered from the British Empire; but notwithstanding the dissolution of our *civil* connection with the parent state, we still hope to retain the *religious polity*; the primitive and evangelical doctrine and discipline, which, at the Reformation, were restored and established in the Church of England.'[103] While many supported the voluntary continuation of ties, Rev. Ebenezer Dibblee doubted that American Anglicans actually were released from the English church and 'all obligation in Spiritualities of Canonical obedience.' Dibblee believed that his colleagues, who mistakenly thought themselves free from all obligations to the Church of England, were making 'wild work in reforming the Liturgy, and Setting an Ecclesiastical Polity & Constitution.' Furthermore, Dibblee feared potential English reaction to the consecration of Samuel Seabury by the nonjuring bishops of Scotland. He worried that the English government, the clergy, and the Society would think them 'all Jacobites' and that consequently future connections would be impaired.[104]

Dibblee's apprehensions did not paralyze the majority of American Anglican clergymen, who believed that the peace of 1783 freed them to pursue their own church structure, even if they wished to maintain most of the beliefs of the English church. The American church naturally looked to its English parent for the consecration of its bishops, but an Act of Parliament was necessary before English prelates could excuse American candidates from the Oath of the King's Supremacy. Such legislation did not pass until June 1786. In the meantime, the Danish church would have ordained Americans, after a subscription to the Thirty-Nine Articles of the Church of England (excepting the political parts), but as William White explained, 'there was no idea of having recourse, in the first instance, to any other quarter than that of the English Episcopacy.'[105] Only after thorough application to English officials had Samuel Seabury sought consecration through the prelates of the Church of Scotland.

While the issue of episcopal consecration for the American church remained unsettled, members debated whether structural or liturgical changes could be initiated before they had acquired a duly constituted bishop. As in the previous campaign in the 1760s for a colonial episcopate, the prevailing opinions of southern and northern churchmen differed dramatically. In the 1780s, two contrary proposals for church development emerged from Connecticut and Philadelphia. The first effort at reorganizing Anglican churches occurred in Maryland in November 1780 at which time organizers employed the name 'Protestant Episcopal Church' to replace their former designation as members of the Church of England. The national church later adopted the same title. While Maryland clergymen and laity tried to organize within their state, Rev. William White of Philadelphia proposed a plan for the federal union of all Anglican churches. White's widely read publication, *The Case of the Episcopal Church in the United States Considered* (1782), recommended amendments to church structure to conform with the new political values of the United States. He believed that the American church should distance itself from the English church, accept the parish as the basic unit of organization, include laymen as part of their church government, and, at least in the beginning, permit the lay-election of an American bishop due to the urgent need for ministers. White's plan did not win the support of many loyalist churchmen from Connecticut and elsewhere who denied the necessity for such radical changes, strongly opposed such a role for the laity in church government, and insisted that the acquisition of a duly constituted bishop was a necessary first step before any other reorganization could occur. At a meeting in Woodbury, Connecticut, on 25 March 1783, attendants articulated their preference for the English system, including the diocese as the unit of organization, and they took preliminary steps to elect a candidate, Jeremiah Leaming or Samuel Seabury, to seek consecration in England.[106]

Contrary to many SPG ministers who advocated the continuation of close ties with England, Rev. William White envisioned a much more independent American church, which, he believed, would comport better with both American independence and a long-standing colonial acceptance of lay participation in the church. Furthermore, the urgencies of securing a bishop for the church to ordain ministers necessitated innovation. *The Case of the Episcopal Church* argued that 'subjection to any spiritual juris- diction, connected with the temporal authority of a foreign state' would be a clear violation of the duties which American citizens owed to the states. The former connection with the Bishop of London, whose authority was derived from the Crown, was 'dissolved by the revolution.' White also explicitly denied the possibility of a purely spiritual relationship between the American Episcopal church and the English church. Even if the Bishop of London no longer required oaths to the English crown, any American 'dependence on his Lordship and his successors in that See would be liable to the reproach of foreign influence, and render episcopalians less qualified than those of other communions, to be entrusted by their coun- try.'[107] The general suspicion of Anglican disloyalty to the American states during the Revolution, if perpetuated, would threaten the survival of the church in the new republic.

Objections to White's plan did not arise entirely from establishmentar- ian principles, but also from the intensely conservative demeanor of the Church of England. In a manner which depicted his reverence for tradi- tional practices, Samuel Seabury described to his diocesan clergy the activities of southern clergy and laity who had begun to revise the liturgy, offices and government of the church. '[T]he authority on which they have acted, is unknown in the Episcopal Church. The government of the Church by Bishops, we hold to have been established by the Apostles, acting under the commission of Christ, and the direction of the Holy Ghost; and therefore is not to be altered by any power on earth, nor indeed by an angel from heaven.' In Seabury's opinion, the task of compiling a liturgy should have been left to the bishops, and, in turn, the liturgy should con- form as nearly as possible to the Book of Common Prayer so as not to deviate from the practices of the primitive church. 'By this conduct we shall secure ourselves against new-fangled notions in religion ... And let us remember, that in religion novelty and truth can scarcely come together: For nothing in religion is now true, that was not true seventeen hundred years ago.'[108] He opposed innovations since he believed that the church should possess the same doctrines, principles, government, and practices as had the Apostles and primitive Christians.

As well as fearing liturgical change, conservatives also believed that the political principle of popular sovereignty should not infiltrate into matters of church government. Typical of a High-Church dichotomization of cler- gymen and laity, Seabury opposed any accommodation of church systems or sermons to 'popular humor or fancy.'[109] Because proposals for liturgical alterations often came from clergy who had supported the Revolution, former loyalists tended to interpret these events as a second phase of imperial dismemberment. After achieving a civil victory, Bela Hubbard warned that rebel Anglican clergy were turning to the church.[110] Thomas Bradbury Chandler firmly denounced any presbyterian or truncated form of episcopacy as the efforts of irresponsible and immoral men who would allow 'genuine Episcopacy' to be 'sacrificed on the Altar of Ecclesiastical Republicanism.' He particularly opposed the presbyterian tendencies of a recent Episcopal Church convention in Virginia which gave excessive authority, he believed, to lay-members and thereby 'robbed Episcopacy of some of its essential rights.'[111] While John Bowden believed the American laity should be included in decisions about prayers and laws, he thought bishops should have an absolute veto over the resolutions of the clergy and the people since he believed the Apostles had invested early bishops with such powers. Consequently, he disapproved of any radical republican alteration to the church's hierarchical structure and cautioned, 'Let us not be influenced by any motive whatsoever, however it may comport with popular ideas, to *deform* the government of Christ's Church. It is to be feared, that absurd notion of conforming the government of the church to that of the state, prevails too much amongst us.'[112] No wonder many ministers opposed a new service, designed to be read every 4 July to commemorate independence, when it appeared as part of the proposed Prayer Book of 1786, a text which was ultimately not accepted. Despite his personal commitment to the revolutionary cause, William White noted how divisive such politically sensitive material could be for the Episcopal Church, an infant organization not yet secure nor sufficiently unified to celebrate the occasion of its birth.[113]

The issue of the new church's relationship with the Church of England or, conversely, its adoption of republican principles crystallized in debate about alterations to the liturgy. Several Anglican ministers, particularly SPG missionaries, opposed liturgical innovations vehemently or, more mildly, cautioned against unnecessary changes. Roger Viets cautioned, 'I intreat you never to admit of any material alterations in your form of public devotion. – Indeed to admit of no other alterations, than such small ones, as revolutions may render absolutely necessary. Even small, unnecessary or wanton innovations, are more dangerous, and more pernicious, than is generally imagined.' Viets revealed not only his great reverence for the liturgy of the church, but also his continued respect for the civil and religious councils of England. As he asked rhetorically, '[i]f the liturgy of our church can be altered for the better, how comes it to pass that the united councils of the church and state in England (the most judicious nation in the world) have not found it out and made the requisite alterations?'[114] Elsewhere, he considered that only one or two Collects would need to be omitted to accommodate American politics.[115]

Anglican conservatism proved a formidable barrier to structural or liturgical change, a reality which the most innovative clergymen recognized in their own treatises. William White and William Smith, in arguing for change, each began with an acknowledgment of the church's prevailing disposition. In his address at the opening of the Convention of the Protestant Episcopal Church in June 1786, Rev. White urged his listeners to act 'with the caution and moderation becoming a church "not given to change."' The church's foundation, which was built by the Apostles, should not be altered dramatically, because God would forbid 'an invariable adherence to anything confessedly resting on man's authority.' Furthermore White appealed to his listeners' sense of community with the Church of England. He hoped that 'the venerable parent tree will not be disgraced by its branches; that a church, which hath stood for ages renowned for her orthodoxy, will not have cause to grieve over any essential deviation, in a new church which hath arisen under her nursing care.' Then White differed from other conservatives in advocating a compromise position in the tradition of the Anglican 'middle way.' The task of remodeling the constitution and government of American Anglicanism necessitated a balance between traditional commitments to 'apostolic usage, and a regard to the duties which become us as citizens of one confederate republic.'[116]

With great eloquence, Rev. William Smith described the intimidating task of reforming the liturgy of the Church of England. Upon first considering the necessary alterations, he explained,

we were struck with the utmost diffidence. We contemplated our church service as an august and beautiful fabric – venerable for its antiquity – venerable from the memory of those glorious, and now glorified, luminaries, saints and martyrs, who laid the foundations of our church on the rock of ages. We stood arrested, as it were, at an awful distance – It appeared almost sacrilege to approach the porch, or lift a hand to touch a single part, to polish a single corner, or to clear it from its rust of years![117]

Smith's description overflows with melodrama, and although he argued in a manner to gain the respect of ultra-conservatives, his allusion to 'sacrilege' may have satirized those who, in his opinion, regarded the liturgy with an idolatrous awe. His own text encouraged considerable liturgical change beyond mere 'polishing.' In fact, Smith underscored the opportunities which civil independence presented for ecclesiastical reform. As he reminded the General Convention, in 1661 six hundred alterations were made and 'if there was reason for those changes at that time, there is *equal,* if not *greater* reason, for some further improvements now.'[118]

Writing much later in 1795, Henry Purcell of South Carolina expressed a great confidence about republicanism's role in modifying the American Episcopal Church, especially through the internalization of egalitarianism and the rejection of privilege. In his discussion of the powers of the prelacy, Purcell disagreed that bishops, whom he described as 'pretenders to a lineal and uninterrupted succession from the apostles,' should have a veto power over the decisions of the clergy and laity. Under the republican form of government, bishops should appear no higher than the clergy and laity in convention 'are disposed to let them. And they, surely, cannot expect that we will so speedily set them up as idols.' Although Purcell opposed the 'consummate vanity' of bishops, he did concede the necessity of the office, if divested of its 'overweening pride' and 'offensive appendages.' Consequently, the peace of 1783 had offered countless blessings to the church, including the possibility of episcopal reformation. As Purcell mused, once the church achieved independence from secular powers in England, why should it 'embarrass' itself by adhering to old and unreformed practices? Instead, he urged, 'let us exhibit ... as great a phenomenon in our *ecclesiastical,* as we have already done in our *civil* capacity.' The American Revolution's principles of independence and egalitarianism suggested the preferred direction of reformation, including the elimination of 'every *iota* of courtly trumpery from our ritual' and 'foreign trappings.' Purcell warned that American Anglicans should not obsequiously send their convention journals to English prelates as if 'we were still appendages, and needed their smiles, or dreaded their frowns.' In his opinion, the continuation of this deference impaired the future of the American church. Republicanism, he thought, 'should have weaned our affections.'[119]

These contentious issues of liturgical change and the extent to which the American church should conform to American political values were explored throughout the 1780s in a series of state and general conventions. Ultimately, the General Convention of 1789 provided the final solution by adopting a constitution and a set of canons, as well as authorizing a new Book of Common Prayer. But in the 13 years between 1776 and 1789, the clergymen of the American Anglican church faced tremendous challenges, which in hindsight may be described as divided allegiances. Personal and local obligations to one's family and congregation often conflicted when disestablishment and the withdrawal of SPG support changed the rules of clerical remuneration. The American Revolution caused individual ministers to re-evaluate their own priorities and reconsider their self-identification with particular nations and church structures. Matters of personal identity became intertwined with these important decisions of church structure and liturgical change. In this time of new beginnings, ministers had to sort out whether they wished to embrace independence in the ecclesiastical sphere, or try to limit the effects of the political revolution on the church. An acceptance of change in the ecclesiastical realm frequently coexisted with wartime patriotism, or more abstractly, a personal disposition which favored cultural and religious innovation. Conversely, a defense of traditional establishmentarian principles, particularly among loyalists, harkened back to the English and colonial past as the preferred model for the church's future. North American Anglicanism of the late eighteenth century and early nineteenth century provided an opportunity for the expression of both points of view: in the new beginnings of the Protestant Episcopal Church of the United States and in the developing structure of the Church of England in Canada.

Epilogue

Denominationalism, voluntarism and patriotism, which coalesced into the new religious paradigm of the post-revolutionary era, influenced all religious groups, including Episcopalians. Denominationalism repudiated the idea that all Christians must be comprehended into a single national church; dependence on the voluntary support of the laity encouraged a democratically governed church; and patriotism united a reverence for national institutions with Christian piety.[1] While this triumvirate offered a general model for all religious traditions in the new republic, individual groups differed in their incorporation of each element. For the American Episcopal Church, these religious principles necessitated not only a rejection of establishmentarianism, but also the adoption of a less hierarchical church structure and a severing of formal ties with the Church of England. The omission of references to the English monarch in the American Book of Common Prayer proved less controversial than the reorganization of the church's structure. Differing interpretations concerning the relative importance of episcopal, clerical, and lay functions seriously inhibited the creation of an Episcopalian church of national scope.

The convention system, which provided the mechanism of ecclesiastical change, closely paralleled the conventions which culminated in the federal constitution of 1787. Both the government of the United States and that of the Protestant Episcopal Church were shaped by the prevailing desire for a strong central government. When the Episcopal Convention met in July 1789, the recent adoption of the national Constitution may have strengthened the church's arguments for a federal union. The General Convention of 1789 had to reconcile three divergent views on church government: a middle and southern states' church with English consecration and a representative clerical and lay convention; a New England church headed by a Scottish-consecrated bishop and governed by a clerical convention; and a Methodist Episcopal Church. A reunion with the Methodists did not occur, but eventually northern and southern strains of Anglicanism quieted their hostilities.[2] Regional tensions persisted, but did not prevent the formation of a national church organization.

A series of compromises during the two sessions of the General Convention of 1789 recognized the validity of Seabury's orders, created a separate House of Bishops with a partial veto, and made the participation of lay deputies optional. At the second session in September, the General Convention gave the House of Bishops a stronger veto and the right to originate legislation. Seabury and New England Anglicanism compromised by accepting lay representation in the convention and agreeing to the omission of the Athanasian Creed. No New England delegates had participated in the General Convention of 1785, but these concessions helped to bring New England Anglicanism back into the fold. The Book of Common Prayer adopted in 1789 also may be interpreted as a compromise since it eliminated several controversial changes of the Proposed Book. The 1789 prayer book restored the Nicene Creed, the full text of the Apostles' Creed, and the word 'regeneration' in the service for baptism.[3]

The precarious episcopal structure in America, which began with the consecration of Samuel Seabury in 1784, found greater stability in 1787 with the English consecrations of William White of Pennsylvania and Samuel Provoost of New York. Suspicions continued due to Seabury's reputation as a Scottish-consecrated bishop and a High-Church loyalist. Conversely, White and Provoost could be characterized as English-style, latitudinarian, and patriot bishops. The request from Massachusetts that their episcopal candidate, Edward Bass, be consecrated by the three American bishops aimed to unify the divergent strains of American Episcopalians. Samuel Parker of Boston and his fellow petitioners agreed that the church in America had a full complement of three bishops and therefore did not need to apply to England for further consecrations. Seabury favored the joint consecration of Bass, but Provoost's opposition to Seabury proved decisive in preventing the union.[4] In 1790, James Madison was consecrated in England as the Bishop of Virginia, and in 1792 Thomas Claggett, the Bishop of Maryland, became the first bishop to be consecrated in America. The four American bishops, three of whom had been consecrated in England, performed the service for Claggett. Subsequently, Robert Smith was consecrated Bishop of South Carolina in 1795, and Edward Bass became the Bishop of Massachusetts and Rhode Island in 1797.

Despite the improved stability of the episcopal structure by the turn of the century, the American Episcopal Church had not yet achieved any truly national representation. In some states, that goal awaited a new generation of Episcopalians. New England had become involved in the national church organization, but North Carolina did not send a representative to the General Convention until 1817, and Georgia was not represented until 1823. The Episcopal Church, accustomed to a parish outlook, experienced some difficulties in extending its vision into the expanding western frontier. Financial difficulties, as well as continuing anti-British sentiment, mitigated against any structured program of expansion. The new American bishops also demonstrated caution in asserting their authority because they wanted to reassure those who distrusted episcopacy.[5]

By the early 1790s, the American Episcopal Church possessed a governing structure, a prayer book, and a national constitution. Its mechanism for the creation of new bishops and the ordination of ministerial candidates had rectified the most obvious institutional flaw of the colonial Church of England: the lack of a colonial episcopate. Subsequently, a new generation of leaders, including Bishops John Henry Hobart and Alexander Viets Griswold, encouraged growth and expansion. Griswold was one of the original sponsors of the Domestic and Foreign Missionary Society of the Protestant Episcopal Church, which the General Convention organized in 1820. Hobart promoted theological education, and although he first favored diocesan seminaries over a general seminary, he became instrumental in the founding of the General Theological Seminary in New York City, which opened in 1822.[6]

From the perspective of the Revolutionary War, the ultimate success of the Episcopalians in reorganizing their church according to federal principles and in creating a constitutional episcopacy acceptable to the republic seemed anything but assured. Between the Declaration of Independence and 1789, Anglican ministers had faced 13 years of doubt and confusion about the direction of their church. During this critical period, the church preserved its ecclesiastical heritage while adapting its structure to fit the new political situation. To some extent, the bishop movement of the 1760s and 1770s endured, since Episcopalians in the 1780s and 1790s still looked to the creation of an episcopacy to complete their church hierarchy. Anglican patriots, however, repudiated the associated principles of establishmentarianism and religious privilege. The Revolution also caused Anglican clergymen to reconsider the nature of their mission and to re-evaluate their duties to the British monarch and the Church of England. The splitting of traditional Anglican civil theology into divergent patriot and loyalist portions provided new foundations for North American Anglicanism. In Canada, establishmentarian and loyalist sentiments combined; in the United States, new religious sensibilities merged with American patriotism.

Having endured the trying times of the war, including revolutionary demands for fast-day prayers or Congressional oaths, the surviving ministers of the Church of England faced fundamental changes in their church and their society. During the war, the depoliticization of the Anglican clergy provided the beginnings of a non-political foundation for the emerging Protestant Episcopal Church, but the post-revolutionary world demanded an acceptance of traits entirely antithetical to traditional Anglicanism. Denominationalism, voluntarism, and religious patriotism formed the cornerstones of American religion in the late eighteenth and early nineteenth centuries. For colonial Anglicans, these ideas posed psychological hurdles since members of the Church of England were most likely to look to English models and precedents; members of established churches had the most to lose from disestablishment; and Anglicanism traditionally affirmed a hierarchical church structure. At first, American Anglicanism divided on these issues, but the exile of loyalist ministers and a series of constitutional compromises ultimately reconciled northern and southern strains of American Anglicanism into an acceptance of a national church organization. The Episcopal Church preserved its ecclesiastical heritage and simultaneously laid a republican foundation for its future development.

Appendix:
Colonial Church of England Ministers, 1775–83

Note that the spelling of surnames varies. Ministers who served more than one colony during their revolutionary career are listed only once.
*Information too scarce to make a positive determination of incumbency.

NEW ENGLAND

Massachusetts

Bass, Edward
Byles, Mather
Caner, Henry
Clark, William
Fisher, Nathaniel
Lewis, Stephen
McGilchrist, William
Nickolls, Robert

Parker, Samuel
Serjeant, Winwood
Thompson, Ebenezer
Troutbeck, John
Walter, William
Weeks, Joshua Wingate
Wheeler, Willard
Winslow, Edward

Connecticut

Andrews, Samuel
Beach, John
Beardsley, John
Bostwick, Gideon
Clarke, Richard
Dibblee, Ebenezer
Fogg, Daniel
Graves, Matthew
Hubbard, Bela
Jarvis, Abraham
Kneeland, Ebenezer
Leaming, Jeremiah

Mansfield, Richard
Marshall, John Rutgers
Newton, Christopher
Nichols, James
Peters, Samuel Andrews
Sayre, James
Sayre, John
Scovil, James
Townsend, Epenetus
Tyler, John
Viets, Roger

Rhode Island

Bisset, George
Fayerweather, Samuel

Graves, John
Usher, John Sr

Maine

Bailey, Jacob
Wiswall, John

New Hampshire

Badger, Moses
Cossit, Rana

MIDDLE COLONIES

New York

Auchmuty, Samuel
Avery, Ephraim
Babcock, Luke
Barker, James
Bloomer, Joshua
Bowden, John
Charlton, Richard
Cooper, Myles
Cutting, Leonard
Doty, John

Inglis, Charles
Lyon, James
Moore, Benjamin
Munro, Henry
Page, Bernard*
Provoost, Samuel
Seabury, Samuel
Stuart, John
Vardill, John*

New Jersey

Ayers, William
Beach, Abraham
Blackwell, Robert
Browne, Isaac
Chandler, Thomas Bradbury
Cooke, Samuel

Frazer, William
Odell, Jonathan
Ogden, Uzal Jr
Panton, George
Preston, John

Pennsylvania (and Delaware)

Barton, Thomas
Batwell, Daniel
Coombe, Thomas
Craig, George
Currie, William
Duché, Jacob
Illing, F. F.*
Magaw, Samuel

Murray, Alexander
Peters, Richard
Reading, Philip
Ross, Aeneas
Smith, William
Stringer, William
Tingley, Samuel
White, William

CHESAPEAKE

Maryland

Addison, Henry
Allen, Bennet
Andrews, John
Barroll, William
Bell, Hamilton Jr
Bell, Hamilton Sr
Berry, Jeremiah
Booth, Bartholomew*
Boucher, Jonathan
Bowie, John
Braithwaite, Thomas
Browne, Richard
Browne, Thomas
Campbell, Isaac
Chase, Thomas
Claggett, Thomas John
Dean, Hugh
Edmiston, William
Eversfield, John
Fendall, Henry
Forbes, John
Gantt, Edward
Gates, Thomas
Goldie, George
Gordon, John
Hanna, William
Harris, Mathias
Harrison, Walter Hanson
Hindman, Jacob H.

Hughes, Philip
Keene, Samuel
Lauder, Francis
Lendrum, Thomas
Love, David
McCormick, Robert
McGill, James
McGowan, Walter
McKinnon, Daniel
McPherson, John
Messenger, John
Mitchell, George
Montgomery, John
Neill, Hugh
Patterson, John
Read, Thomas
Rosse, John
Scott, John
Sloane, Samuel
Stephen, John
Tabbs, Moses
Thompson, William
Thornton, Thomas
Threkeld, Joseph*
Walker, Philip
West, William
Williamson, Alexander II
Wilmer, James Jones
Worsley, George H.

Virginia

Agar, William
Agnew, John
Andrews, Robert
Andrews, William
Aven, Archibald
Avery, Isaac
Baker, Thomas*
Balmaine, Alexander
Barnett, John*
Barret, Robert
Blagrove, Benjamin
Bland, William

Bracken, John
Braidfoot, John
Brander, John
Brooke, Clement
Bruce, John
Brunskill, John
Buchan, Robert
Buchanan, John
Burges, John Henry
Butler, Samuel*
Cameron, John
Camm, John

Camp, Ichabod
Campbell, Archibald
Campbell, John*
Carter, Jesse
Clay, Charles
Cocke, John*
Cordell, John
Coutts, William
Craig, James (Fauquier County)
Craig, James (Lunenburg County)
Cruden, Alexander
Currie, David
Dade, Townshend
Davenport, John
Davies, Price
Davis, Thomas Jr
Davis, Thomas Sr
Davis, William
Dick, Archibald
Dickson, Robert
Dixon, John
Douglas, William
Dunbar, Hancock
Duncan, William
Dunlap, William
Emmerson, Arthur
Fanning, William
Field, Thomas
Fontaine, James Maury
Giberne, Isaac William
Gordon, Alexander
Grayson, Spence
Griffith, David
Gurley, George
Gwatkin, Thomas
Gwilliam, Lewis
Hall, Thomas
Hamilton, Arthur
Harrison, William
Henley, Samuel
Henry, Patrick
Herdman, James
Holt, John White
Hopkinson, Thomas*
Hubard, William
Hurt, John
Jarratt, Devereux
Johnson, Thomas
Jones, Edward

Jones, Emmanuel Jr*
Jones, Emmanuel III
Jones, John
Kenner, Rodham Jr
Klug, Samuel
Leigh, William
Leland, John Jr
Leland, John Sr
Lunan, Patrick
Lundie, Thomas
Lyon, John
Lyth, John
Madison, James
Manning, Nathaniel
Marye, James Jr
Massey, Lee
Matthews, John
Maury, Matthew
Maccartney, James
McCroskey, Samuel Smith
McKay, Fitzhugh
McKay, William
MacRae, Christopher
McRoberts, Archibald
Milner, John*
Morton, Andrew
Muhlenberg, John Peter Gabriel
Nixon, William*
Ogilvie, John
Peasley, William
Price, Thomas
Reade, Robert
Rowland, John Hamilton
Saunders, John Hyde
Scott, James
Sebastian, Benjamin
Selden, Miles
Selden, William
Semple, James
Shield, Samuel
Skyring, Henry
Smith, Adam
Smith, Thomas
Stevenson, James
Stuart, William
Sturgis, Daniel
Thompson, James
Thruston, Charles Mynn
Todd, Christopher

Townsend, Jacob
Vere, William
Waugh, Abner
White, Alexander

Wilkinson, Thomas
Willie, William
Wilson, Francis
Wingate, John

LOWER SOUTH

North Carolina

Alexander, John*
Blount, Nathaniel
Burgess, Thomas Sr
Cupples, Charles
Earl, Daniel
Ford, Hezekiah

Micklejohn, George
Pettigrew, Charles
Reed, James
Taylor, Charles Edward
Wills, John

South Carolina

Blackburn, Benjamin
Bullman, John
Cooper, Robert
Ellington, Edward
Finlay, Alexander
Foulis, James
Garden, Alexander
Graham, William Eastwick
Harrison, James
Hart, Samuel
Jenkins, Edward

Lewis, John
Lucius, Samuel Frederick
Moreau, Charles F.
Pearce, Offspring
Percy, William
Purcell, Henry
Purcell, Robert
Smith, Robert
Stuart, James
Turquand, Paul
Warren, Samuel Fenner

Georgia

Brown, James
Seymour, James
Smith, Haddon
Stewart, John

Notes

CHAPTER 1 INTRODUCTION

1. Thomas Paine, *The American Crisis*, no. 1 (December 23, 1776), 1.
2. William Smith to SPG, 10 July 1775, *Hist. Coll.* II, 475; Samuel Magaw, *A Sermon Delivered in St. Paul's Church, on Saturday, December 27, 1783* (Philadelphia: Hall and Sellers, 1784), 27; John Wolfe Lydekker, *The Life and Letters of Charles Inglis: His Ministry in America and Consecration as First Colonial Bishop, from 1759 to 1787* (New York: Macmillan, 1936), 157; and Henry Caner to SPG, 25 Sept. 1770, SPG Journals XVIII, 466.
3. Samuel Johnson to SPG, York Town, 25 November 1776, *Hist. Coll.* II, 488.
4. William Meade, *Old Churches, Ministers and Families of Virginia* I–II (Baltimore: Genealogical Publishing Company, 1966), II, 35–8; Otto Lohrenz, 'The Virginia Clergy and the American Revolution' (unpublished PhD diss., University of Kansas, 1970), 67–8.
5. *DAB* II, 474; Anne Y. Zimmer, *Jonathan Boucher: Loyalist in Exile* (Detroit, MI: Wayne State University Press, 1978), 173–5.
6. Lohrenz, 'The Virginia Clergy and the American Revolution,' 72–3, 99; and Lohrenz, 'Parson and Patrons: The Clerical Career of Thomas Johnston of Maryland and Virginia,' *AEH* 58 (1989) 169–95.
7. Samuel Seabury Jr to SPG, New York, 29 March 1777, SPG Ser B, II, 191; Henry Caner to SPG, Boston, 14 April 1776, SPG Ser B, XXII, 135.
8. Howard L. Applegate, 'Anglican Chaplains Serving the American Revolutionary Army, 1775–1783,' *HMPEC* 30 (1961), 138–40.
9. Lohrenz, 'The Virginia Clergy and the American Revolution,' 212; Meade, *Old Churches, Ministers and Families of Virginia* I, 20–1; and Thomas Nelson Rightmyer, 'The Holy Orders of Peter Muhlenberg,' *HMPEC* 30 (1961), 183–97.
10. William Gibson, ' "Pious Decorum": Clerical Wigs in the Eighteenth-Century Church of England,' *AEH* 65 (1996), 145–61; John Walsh and Stephen Taylor, 'Introduction: the Church and Anglicanism in the "long" eighteenth century,' in *The Church of England c.1689 – c.1833: From Toleration to Tractarianism*, John Walsh, Colin Haydon, and Stephen Taylor, eds (Cambridge: Cambridge University Press, 1993), 7; and Paul Langford, 'The English Clergy and the American Revolution,' in *The Transformation of Political Culture: England and Germany in the Late Eighteenth Century*, Eckhart Hellmuth, ed. (London: Oxford University Press, 1990), 304; Viviane Barrie-Curien, 'Clerical Recruitment and Career Patterns in the Church of England during the Eighteenth Century,' in *Crown and Mitre: Religion and Society in Northern Europe Since the Reformation*, W. M. Jacob and Nigel Yates, eds (Woodbridge: Boydell Press, 1993), 97.
11. J. M. Bumsted, ' "Things in the Womb of Time": Ideas of American Independence, 1633–1763,' *WMQ*, 3d Ser. (1974), 533–64; Max Savelle, 'Nationalism and Other Loyalties in the American Revolution,' *AHR*, 67

(1961–2), 901–23; and John Murrin, 'A Roof Without Walls: The Dilemma of American National Identity,' *Beyond Confederation: Origins of the Constitution and American National Identity*, Richard Beeman et al., eds (Chapel Hill: University of North Carolina Press, 1987), 333–48.

12. On the moral dimension see Gordon Wood, *The Creation of the American Republic, 1776–1787* (New York: W.W. Norton, 1969), chapter 3. On the evangelical emphasis see Jon Butler, 'Coercion, Miracle, Reason: Rethinking the American Religious Experience in the Revolutionary Age,' in *Religion in a Revolutionary Age*, Ronald Hoffman and Peter J. Albert, eds (Charlottesville: University of Virginia Press, 1994), esp. 1–3.

13. John F. Woolverton, *Colonial Anglicanism in North America* (Detroit, MI: Wayne State University Press, 1984), 34.

14. Harry S. Stout, *The New England Soul: Preaching and Religious Culture in Colonial New England* (New York: Oxford University Press, 1986), 3–4, 6–7; and Richard D. Brown, 'Rural Clergymen and the Communication Networks of 18th-Century New England,' *Knowledge is Power: The Diffusion of Information in Early America, 1700–1865* (New York: Oxford University Press, 1989), 65–81.

15. Rhys Isaac, *Transformation of Virginia, 1740–1790* (Chapel Hill: University of North Carolina Press, 1982), 58–114.

16. Edmund Burke, *Burke's Speech on Conciliation with America*, Sidney Carleton Newsom, ed. (New York: Macmillan, 1920), 29.

17. Perry Miller, *The New England Mind: The Seventeenth Century* (Cambridge, MA: The Belknap Press of Harvard University Press, 1939), 398–431. See also John Wingate Thornton, *The Pulpit of the American Revolution* (Boston, MA: D. Lothrop, 1876), xxxviii.

18. E. S. Morgan, 'The Puritan Ethic and the American Revolution,' in his *The Challenge of the American Revolution* (New York: W.W. Norton, 1976), 89–95.

19. Leonard J. Kramer, 'Muskets in the Pulpit: 1776–1783,' *Journal of the Presbyterian Historical Society* 31 (1953), 229–44, esp. 229, and continued in *JPHS* 32 (1954), 37–51; his 'Presbyterians Approach the American Revolution,' *Journal of the Presbyterian Historical Society* 31 (1953), 71–86, 167–80; and Mark Noll, *Princeton and the Republic, 1768–1822* (Princeton, NJ: Princeton University Press, 1989), 28–58.

20. Rhys Isaac, 'Preachers and Patriots: Popular Culture and the Revolution in Virginia,' in *The American Revolution: Explorations in the History of American Radicalism*, Alfred F. Young, ed. (DeKalb: Northern Illinois University Press, 1976), 127–56; and William McLoughlin, *Soul Liberty: the Baptists' Struggle in New England, 1630–1833* (Providence, RI: Brown University Press, 1991), 178–95.

21. Arthur J. Mekeel, 'The Relation of the Quakers to the American Revolution,' *Quaker History* 65 (Spring, 1976), 3–18; Joseph S. Tiedemann, 'Queens County, New York: Quakers in the American Revolution: Loyalists or Neutrals?' *HMPEC* 52 (1983), 215–27; and Peter Brock, *Pacifism in the United States: From the Colonial Era to the First World War* (Princeton, NJ: Princeton University Press, 1968), 183–258, 259–84.

22. Allan Raymond, ' "I Fear God and Honour the King": John Wesley and the American Revolution,' *CH* 45 (1976), 316–28.

23. Charles H. Metzger, *Catholics and the American Revolution* (Chicago: Loyola University Press, 1962), 267–79, esp. 277. Metzger argued that the vast majority of Catholics were patriots, but he also discusses Catholic loyalism.
24. Such is the approach of Mark A. Noll, *Christians in the American Revolution* (Washington, DC: Christian University Press, 1977), 75.
25. Alan E. Heimert, *Religion and the American Mind: From the Great Awakening to the Revolution* (Cambridge, MA: Harvard University Press, 1966), *passim*; and John M. Murrin, 'No Awakening, No Revolution? More Counterfactual Speculations,' *Reviews in American History* 11 (1983), 161.
26. Timothy Tackett, *Religion, Revolution and Regional Culture in Eighteenth-Century France: The Ecclesiastical Oath of 1791* (Princeton, NJ: Princeton University Press, 1986).
27. W. W. Sweet, 'The Role of the Anglicans in the American Revolution,' *Huntingdon Library Quarterly* 11 (1948), 52; and David L. Holmes, 'The Episcopal Church and the American Revolution,' *HMPEC* 47 (1978), 265.
28. S. D. McConnell, *History of the American Episcopal Church from the Planting of the Colonies to the End of the Civil War* (London: Sampson, Low, Marston, Searle and Rivington, 1891), 205. On relations between the laity and clergy in England, see W. M. Jacob, *Lay People and Religion in the Early Eighteenth Century* (Cambridge: Cambridge University Press, 1996), 20–51.
29. For instance, both terms can be found in T. B. Chandler, et al., *An Address from the Clergy of New-York and New-Jersey, to the Episcopalians in Virginia; occasioned by some late transactions in that colony relative to an American Episcopate* (New York: Hugh Gaine, 1771), 1–2 and title.

CHAPTER 2   THE PRE-REVOLUTIONARY COLONIAL
CHURCH OF ENGLAND

1. Jon Butler, 'Magic, Astrology, and the Early American Religious Heritage, 1600–1760,' *AHR* 84 (1979), 317–46, esp. 318; Thomas Tanselle, 'Some Statistics on American Printing,' *The Press & the American Revolution*, Bernard Bailyn and John B. Hench, eds (Boston: Northeastern University Press, 1981), 326–30; Patricia U. Bonomi, *Under the Cope of Heaven: Religion, Society, and Politics in Colonial America* (New York: Oxford University Press, 1988), 3, 14–37; Jon Butler, *Awash in a Sea of Faith: Christianizing the American People* (Cambridge, MA: Harvard University Press, 1990), 100–1, 128. On decline, see the opposing opinions of William W. Sweet, *The Story of Religion in America* (New York: Harper, 1950, orig. publ. 1930), 322; and Douglas H. Sweet, 'Church Vitality and the American Revolution: Historiographical Consensus and Thoughts Towards a New Perspective,' *CH* 45 (1976), 341–57.
2. Alan Smith, *The Established Church and Popular Religion 1750–1850* (London: Longman, 1971), 8; John F. Woolverton, *Colonial Anglicanism in North America* (Detroit, MI: Wayne State University Press, 1984), 16–17.

3. J. C. D. Clark, *English Society, 1688–1832* (Cambridge: Cambridge University Press, 1985), 216–35, esp. 219.
4. Woolverton, *Colonial Anglicanism in North America*, 185–6; E. R. Norman, *Church and Society in England, 1770–1970* (London: Oxford University Press, 1976), 15–16; and Horton Davies, *Worship and Theology in England: From Watts and Wesley to Maurice, 1690–1850* III (Princeton, NJ: Princeton University Press, 1961), 19–37, esp. 29; Ian Green, 'Anglicanism in Stuart and Hanoverian England,' in *A History of Religion in Britain: Practice and Belief from Pre-Roman Times to the Present*, Sheridan Gilley and W. J. Sheils, eds (Oxford: Blackwell, 1994), 168–87.
5. Richard Brown, *Church and State in Modern Britain, 1700–1850* (London: Routledge, 1991), 100; Smith, *The Established Church and Popular Religion*, 10; Stephen H. Applegate, 'The Rise and Fall of the Thirty-Nine Articles: An Inquiry into the Identity of the Protestant Episcopal Church in the United States,' *HMPEC* 50 (1981), 409–16; and David L. Holmes, *A Brief History of the Episcopal Church* (Valley Forge, PA: Trinity Press International, 1993), 9–18.
6. Henry Caner, *The Firm Belief of a Future Reward A Powerful Motive to Obedience and a Good Life: A Sermon Preached at Christ Church in Boston, August 20, 1765 at the Funeral of the Rev. Timothy Cutler* (Boston, MA, 1765), 19.
7. Gerald J. Goodwin, 'The Anglican Middle Way In Early Eighteenth-Century America: Anglican Religious Thought in the American Colonies, 1702–1750' (unpublished PhD diss., University of Wisconsin, 1965), 323, 328, 346–7; Woolverton, *Colonial Anglicanism in North America*, 182–3; Brown, *Church and State in Modern Britain*, 99–100.
8. Robert D. Cornwall, 'The Church and Salvation: An Early Eighteenth-Century High Church Anglican Perspective,' *AEH* 62 (1993), 175–91.
9. Woolverton, *Colonial Anglicanism*, 181; and Gerald J. Goodwin, 'The Anglican Reaction to the Great Awakening,' *HMPEC* 35 (1966), 352–6.
10. Henry Caner, *A Discourse Concerning the Publick Worship of God* (Newport, RI, 1748), 44.
11. John Tyler, *The Sanctity of a Christian Temple: Illustrated in a Sermon, At the Opening of Trinity-Church in Pomfret, on Friday, April 12, 1771* (Providence, RI, 1771), 29–31, 33.
12. Thomas J. Curry, *The First Freedoms: Church and State in America to the Passage of the First Amendment* (New York: Oxford University Press, 1986), 105. See also Bonomi, *Under the Cope of Heaven*, 31.
13. Sydney Ahlstrom, *A Religious History of the American People* (New Haven, CT: Yale University Press, 1972), 218; and Woolverton, *Colonial Anglicanism*, 19.
14. Elizabeth Davidson, *Establishment of the English Church in Continental American Colonies* (Durham, NC: Duke University Press, 1936), 79–86.
15. Arthur Pierce Middleton, 'The Colonial Virginia Parish,' *HMPEC* 40 (1971), 433–4.
16. William H. Seiler, 'The Anglican Parish Vestry in Colonial Virginia,' *Journal of Southern History* 22 (1956), 329–37; Gerald E. Hartagen, 'The Vestries and Morals in Colonial Maryland,' *Maryland Historical Magazine* 63 (1968), 360–78; Alan D. Watson, 'The Anglican Parish in Royal North

Carolina, 1729–1775,' *HMPEC* 48 (1979), 314–15; Alan L. Clem, 'The Vestries and Local Government in Colonial Maryland,' *HMPEC* 31 (1962), 224; Gerald E. Hartagen, 'The Anglican Vestry in Colonial Maryland: A Study in Corporate Responsibility,' *HMPEC* 40 (1971), 319; Bordon W. Painter, Jr, 'The Vestry in Colonial New England,' *HMPEC* 44 (1975), 385–9.

17. Arthur Pierce Middleton, 'The Colonial Virginia Parish,' *HMPEC* 40 (1971), 436; and Spencer Ervin, 'The Establishment, Government and Functioning of the Church in Colonial Virginia,' *HMPEC* 26 (1957), 65–110.

18. Middleton, 'Colonial Virginia Parish,' 436.

19. Michael T. Malone, 'Sketches of the Anglican Clergy Who Served in North Carolina during the Period, 1765–1776,' *HMPEC* 39 (1970), 140; Gerald E. Hartagen, 'Vestry and Clergy in the Anglican Church of Colonial Maryland,' *HMPEC* 37 (1968), 371–96; Davidson, *The Establishment of the English Church in Continental American Colonies*, 25–9; and Painter, 'Vestry in Colonial New England,' 396–405.

20. Ahlstrom, *A Religious History of the American People*, 188–9; James Thayer Addison, *The Episcopal Church in the United States, 1789–1931* (Hamden, CT: Archon Books, 1969), 29; and Raymond W. Albright, *A History of the Protestant Episcopal Church* (New York: Macmillan, 1964), 19–20.

21. William Warren Sweet, *Religion in Colonial America* (New York: Charles Scribner's Sons, 1942), 31–2; Woolverton, *Colonial Anglicanism*, 78.

22. Addison, *The Episcopal Church in the United States*, 33–4; Arthur Pierce Middleton, 'Toleration and the Established Church in Maryland,' *HMPEC* 53 (1984), 15; Albright, 29.

23. Clifton E. Olmstead, *History of Religion in the United States* (Englewood Cliffs, NJ: Prentice-Hall, 1960), 54; W. W. Sweet, *Religion in Colonial America*, 39; and S. Charles Bolton, *Southern Anglicanism: The Church of England in Colonial South Carolina* (Westport, CT: Greenwood, 1982), 36.

24. Woolverton, *Colonial Anglicanism*, 169; Paul Conkin, 'The Church Establishment in North Carolina, 1765–1776,' *North Carolina Historical Review* 32 (1955), 1–30; Davidson, *The Establishment of the English Church in Continental American Colonies*, 55–7; Sarah McCulloh Lemmon, 'The Genesis of the Protestant Episcopal Diocese of North Carolina, 1701–1823,' *North Carolina Historical Review* 28 (1951), 426–30.

25. Olmstead, *History of Religion in the United States*, 55; and Addison, *The Episcopal Church in the United States*, 39.

26. Samuel Clyde McCulloch, 'The Foundation and Early Work of the Society for the Propagation of the Gospel in Foreign Parts,' *HMPEC* 20 (1951), 121–35; McCulloch, 'The Foundation and Early Work of the Society for Promoting Christian Knowledge,' *HMPEC* 12 (1943), 215–24; William A. and Phyllis W. Bultmann, 'The Roots of Anglican Humanitarianism: A Study of the Membership of the S.P.C.K. and the S.P.G., 1699–1720,' *HMPEC* 33 (1964), 3–48; and Frank J. Klingberg, 'Contributions of the S.P.G. to the American Way of Life,' *HMPEC* 12 (1943), 217.

27. E. Clowes Chorley, 'The Beginnings of the Church in the Province of New York,' *HMPEC* 13 (1944), 7–25; and Woolverton, *Colonial Anglicanism*, 125.

28. Olmstead, *History of Religion in the United States*, 56–7; Addison, *The Episcopal Church in the United States*, 47; Ahlstrom, *A Religious History of the American People*, 216; Louis C. Washburn, 'The Church in

Pennsylvania,' *HMPEC* 4 (1935), 118; Woolverton, *Colonial Anglicanism*, 134; and Deborah Mathias Gough, *Christ Church, Philadelphia: The Nation's Church in a Changing City* (Philadelphia, PA: University of Pennsylvania Press, 1995), 5–21.

29.   Ahlstrom, *A Religious History of the American People*, 215, 223–4; Edgar Legare Pennington, 'Anglican Beginnings in Massachusetts,' *HMPEC* 10 (1941), 280; Samuel M. Garrett, 'George Muirson and the Mission into Connecticut,' *HMPEC* 43 (1974), 125–68; and Glenn Weaver, 'Anglican–Congregationalist Tensions in Pre-Revolutionary Connecticut,' *HMPEC* 26 (1957), 269–78.

30.   Jon Butler, *Awash in a Sea of Faith*, 100–1.

31.   Butler, *Awash in a Sea of Faith*, 109–13; Rhys Isaac, *The Transformation of Virginia, 1740–1790* (New York: W.W. Norton, 1982), 58–9; and Woolverton, *Colonial Anglicanism*, 28.

32.   Frederick V. Mills, 'Anglican Expansion in Colonial America, 1761–1775,' *HMPEC* 39 (1970), 316–19; and Albright, *A History of the Protestant Episcopal Church*, 25.

33.   Mills, 'Anglican Expansion,' 316–19.

34.   Mills, 'Anglican Expansion,' 319–20.

35.   Woolverton, *Colonial Anglicanism*, 25; and Joan R. Gundersen, 'The Search for Good Men: Recruiting Ministers in Colonial Virginia,' *HMPEC* 49 (1979), 455–8.

36.   Matthew Graves to Bishop Sherlock, New London, Connecticut, 20 July 1750, Fulham Papers, I, 288.

37.   Thomas Dawson to Bishop Sherlock, 10 June 1755, William and Mary College, Fulham Papers, XIII, 186–7; and Bishop of London to Dr Doddridge, 11 May 1751, London, *Hist. Coll.* I, 373.

38.   Frederick V. Mills Sr, 'The Protestant Episcopal Churches in the United States 1783–1789: Suspended Animation or Remarkable Recovery?' *HMPEC* 46 (1977), 153–6. Mills estimated there were 286 Anglican clergymen in America in 1774. For 1792 estimates, see Holmes, *A Brief History of the Episcopal Church*, 60.

39.   Mills, 'Protestant Episcopal Churches in the U.S. 1783–1789: Suspended Animation or Remarkable Recovery?' 152, 161–2, 169.

40.   Gerald J. Goodwin, 'Christianity, Civilization, and the Savage: The Anglican Mission to the American Indian,' *HMPEC* 42 (1973), 98–9.

41.   Barton to SPG, 20 October 1757, SPG Journals XIV, 80–1 on 'savagery'; Barton to SPG, 10 November 1766, SPG Journals XVII, 281–2; Barton to SPG, 6 November 1769, SPG Journals XVIII, 333–4; and Barton to SPG, 28 June 1763, *Hist. Coll.* II, 348.

42.   John Calam, *Parsons and Pedagogues: The S.P.G. Adventure in American Education* (New York: Columbia University Press, 1971), 11.

43.   Robert A. Bennett, 'Black Episcopalians: A History from the Colonial Period to the Present,' *HMPEC* 43 (1974), 231–3; and John C. Van Horne, 'Impediments to the Christianization and Education of Blacks in Colonial America: The Case of the Associates of Dr. Bray,' *HMPEC* 50 (1981), 248.

44.   Rev. Mr Leaming to SPG, Norwalk, Connecticut, 25 March 1762; SPG Journals XV, 236; and Van Horne, 'Impediments to the Christianization and Education of Blacks,' 246–65, esp. 249–50.

45. Denzil T. Clifton, 'Anglicanism and Negro Slavery in Colonial America,' *HMPEC* 39 (1970), 61–3; Albright, *A History of the Protestant Episcopal Church*, 77.

46. Mr Moreau to SPG, 19 October 1750, SPG Journals XII, 4; Robert M. Kingdon, 'Why Did the Huguenot Refugees in the American Colonies Become Episcopalians?' *HMPEC* 49 (1980), 317–29; and Jon Butler, *The Huguenots in America: A Refugee People in New World Society* (Cambridge, MA: Harvard University Press, 1983), 77–8, 199–208.

47. Albright, *A History of the Protestant Episcopal Church*, 91; and Nelson R. Burr, 'The Episcopal Church and the Dutch in Colonial New York and New Jersey, 1664–1784,' *HMPEC* 19 (1950), 95–109.

48. William Smith to Bishop of London, Philadelphia, 18 December 1766, *Hist. Coll.* II, 411; and Smith to Archbishop of Canterbury, 20 June 1768, Hawks Mss in Hawks Coll., AEC, RG117–60–52; and Nelson H. Burr, 'The Early History of the Swedes and the Episcopal Church in America,' *HMPEC* 7 (1938), 123.

49. Richard Peters, *A Sermon, Preached in the New Lutheran Church of Zion, in the City of Philadelphia, at the Instance of the Ministers, Wardens, and Vestry-Men, of the Incorporated Congregation of St. Michael's, on the 26th Day of June, 1769* (Philadelphia, 1769), 9. See also Richard Peters to the Bishop of London, Philadelphia, 30 August 1768, *Hist. Coll.* II, 433.

50. Thomas Barton to SPG, Lancaster, PA, 16 November 1764, SPG Journals XVI, 335.

51. Barton to SPG, Lancaster, Pennsylvania, 8 November 1762, *Hist. Coll.* II, 343; and Barton to SPG, 16 November 1764, SPG Journals XVI, 335.

52. Rev. Mr Peters to SPG, 13 April 1761, SPG Journals XV, 141–2.

53. Matthew Graves to SPG, 20 February 1763, SPG Journals XVI, 41.

54. Rev. Mr Bass to SPG, 24 March 1760, SPG Journals XIV, 305.

55. Thomas Barton to SPG, 8 November 1762, Lancaster, Pennsylvania, *Hist. Coll.* II, 343; and Alfred W. Newcombe, 'The Appointment and Instruction of S.P.G. Missionaries,' *CH* 5 (1936), 355.

56. Dawson to Bishop of London, *Hist. Coll.* I, 384–5. See also Thomas Dawson to Bishop of London, undated *c.*1750, *Hist. Coll.* I, 386.

57. Calculations based on Figures 3–9 in Edwin Scott Gaustad, *Historical Atlas of Religion in America Revised Edition* (New York: Harper & Row, 1976), 1–10.

58. Woolverton, *Colonial Anglicanism*, 27–29, 242 n.36.

59. Bonomi, *Under the Cope of Heaven*, 54; Beach to SPG, 1 April 1751, SPG Journals IV, 64–5; Beach to SPG, 22 April 1760, SPG Journals XIV, 304–5; and Badger to SPG, 5 August 1768, Portsmouth, New Hampshire, SPG Journals XVIII, 38.

60. Gathering this information from innumerable sources would prove a herculean task, if not for the published compilations of Frederick L. Weis. Although biographers and church historians have noted individual errors and omissions in these texts, those mistakes do not detract appreciably from their usefulness in this endeavor. See Frederick Lewis Weis, *The Colonial Churches and the Colonial Clergy of the Middle and Southern Colonies, 1607–1776* (Lancaster, MA, 1938); *The Colonial Clergy and the Colonial Churches of New England, 1620–1776* (Lancaster, MA, 1936); *The Colonial*

Clergy of Maryland, Delaware and Georgia (Baltimore: Genealogical Publishing Co., 1978); *The Colonial Clergy of Virginia, North Carolina and South Carolina* (Boston, 1955); and 'Colonial Clergy of the Middle Colonies, 1628–1776,' *American Antiquarian Society Proceedings* 66 (1956), 167–351. For the use of their research of these Weis collections, I am indebted to John M. Murrin, Mary Murrin and Gregory Dowd.

61.   James Potter, 'The Growth of Population in America, 1700–1860,' in *Population in History: Essays in Historical Demography*, D. V. Glass and D. E. C. Eversley, eds (London: Edward Arnold, 1965), 631–40.

62.   Charles Woodmason, *The Carolina Backcountry on the Eve of the Revolution: The Journal and Other Writings of the Charles Woodmason, Anglican Itinerant*, Richard J. Hooker, ed. (Chapel Hill: University of North Carolina Press, 1953), 13; Bonomi, *Under the Cope of Heaven*, 40, 126; and Woolverton, *Colonial Anglicanism*, 28.

63.   Dobbs to SPG, 13 December 1754, Newburn, NC [*sic*], SPG Journals XIII, 40; Smith to Archbishop of Canterbury, 19 October 1754, Smith Mss in Hawks Coll., AEC, S, I, 8-6-47; and Richard Terrick, Bishop of London, to William Smith, 7 September 1772, Smith Mss in Hawks Coll., AEC, S, I, 76-7-11.

64.   On the favorable occupancy rate at mid-century, see Joan R. Gundersen, 'The Search for Good Men: Recruiting Ministers in Colonial Virginia,' *HMPEC* 48 (1979), 454. See also Gundersen, *The Anglican Ministry in Virginia 1723–1766: A Study of a Social Class* (New York: Garland, 1989); and Woolverton, *Colonial Anglicanism*, 29.

65.   Olmstead, *History of Religion in the United States*, 51; George J. Cleaveland, *Up From Independence: The Episcopal Church in Virginia* (Orange, VA: Green Publishers, 1976), 25; Lawrence L. Brown, 'Henry Compton, 1632–1713; Bishop of London, 1675–1713; Pioneer Leader in the Expansion of the Anglican Communion,' *HMPEC* 25 (1956), 51. Note that all of issue No.1 of *HMPEC* in 1956 features articles on Henry Compton.

66.   J. H. Bennett, Jr, 'English Bishops and Imperial Jurisdiction, 1660–1725,' *HMPEC* 32 (1963), 178, 179–80, 185; and Addison, *The Episcopal Church in the United States*, 30.

67.   Bishop of London to Dr Doddridge, 11 May 1751, *Hist. Coll.* I, 373.

68.   Dan M. Hockman, 'Commissary William Dawson and the Anglican Church in Virginia, 1743–1752,' *HMPEC* 54 (1985), 126; Addison, *The Episcopal Church in the United States*, 31; Parke Rouse, Jr, 'James Blair of Virginia,' *HMPEC* 43 (1974), 189–93; Olmstead, *History of Religion in the United States*, 51–3; and Quentin Begley Keen, 'The Problems of a Commissary: The Reverend Alexander Garden of South Carolina,' *HMPEC* 20 (1951), 136–55.

69.   Albright, *A History of the Protestant Episcopal Church*, 40, 50; Mary Plummer Salsman, 'The Reverend Roger Price (1696–1772) Commissary to New England,' (revised by Walter H. Stowe), *HMPEC* 14 (1945), 193–229.

70.   Hugh Neill to SPG, 8 June 1761, *Hist. Coll.* II, 326–7; and Samuel Seabury, Jr to SPG, 28 March 1760, SPG Journals XV, 21–2; and for an exceptional opinion on confirmation, see George Craig to –, 27 July 1760, *Hist. Coll.* II, 293.

71.   Richard Peters to Bishop of London, 14 November 1766, *Hist. Coll.* II, 409.

72. Douglass Adair, ed., 'The Autobiography of the Reverend Devereux Jarratt, 1732–1763,' *WMQ* 3rd Ser., 9 (1952), 379. See also David L. Holmes, ed., *The Life of the Reverend Devereux Jarratt* (Cleveland, OH: Pilgrim Press, 1995).
73. David C. Humphrey, 'Anglican "Infiltration" of Eighteenth Century Harvard and Yale,' *HMPEC* 43 (1974), 248, 251.
74. Henry Caner to Archbishop of Canterbury, 7 April 1759, *Hist. Coll.* III, 452–3.
75. Johnson to SPG, 25 March 1754, SPG Journals XII, 376–7; and Rev. Pundersen to SPG, 26 March 1755, SPG Journals XIII, 58.
76. Thomas Barton to SPG, 6 December 1760, *Hist. Coll.* II, 294.
77. Ahlstrom, *A Religious History of the American People*, 222; and Calam, *Parsons and Pedagogues, passim.*
78. Susan Louise Patterson, 'Biographical Sketches of Anglican Clergymen Trained at the College of William and Mary, 1726–1776: A Study of James Blair's Plan and its Result' (unpublished MA thesis, Department of History, College of William and Mary, Williamsburg, Virginia, 1973), esp. vi.
79. One study of the 409 licensees to the colonies estimates that of the 253 certified between 1761 and 1775, data exists on 63, 31 of which were educated in the colonies and nine in the mother country. See Frederick V. Mills, 'Anglican Expansion in Colonial America,' 322–3.
80. James Potter, 'Growth of Population,' 640; and Robert V. Wells, *The Population of the British Colonies in America before 1776* (Princeton, NJ: Princeton University Press, 1975), 260, 284.
81. Richard Peters to Archbishop of Canterbury, 17 October 1763, *Hist. Coll.* II, 391; and Ahlstrom, *A Religious History of the American People*, 223.
82. Neill's opinions are contained in a letter of the Archbishop of Canterbury to Jacob Duché, 16 September 1763, *Hist. Coll.* II, 390.
83. Donald F. M. Gerardi, 'The King's College Controversy, 1753–1756 and the Ideological Roots of Toryism in New York,' *Perspectives in American History* XI (1977–8), 147–96. John M. Mulder, 'William Livingston: Propagandist Against Episcopacy,' *Journal of Presbyterian History* 54 (1976), 90; Curry, *The First Freedoms*, 121–2; Don R. Gerlach and George E. DeMille, 'Samuel Johnson: Praeses Collegii Regis, 1755–1763,' *HMPEC* 44 (1975), 417–36.
84. Clergy of Philadelphia to Bishop of London, 30 April 1760, Philadelphia, *Hist. Coll.* II, 318.
85. Dobbs to SPG, 29 March 1764, Cape Fear Brunswick, SPG Journals XVI, 165.
86. Carol Van Voorst, *The Anglican Clergy in Maryland, 1692–1776* (New York: Garland, 1989), 204–18, esp. 206, 311–12. See also David C. Skaggs and Gerald E. Hartdagen, 'Sinners and Saints: Anglican Clerical Conduct in Colonial Maryland,' *HMPEC* 47 (1978), 184. Lower estimates in Nelson Waite Rightmyer, 'The Character of the Anglican Clergy in Colonial Maryland,' *HMPEC* 19 (1950), 128.
87. Gundersen, 'The Search for Good Men,' 454.
88. Gundersen, *The Anglican Ministry in Virginia*, 119–47, esp. 125, 141.
89. Van Voorst, *The Anglican Clergy in Maryland*, 311–12.
90. David Curtis Skaggs, 'Thomas Cradock's Sermon on the Governance of Maryland's Established Church,' *WMQ* 3rd Ser., 27 (1970), 650. See also

Skaggs, 'The Chain of Being in Eighteenth Century Maryland: The Paradox of Thomas Cradock,' *HMPEC* 45 (1976), 161–3.
91. Gerald J. Goodwin, 'The Anglican Reaction to the Great Awakening,' *HMPEC* 35 (1966), 348, 356.
92. Jarratt, *Sermons on the Various and Important Subjects in Practical Divinity* (1793–4), as quoted in Gundersen, *The Anglican Ministry*, 119.
93. Gundersen, *The Anglican Ministry in Virginia*, 119; and Rightmyer, 'Character of the Anglican Clergy of Colonial Maryland,' 122, 131.
94. Chandler to Bishop of London, 21 October 1767, Elizabeth Town, New Jersey, *Hist. Coll.* IV, 335.
95. Bernard to SPG, 24 March 1759, Amboy, New Jersey, SPG Journals XIV, 189.
96. Rightmyer, 'Character of the Anglican Clergy of Colonial Maryland,' 129; Francis L. Hawks, *Contributions to the Ecclesiastical History of the United States* (New York, 1836–9) I, 114; and Rhys Isaac, 'Religion and Authority: Problems of the Anglican Establishment in Virginia in the Era of the Great Awakening and the Parsons' Cause,' *WMQ* 3rd Ser., 30 (1973), 10.
97. William Waller Hening, ed., *The Statutes at Large: Being a Collection of all the Laws of Virginia, from the First Session of the Legislature, in the Year 1619* I–XII (Charlottesville, VA: University Press of Virginia, 1969, orig. publ. Richmond, 1823), VI, 568–9; VII, 240; Isaac, 'Religion and Authority,' 12.
98. Hawks, *Contributions* I, 117–19; A. Shrady Hill, 'The Parson's Cause,' *HMPEC* 46 (1977), 15; and Francis Godwin James, 'Clerical Incomes in Eighteenth Century England, *HMPEC* 18 (1949), 315.
99. Rhys Isaac, 'Religion and Authority,' 16–21; and Hawks, *Contributions* I, 119.
100. Francis L. Hawks, *Contributions* II, 246–7, 250; Nelson Rightmyer, 'The Anglican Church in Maryland: Factors Contributory to the American Revolution,' *CH* 19 (1950), 191, 196.
101. Hawks, *Contributions* II, 253; and Rightmyer, 'Anglican Church in Maryland,' 197. In 1773 compromise legislation was reached which set the tax at 30 pounds of tobacco per poll.
102. James, 'Clerical Incomes in Eighteenth Century England,' 314.
103. Henry Caner to Bishop Gibson, 18 September 1730, Fairfield, Connecticut, Fulham Papers I, 243–4.
104. Browne to SPG, 12 December 1760, SPG Journals XV, 72.
105. Browne to SPG, 6 April 1768, Newark, New Jersey, SPG Journals XVII, 526–7.
106. Bloomer to SPG, 18 February 1771, SPG Journals XIX, 47–8.

CHAPTER 3   THE BISHOP CONTROVERSY

1. John Adams to Dr Jedidiah Morse, 2 December 1815, in Charles Francis Adams, ed., *The Works of John Adams, Second President of the United States: With a Life of the Author, Notes and Illustrations* (Boston, MA: Little, Brown, 1856) X, 185.
2. Perry Miller 'Crisis and Americanization,' in *The Great Awakening: Event and Exegesis*, Darrett B. Rutman, ed. (Huntington, NY: Robert E. Krieger

Publishing Company, 1977, orig. publ. 1970), 139–56; Alan Heimert, *Religion and the American Mind from the Great Awakening to the Revolution* (Cambridge, MA: Harvard University Press, 1966), *passim*; and Alan Heimert and Perry Miller, eds, *The Great Awakening: Documents Illustrating the Crisis and Its Consequences* (Indianapolis: Bobbs-Merrill, 1967), lxi; John M. Murrin, 'No Awakening, No Revolution? More Counterfactual Speculations,' *Reviews in American History* 11 (1983), 161; William G. McLoughlin, ' "Enthusiasm for Liberty": The Great Awakening as the Key to the Revolution,' *American Antiquarian Society Proceedings* 87 (1977), 69–95; and Philip Lawson, *The Imperial Challenge: Quebec and Britain in the Age of the American Revolution* (Montreal: McGill-Queen's University Press, 1989), 126–45.

3. Ebenezer Baldwin, 'An Appendix Stating the Heavy Grievances the Colonies Labor Under...' (31 August 1774), in Jack P. Greene, ed., *Colonies to Nation 1763–1789: A Documentary History of the American Revolution* (New York: W. W. Norton, 1975), 213–20, esp. 213.

4. Scholars differ on the influence of the bishop controversy on the coming of the Revolution. See Carl Bridenbaugh, *Mitre and Sceptre: Transatlantic Faiths, Ideas, Personalities, and Politics. 1689–1775* (New York: Oxford University Press, 1962), xiv, 320; McLoughlin, 'Enthusiasm for Liberty,' 47; Frederick V. Mills, Sr, 'The Colonial Anglican Episcopate: A Historiographical Review,' *AEH* 62 (1992), 342; and Winthrop S. Hudson, *Religion in America* (New York: Charles Scribner's Sons, 1965), 92; Jon Butler, *Awash in a Sea of Faith: Christianizing the American People* (Cambridge, MA: Harvard University Press, 1990), 195–7; Patricia U. Bonomi, *Under the Cope of Heaven: Religion, Society, and Politics in Colonial America* (New York: Oxford University Press, 1986), 199; and Arthur Lyon Cross, *The Anglican Episcopate and the American Colonies* (New York: Longmans, Green, 1902), 214.

5. Bernard Bailyn, *The Ideological Origins of the American Revolution* (Cambridge, MA: Belknap Press, 1976, orig. publ. 1967), 96–8; and Gordon S. Wood, 'Rhetoric and Reality in the American Revolution,' *WMQ* 3rd Ser., 23 (1966), 3–32.

6. Bridenbaugh, *Mitre and Sceptre*, 57, 214. For a critique of Bridenbaugh, see William H. Hogue, 'The Religious Conspiracy Theory of the Anglican Revolution: Anglican Motive,' *CH* 45 (1976), 277–92.

7. See Leonard J. Trinterud, *The Forming of an American Tradition: A Re-examination of Colonial Presbyterianism* (Freeport, NY: Books for Libraries Press, 1949), 229–41. Trinterud's chapter, 'The Threat of Anglican Establishment,' does not consider any non-political reasons in the Anglican campaign for a resident bishop.

8. On the evangelical perspective critical to Anglicanism, see Joan R. Gundersen, *The Anglican Ministry in Virginia, 1723–1766: A Study of a Social Class* (New York: Garland, 1989), i–iii. See also John Walton, 'Tradition of the Middle Way: The Anglican Contribution to the American Character,' *HMPEC* 44 (1975) 5 (Extra), 7–9.

9. On sectarian divisions in the colonies, see J. C. D. Clark, *The Language of Liberty* (Cambridge: Cambridge University Press, 1994), xii, 203–17, 339–40. Clark reinforces Bridenbaugh's claims that religious causation was

central to the Revolution, but also Alan Heimert's analysis of the participants. See Heimert, *Religion and the American Mind from the Great Awakening to the Revolution* (Cambridge, MA: Harvard University Press, 1966). Whereas Bailyn emphasized oppositional and secular political ideas, Clark focused mainly on underlying religious antagonisms between Anglicans and dissenters as a fundamental cause of the Revolution.

10. Hogue, 'The Religious Conspiracy Theory of the American Revolution: Anglican Motive,' 277–8, 292; Donald F. M. Gerardi, 'The Episcopate Controversy Reconsidered: Religious Vocation and Anglican Perceptions of Authority in Mid-Eighteenth-Century America,' *Perspectives in American History* 3 (1987), 81–114: and Butler, *Awash in a Sea of Faith*, 197.

11. Frederick V. Mills, Sr, 'The Internal Anglican Controversy Over an American Episcopate, 1763–1775,' *HMPEC* 44 (1975), 257–76; Mills, *Bishops by Ballot: An Eighteenth-Century Ecclesiastical Revolution* (New York: Oxford University Press, 1978), 100–6; Carol Van Voorst, *The Anglican Clergy in Maryland, 1692–1776* (New York: Garland, 1989), 78–87; and S. Charles Bolton, *Southern Anglicanism: The Church of England in Colonial South Carolina* (Westport, CT: Greenwood Press, 1982), 121–53, 156.

12. J. C. D. Clark, *English Society, 1688–1832* (Cambridge: Cambridge University Press, 1985), 7, 216–35.

13. François-Xavier de Montmorency Laval was named Bishop Laval, the first Bishop of Quebec in 1674, and the Franciscan Juan de Zumárraga was appointed the first Bishop of Mexico in 1527. See W. J. Eccles, *France in America,* rev. edn (East Lansing, MI: Michigan State University Press, 1990), 56–7; and Mark A. Noll, *A History of Christianity in the United States and Canada* (Grand Rapids, MI: William B. Eerdmans, 1992), 23.

14. Samuel Auchmuty to Samuel Johnson, 27 August 1766, Hawks Mss in Hawks Coll., AEC, RG 117-60-9.

15. William Wilson Manross, *A History of the American Episcopal Church* (New York: Morehouse-Gorham, 1950), 154, 159–60; Bridenbaugh, *Mitre and Sceptre*, 27; and Raymond W. Albright, *A History of the Protestant Episcopal Church*, (New York: Macmillan, 1964) 97–8.

16. Manross, *A History of the American Episcopal Church*, 161; Bridenbaugh, *Mitre and Sceptre*, 31–53; Edgar Legare Pennington, 'The S.P.G. Anniversary Sermons, 1703–1783,' *HMPEC* 20 (1951), 10–43; Don R. Gerlach, 'Champions of an American Episcopate: Thomas Secker of Canterbury and Samuel Johnson of Connecticut,' *HMPEC* 41 (1972), 381–414; Norman Sykes, *From Sheldon to Secker: Aspects of English Church History, 1660–1768* (Cambridge: Cambridge University Press, 1959), 205–10; and Geoffrey Yeo, 'A Case Without Parallel: The Bishops of London and the Anglican Church Overseas, 1660–1748,' *JEH* 44 (1993), 450–75.

17. Manross, *A History of the American Episcopal Church*, 164; and Bonomi, *Under the Cope of Heaven*, 199.

18. Mills, *Bishops by Ballot*, 42–4; and Bridenbaugh, *Mitre and Sceptre*, 246.

19. Thomas Bradbury Chandler, *The Appeal Defended: or, the proposed American Episcopate Vindicated, in Answer to the Objections and Misrepresentations of Dr. Chauncy and Others* (New York, Hugh Gaine, 1771), 2.

20. William Smith to Bishop of London, 6 May 1768, Fulham Papers XXII, 11.

21. Bridenbaugh, *Mitre and Sceptre*, 298–301; and Albright, *A History of the Protestant Episcopal Church*, 106–8.

22. William Smith to Secretary, SPG, 6 May 1768, *Hist. Coll.* II, 427.
23. Peters to Bishop of London, 14 November 1766, *Hist. Coll.* II, 410; Mills, *Bishops by Ballot*, 62–70. See also Samuel Auchmuty to Samuel Johnson, 3 January 1767, Hawks Mss in Hawks Coll., AEC, RG117-60-10.
24. Mills, *Bishops by Ballot*, 89–92; and Van Voorst, *The Anglican Clergy in Maryland*, 78–87, esp. 86. Van Voorst states that of the 56 Anglican clergymen in Maryland in 1770, only 11 favored an episcopate.
25. Hugh Neill to Bishop of London, 20 September 1768, *Hist. Coll.* IV, 338. Likewise, Thomas John Claggett to Bishop of London, 20 September 1769, *Hist. Coll.* IV, 340–1.
26. For the Maryland petitions on episcopacy, see William H. Browne, ed., *Archives of Maryland: Proceedings of the Council of Maryland*, 32 vols (Baltimore, MD: Maryland Historical Society, 1912), XXXII, 379–84. See also Jonathan Boucher, ed. *Reminiscences of an American Loyalist, 1738–1789*, Jonathan Bouchier, ed. (Boston MA: Houghton Mifflin, 1925), 65.
27. Camm to William Smith, 3 June 1774, Hawks Mss in Hawks Coll., AEC, RG 117-60-12. See also Thad W. Tate, 'The Coming of the Revolution in Virginia: Britain's Challenge to Virginia's Ruling Class, 1763–1776,' *WMQ* 3rd Ser., 39 (1962), 326–33.
28. George W. Pilcher, 'Virginia Newspapers and the Dispute Over the Proposed Colonial Episcopate, 1771–1772,' *The Historian* 23 (1960), 99; Pilcher, 'The Pamphlet War on the Proposed Virginia Anglican Episcopate, 1767–1775,' *HMPEC* 30 (1961); and Paul K. Longmore, '"All Matters and Things Relating to Religion and Morality": The Virginia Burgesses' Committee for Religion, 1769 to 1775,' *Journal of Church and State* 38 (1996), 785–91. Gwatkin and Henley's publication also responded to the proceedings of the Anglican convention and their receipt of *An Address from the Clergy of New-York and New-Jersey, to the Episcopalians in Virginia* (New York: Hugh Gaine, 1771), which was signed by T. B. Chandler, Myles Cooper, and other ministers.
29. The House of Burgesses' statement is reproduced in Pilcher, 'Virginia Newspapers and the Dispute Over the Proposed Colonial Episcopate,' 106.
30. Thomas Gwatkin and Samuel Henley, *A Letter to the Clergy of New York and New Jersey, Occasioned by an Address to the Episcopalians in Virginia* (Williamsburg: Purdie & Dixon, 1772), 23.
31. Gwatkin and Henley, *A Letter to the Clergy of New York and New Jersey*, 14.
32. John Gordon to –, 11 October 1770, Vertical File, EDLM.
33. Mills, *Bishops by Ballot*, 128.
34. Bolton, *Southern Anglicanism* 121–53, esp. 156.
35. Thomas Bradbury Chandler, *A Free Examination of the Critical Commentary on Archbishop Secker's Letter to Mr. Walpole* (New York: Hugh Gaine, 1774) 80–1.
36. Charles Inglis to SPG, 1 December 1766, *Hist. Coll.* V, 124.
37. Connecticut Clergy to Richard Terrick, 8 October 1766, Fulham Papers I, 308–9.
38. Chandler et al., *An Address From the Clergy of New-York and New-Jersey*, 5. A similar opinion in Thomas, Bishop of Oxford to Horatio Walpole, 9 January 1750/1, Lambeth Palace Misc., reel 5, MS 2589, 52.
39. William Willie to Bishop of London, 19 June 1772, Fulham Papers XXVI, 148–9.

40. James Horrocks to Bishop Terrick, 8 October 1771, Fulham Papers XIV, 213–14.

41. Other individuals who had been raised as dissenters include Samuel Johnson, Samuel Seabury Sr, Jeremiah Leaming, Agur Treadwell, Richard Mansfield, Samuel Andrews, and Thomas Bradbury Chandler. See Mills, *Bishops by Ballot*, 12; and Richard Mansfield, *A Funeral Upon the Decease of the Reverend John Beach* (New Haven, CT: T. and S. Green, 1782), 16.

42. Henry Caner, *The Firm Belief of a Future Reward a Powerful Motive to Obedience and a Good Life. A Sermon Preached at Christ Church in Boston, August 20, 1765. At the Funeral of the Rev. Timothy Cutler, D.D. Late Rector of Said Church* (Boston, MA: Thomas and John Fleet, 1765), 17–19.

43. Matthew Graves to Bishop of London, 1 April 1768, Fulham Papers XXII, 179. On his own personal sacrifices, see John Beach, *A Friendly Expostulation, with all persons concern'd in publishing a late pamphlet, entitled, the real advantages which ministers and people may enjoy, especially in the colonies by conforming to the Church of England* (New York: John Holt, 1763), 9–11.

44. Cross, *The Anglican Episcopate and the American Colonies*, 257–8. See also James Thayer Addison, *The Episcopal Church in the United States, 1789–1931* (Hamden, CT: Archon Books reprint, 1969, orig. publ. 1951), 50; and David L. Jacobson, 'The King's Four Churches: The Established Churches of America, England, Ireland, and Scotland in the Early Years of George III,' *AEH* 59 (1990), 184.

45. Mills, *Bishops by Ballot*, 32–3.

46. Chandler to Bishop Terrick, 10 July 1766, Fulham Papers VI, 162–3. For another appeal, see the petition of the clergy of Massachusetts, New Hampshire, and Rhode Island to Bishop Terrick, 22 September 1768, Fulham Papers VI, 68.

47. Martyn to Bishop Terrick, 20 October 1765, Fulham Papers X, 160–1.

48. Evarts B. Greene, 'The Anglican Outlook on the American Colonies in the Early Eighteenth Century,' *AHR* 20 (1914–15), 85; Albright, *A History of the Protestant Episcopal Church*, 98; and Stephen Taylor, 'Whigs, Bishops and America: The Politics of Church Reform in Mid-Eighteenth-Century England,' *Historical Journal* 36 (1993), 331–56.

49. Horatio Walpole to Bishop Sherlock, 29 May 1750, Appendix A in Cross, *The Anglican Episcopate and the American Colonies*, 323–5. See Manross, *A History of the American Episcopal Church* 156–8; Jack M. Sosin, 'The Proposal in the Pre-Revolutionary Decade for Establishing Anglican Bishops in the Colonies,' *JEH* 13 (1962), 78; Mills, 'The Colonial Anglican Episcopate,' 332; and Bridenbaugh, *Mitre and Sceptre*, 83–115; and Mills, *Bishops by Ballot*, 28–34.

50. Taylor, 'Whigs, Bishops and America', 331–3.

51. Taylor, 'Whigs, Bishops and America,' 337–8, 348–53. Taylor also suggests that while SPG missionaries from New England pressed for bishops for 'political reasons,' English bishops advanced only pastoral arguments.

52. Richard Terrick, Bishop of London, to Episcopal Clergy of Connecticut, 18 February 1765, Hawks Mss in Hawks Coll., AEC, RG 117-61-63. From London, Thomas Coombe reported that many bishops shared this cautious

attitude. Coombe to William Smith, 12 March 1770, Smith Mss in Hawks Coll., AEC, S, I, 70-7-5.

53. Manross, *A History of the American Episcopal Church*, 155–6. In November 1784 Samuel Seabury Jr secured consecration as the first colonial bishop in the new republic from Scottish non-juring bishops. See *DAB* XVI, 528–30.

54. Norman Sykes, *Church and State in England in the XVIIIth Century* (New York: Octagon Books, 1975), 77; and his *From Sheldon to Secker: Aspects of English Church History, 1660–1768* (Cambridge: Cambridge University Press, 1959), 193.

55. Jon Butler, *Awash in a Sea of Faith*, 197; Bridenbaugh, *Mitre and Sceptre*, 210–11.

56. John Wingate Thornton, *The Pulpit of the American Revolution: Or, The Political Sermons of the Period of 1776* (Boston: D. Lothrop, 1876), xxx. See also H. G. G. Herklots, *The Church of England and the American Episcopal Church: from the first Voyages of Discovery to the first Lambeth Conference* (London: A.R. Mowbray, 1966), 79.

57 Manross, *A History of the American Episcopal Church*, 158. See also Sosin, 'The Proposal in the Pre-Revolutionary Decade for Establishing Anglican Bishops,' 76.

58. Samuel Johnson 'A Short Vindication of the Society', in Henry Caner, *A Candid Examination of Dr. Mayhew's Observations on the charter and conduct of the Society for the Propagation of the Gospel in Foreign Parts* (Boston, MA: Thomas and John Fleet, 1763), 88.

59. Secker, Archbishop of Canterbury, to Johnson, 27 September 1758, Smith Mss in Hawks Coll., AEC, S, I, 25-6-64.

60. Bernhard Knollenberg, *Origin of the American Revolution: 1759–1776* (New York: Macmillan 1960), 83. On the financing of colonial bishops, see Thomas Bradbury Chandler, *An Appeal to the Public, in Behalf of the Church of England in America* (New York: James Parker, 1767), 97–108; and Charles Inglis, *A Vindication of the Bishop of Landaff's Sermon* (New York: J. Holt, 1768), 80.

61. John Adams, *Works* X, 185.

62. Chandler et al., *An Address from the Clergy of New-York and New-Jersey, to the Episcopalians in Virginia*, 37.

63. Archbishop Drummond, 'Thoughts Upon the Present State of the Church of England in America,' June 1764, Lambeth Palace Misc., reel 5, MS 2589, 85–9.

64. Bernard Bailyn, *The Ideological Origins of American Politics*, 97; and James H. Hutson, 'The Origins of "The Paranoid Style in American Politics": Public Jealousy from the Age of Walpole to the Age of Jackson,' *Saints and Revolutionaries: Essays on Early American History*, David D. Hall et al., eds (New York: W.W. Norton, 1984), 345–6.

65. So Thomas Bradbury Chandler characterized his opponents in *The Appeal Defended*, 2.

66. John M. Mulder, 'William Livingston: Propagandist Against Episcopacy,' *Journal of Presbyterian History* 54 (1976), 90.

67. *For the Information of the Publick. As it has been asserted, in defiance of truth, that no Application was ever made for an American bishop, the*

following extract from the introduction to Doctor Chandler's Appeal to the public, in behalf of the Church of England in America, it is thought will be of service (New York, 1768) broadside, Evans Early American Imprints, 10898.

68. Hogue, 'The Religious Conspiracy Theory of the American Revolution,' 277–92, esp. 291; and Jerald C. Brauer, *Protestantism in America*, rev. edn (Philadelphia, PA: Westminster Press, 1965), 67.

69. Robert Bruce Mullin, *Episcopal Vision/American Reality: High Church Theology and Social Thought in Evangelical America* (New Haven, CT: Yale University Press, 1986), xiii–xiv. See also Peter Doll, 'The Idea of the Primitive Church in High Church Ecclesiology from Samuel Johnson to J. H. Hobart,' *AEH* 65 (1996), 6–43.

70. Jeremiah Leaming, *A Defence of the Episcopal Government of the Church: Containing Remarks on Two Late, Noted Sermons on Presbyterian Ordination* (New York: John Holt, 1766), 50–63, esp. 57.

71. Samuel Johnson's preface to John Beach, *A Calm and Dispassionate Vindication of the Professors of the Church of England, against the Abusive Misrepresentations and Salacious Argumentations of Mr. Noah Hobart, in his late address to them* (Boston, MA: J. Draper, 1749), vii.

72. John Beach, *A Continuation of the Calm and Dispassionate Vindication of the Professors of the Church of England* (Boston, MA, 1751), 81–2.

73. See John Beach, *An Appeal to the Unprejudiced* (Boston, MA, 1737); Jeremiah Leaming, *A Defence of the Episcopal Government of the Church;* his *A Second Defence, of the Episcopal Government, of the Church, Containing Remarks, on the Objections Advanced by Mr. Noah Welles Against the Church of England* (New York: John Holt, 1770); and his *Dissertations upon Various Subjects, which May Be Well Worth the Attention of Every Christian; and of Real Service to the Sincere Inquirer After True Religion* (New Haven, CT: Thomas and Samuel Green, 1788), esp. sections II–IV.

74. Hogue, 'The Religious Conspiracy Theory,' 282. On post-revolutionary debate on the origins of episcopacy, see John Bowden, *A Letter, from John Bowden, A.M. Rector of St. Paul's Church, Norwalk, to the Reverend Ezra Stiles, D.D. LL.D. president of Yale-College. Occasioned by some passages concerning church government, in an ordination sermon, preached, at New-London, May 17, 1787* (New Haven, CT: Thomas and Samuel Green, 1788), 42.

75. J. Leaming, *A Defence of the Episcopal Government of the Church*, 16–23, 47; and his *A Second Defence, of the Episcopal Government*, 43–4.

76. Jonathan Mayhew, *Observations on the Charter and Conduct of the SPG* (Boston, 1763); Henry Caner, *A Candid Examination of Dr. Mayhew's Observations* (Boston, 1763); and Arthur Browne, *Remarks on Dr. Mayhew's Incidental Reflections Relative to the Church of England, as Contained in his Observations* (Portsmouth, 1763).

77. Thomas Secker, *An Answer to Dr. Mayhew's Observations* (Boston, 1764), passim. See also Cross, *Anglican Episcopate*, 144–60; Bridenbaugh, *Mitre and Sceptre*, 224–9; Mills, *Bishops by Ballot*, 31; and Richard James Hooker, 'The Mayhew Controversy,' *CH* V (1936), 255.

78. Chandler, *An Appeal to the Public*, i–ii, 3–12.

79. Henry Addison, John McPherson, Isaac Campbell, William Brogden to Bishop of London, September 1768, Fulham Papers XXII, 13.
80. William Willie to Bishop of London, 19 June 1772, Fulham Papers XXVI, 148–9.
81. Samuel Johnson, John Beach, James Wetmore, Joseph Lamson, Ebenezer Dibblee, and Richard Mansfield to SPG, 1751, Fulham Papers I, 292.
82. Chandler, *Appeal*, 114–5.
83. Clergy of Connecticut to SPG, Fulham Papers I, 292.
84. Jeremiah Leaming for the Clergy of Connecticut to Richard Terrick, Bishop of London, 19 May 1771, Fulham Papers I, 317.
85. George Craig to SPG, 7 November 1767, *Hist. Coll.* II, 423.
86. Henry Barnes to Bishop Terrick, 25 September 1769, Fulham Papers VI, 73.
87. Daniel Dulany to Lord Baltimore [6th], 1766, Revolutionary War Collection, MHS, Mss 1814.
88. William Knox to William Pitt, 1786, Fulham Papers I, 102.
89. Samuel Auchmuty, Thomas Chandler, John Ogilvie, and Charles Inglis to the Earl of Hillsborough, October 1771 as quoted in Sosin, 'The Proposal in the Pre-Revolutionary Decade for Establishing Anglican Bishops in the Colonies,' 82–3.
90. As quoted in Cross, *The Anglican Episcopate and the American Colonies*, 345.
91. For a variety of opinions on possible motives, see Bridenbaugh, *Mitre and Sceptre*, 292; Jack Sosin, 'The Proposal in the Pre-Revolutionary Decade for Establishing Anglican Bishops in the Colonies,' 79–81; and Samuel Clyde McCulloch, 'Thomas Bradbury Chandler: Anglican Humanitarian in Colonial New Jersey,' in *British Humanitarianism: Essays Honoring Frank J. Klingberg*, Samuel Clyde McCulloch, ed. (Philadelphia, PA: Church Historical Society, 1950), 112.
92. Jonathan Mayhew, *Observations on the Charter and Conduct of the Society for the Propagation of the Gospel in Foreign Parts* (Boston, 1763); Thomas Secker, Archbishop of Canterbury, *An Answer to Dr. Mayhew's Observations* (Boston, 1764); Don R. Gerlach, 'Champions of an American Episcopate: Thomas Secker of Canterbury and Samuel Johnson of Connecticut,' *HMPEC* 41 (1972), 384, 396.
93. Beach, *A Continuation of the Calm and Dispassionate Vindication*, 67.
94. Samuel Johnson, preface to John Beach, *A Calm and Dispassionate Vindication of the Professors of the Church of England*, v–vi.
95. Henry Caner to Bishop Sherlock, 6 May 1751, Fulham Papers VI, 8.
96. Chandler, *The Appeal Defended*, 265.
97. Chandler, *Appeal*, 79–80.
98. Chandler, *A Free Examination of the Critical Commentary on Archbishop Secker's Letter to Mr. Walpole* 33–4, esp. 38.
99. Chandler et al., *An Address from the Clergy of New-York and New-Jersey, to the Episcopalians in Virginia*, 9–32, esp. 12–15.
100. Bishop of London to –, December 1707, Lambeth Palace Misc., reel 1, item 18.
101. Connecticut Clergy to SPG, 1751, Fulham Papers I, 292.
102. Clergy of New Jersey and New York to Bishop Terrick, 2 October 1765, Fulham Papers VI, 156–7.
103. John Ross to Secretary, SPG, 6 July 1771, *Hist. Coll.* II, 457.

104. Petition of the Clergy of Connecticut to Richard Terrick, Bishop of London, 8 October 1766, Fulham Papers I, 309.
105. Inglis, *A Vindication of the Bishop of Landaff's Sermon*, 82.
106. Samuel Andrews, *A Sermon preached at Litchfield, in Connecticut, before a voluntary convention of the clergy of the Church of England of several provinces in America, June 13, 1770* (New Haven, CT, 1770), 12.
107. Jeremiah Leaming for the Clergy of Connecticut to Richard Terrick, Bishop of London, 29 May 1771, Fulham Papers I, 317.
108. Caner to Bishop Sherlock, 31 January 1750, Fulham Papers V, 330–1.
109. McGilchrist to SPG, 31 July 1765, *Hist. Coll.* III, 519. For another Anglican opinion on the irrationality of dissenting arguments, see Thomas Bradbury Chandler, *The Appeal Farther Defended: In Answer to the Farther Misrepresentations of Dr. Chauncy* (New York: Hugh Gaine, 1771), 111–14.
110. Chandler, *Appeal*, 114, 117.
111. Chandler, *The Appeal Defended*, 266.
112. Chandler, *A Free Examination of the Critical Commentary on Archbishop Secker's Letter to Mr. Walpole*, 54.
113. John F. Woolverton, *Colonial Anglicanism in North America* (Detroit, MI: Wayne State University Press, 1984), 19.
114. Clergy of Connecticut to Richard Terrick, Bishop of London, 8 October 1766, Fulham Papers I, 309.
115. Pennsylvania clergy (signed by William Smith), to Bishop Terrick, 31 May 1765, Fulham Papers VIII, 17–18.
116. William Smith to Bishop Terrick, 22 October 1768, Fulham Papers VIII, 40–1.
117. John Andrews, *Two Sermons on Public Occasions* (Philadelphia, PA: W. Young, 1788), 51.
118. Chandler et al., *An Address From the Clergy of New-York and New-Jersey, to the Episcopalians in Virginia*, 44–6.
119. Chandler, *Appeal*, 34.
120. Chandler, *A Free Examination of the Critical Commentary on Archbishop Secker's Letter to Mr. Walpole*, vi, x, 19–22; and Robert Leroy Hilldrup, ed., 'The Need of a Bishop in Virginia in 1756 as Seen by a Layman; a Letter of Graham Frank to Thomas Sherlock, Bishop of London,' *HMPEC* 26 (1957), 170.
121. William Duke, *Observations on the Present State of Religion in Maryland* (Baltimore, MD: Samuel & John Adams, 1795), 39–40.
122. Chandler et al., *An Address From the Clergy of New-York and New-Jersey, to the Episcopalians*, 48.
123. Chandler et al., *An Address from the Clergy of New-York and New-Jersey*, 49–52.
124. On Atlantic travel, see I.K. Steele, *The English Atlantic, 1675–1740: An Exploration of Communication and Community* (New York: Oxford University Press, 1986), esp. 11–16.
125. Rev. Thomas Coombe Jr to Thomas Coombe Sr., London, 6 June 1770 and 8 October 1770, in Coombe Family Papers, HSP, Mss 1993.
126. Johnson to SPG, 12 November 1766, Stratford, Connecticut, SPG Journals XVII, 271–2; and Mary Kent Davey Babcock, 'Difficulties and Dangers of Pre-Revolutionary Ordinations,' *HMPEC* 12 (1943), 225–41.

1 6   9 7 6 9 9 1 1 1 1 1 6 6 7 9 7 6 1 1 1 17 16 1

127. Samuel Johnson to Bishop Sherlock, 25 September 1751, Stratford, Connecticut, Fulham Papers I, 293–4. Johnson claimed that five of 25 candidates died.
128. Bishop of Oxford to Horatio Walpole, 9 January 1750/1, Lambeth Palace Misc., reel 5, MS 2589, 45; and Edmund Gibson, Bishop of London, 'A Memorial Concerning the Sending of Bishops to the English Plantations Abroad,' Lambeth Palace Misc., reel 5, MS 2589, 32.
129. Babcock, 'Difficulties and Dangers of Pre-revolutionary Ordinations,' 233; and Johnson to SPG, 21 December 1757, SPG Journals XIV, 68–71.
130. Quoted in E. Edward Beardsley, *The History of the Episcopal Church in Connecticut* I (New York: Hurd and Hougton, 1865), 184. Full text in Samuel Johnson to Bishop of Oxford, 5 December 1757, Lambeth Palace Misc., reel 2, 111.
131. This common opinion is expressed in George Craig to SPG, 25 June 1766, *Hist. Coll.* II, 405–6.
132. Hugh Neill to SPG, 19 May 1766, Oxford, Pennsylvania, *Hist. Coll.* II, 404.
133. Douglas Adair, ed., 'The Autobiography of the Reverend Devereux Jarratt, 1732–1763,' *WMQ* 3rd Ser., 9 (1952), 383.
134. Thomas Barton to SPG, 10 November 1766, Lancaster, Pennsylvania, *Hist. Coll.* II, 408
135. Chandler et al., *An Address from the Clergy of New-York and New-Jersey*, 46–7.
136. Chandler, *Appeal*, 55.
137. Chandler, *Appeal*, 44; and Pennsylvania clergy to Bishop of London, 10 January 1762, Hawks Mss in Hawks Coll., AEC, RG 117-60-43.
138. Beach to SPG, 14 April 1768, SPG Journals XVII, 523. For a similar opinion, see Edmund Gibson, Bishop of London, 'Memorial Concerning the Sending of Bishops to the English Plantations Abroad,' c.1745 Lambeth Palace Misc., reel 5, MS 2589, 32.
139. Winslow to SPG Secretary, 30 June 1768, *Hist. Coll.* III, 540–1.
140. See William W. Sweet, *The Story of Religions in America*, rev. edn (New York: Harper, 1950; orig. publ. 1930), 174–5. See also David L. Holmes, 'The Episcopal Church and the American Revolution,' *HMPEC* 47 (1978), 265.
141. Thomas Barton to SPG, 10 November 1766, *Hist. Coll.* II, 408.

CHAPTER 4   THE POLITICAL PHILOSOPHIES OF THE TWO EXTREMES

1. Perry Miller, *The New England Mind: The Seventeenth Century* (Cambridge, MA: The Belknap Press of Harvard University Press, 1939), 398–431; C. H. Van Tyne, 'Influence of the Clergy, and of Religious and Sectarian Forces, on the American Revolution,' *AHR* 19 (1913), 44–64; Alice M. Baldwin, *The New England Clergy and the American Revolution* (Durham, NC: Duke University Press, 1928), *passim*; Edmund S. Morgan, 'The Puritan Ethic and the American Revolution,' *WMQ* 3rd Ser., 24 (1967), 3–43; Ruth H. Bloch, 'Religion and Ideological Change in the American Revolution,' in *Religion and American Politics: From the*

Colonial Period to the 1980s, Mark A. Noll, ed. (New York: Oxford University Press, 1990), 44–61; Mark A. Noll, 'The American Revolution and Protestant Evangelicalism,' *The Journal of Interdisciplinary History* 23 (1993), 615–38; and Sarah J. Purcell, '"Spread this Martial Fire": The New England Patriot Clergy and Civil Military Inspiration,' *Journal of Church and State* 38 (1996), 621–38.

2. William W. Rankin, 'Anglican Attitudes and Behaviors Concerning War,' in *The Anglican Moral Choice*, Paul Elmen, ed. (Wilton, CT: Morehouse-Barlow, 1983); J. William Frost, *A Perfect Freedom: Religious Liberty in Pennsylvania* (University Park, PA: Pennsylvania State University Press, 1993, orig. publ. Cambridge University Press, 1990), 29–59; Walter Herbert Stowe, 'A Study in Conscience: Some Aspects of the Relations of the Clergy to the State,' *HMPEC* 19 (1950), 301–4; Glenn T. Miller, 'Fear God and Honor the King: The Failure of Loyalist Civil Theology in the Revolutionary Crisis,' *HMPEC* 47 (1978), 221–42. On passive obedience, see Robert Hole, *Pulpits, Politics and Public Order in England, 1760–1832* (Cambridge: Cambridge University Press, 1989), 11–13, 19–21; Robert D. Cornwall, *Visible and Apostolic: The Constitution of the Church in High Church Anglican and Non-Juror Thought* (Newark, DE: University of Delaware Press, 1993), 73–5, 78, 81–2; J. C. D. Clark, *English Society, 1688–1832* (Cambridge: Cambridge University Press, 1985), 136; and his *The Language of Liberty 1660–1832* (Cambridge: Cambridge University Press, 1994), 155–6, 188–9.

3. James E. Bradley, *Popular Politics and the American Revolution in England: Petitions, the Crown, and Public Opinion* (Macon, GA: Mercer University Press, 1986), 89, 147, 180, 192–3.

4. Bradley, *Popular Politics and the American Revolution in England*, 193, 201; Paul Langford, 'The English Clergy and the American Revolution,' in *The Transformation of Political Culture: England and Germany in the Late Eighteenth Century*, Eckhart Hellmuth, ed. (London: Oxford University Press, 1990), 275–6, 281–2; William Gibson, *Church, State and Society, 1760–1850* (New York: St. Martin's Press, 1994), 41–6; and Henry P. Ippel, 'British Sermons and the American Revolution,' *Journal of Religious History* XII (1982), 197. Ippel calculated that of the 95 sermons which specifically referred to the war, 79 supported the British government against the colonies.

5. Philip Grant Davidson, *Propaganda and the American Revolution 1763–1783* (New York: Norton, 1973, orig. publ. 1943), 249; Mark A. Noll, *Christians in the American Revolution* (Washington, DC: Christian University Press, 1977), 51.

6. Bruce E. Steiner, *Samuel Seabury 1729–1796: A Study in the High Church Tradition* (Oberlin, OH: Ohio University Press, 1971), 127–76; and Seabury, *Letters of a Westchester Farmer 1774–1775*, Clarence H. Vance, ed. (New York: DaCapo Press, 1970).

7. Thomas Bradbury Chandler, *A Friendly Address to All Reasonable Americans, on the Subject of Our Political Confusions: in which the Necessary Consequences of Violently Opposing the King's Troops, and of a General Non-Importation are Fairly Stated* (Boston, MA: Mills and Hicks, 1774); *The American Querist: or, Some Questions Proposed Relative to the Present Disputes Between Great Britain, and Her American Colonies.*

By a North American (New York: James Rivington, 1774); and *What Think Ye of the Congress Now? Or, An Inquiry, How Far the Americans are Bound By and Execute the Decisions of, the Late Congress?* (New York: James Rivington, 1775).

8. Jonathan Boucher, *Reminiscences of an American Loyalist 1738–1789*, Jonathan Bouchier, ed. (Boston, MA: Houghton & Mifflin, 1925), 113; and *DAB* II, 474.

9. Early church historians recognized Anglican patriotism, including: William Warren Sweet, 'Anglicans in the Revolution,' *The Huntington Library Quarterly* 11 (1947–8), 52; and William Stevens Perry (reprinted with an introduction by Lawrence L. Brown), 'The Alleged "Toryism" of the Clergy of the Colonial Church at the Breaking Out of the Revolution: An Historical Examination,' *HMPEC* 45 (1976), 133–44.

10. G. MacLaren Brydon, 'The Clergy of the Established Church in Virginia and the Revolution,' *VMHB* 41 (1933), 242; and Thomas Nelson Rightmyer, 'The Holy Orders of Peter Muhlenburg,' *HMPEC* 30 (1961), 183–96; *DAB* XIII, 311–13; William Meade, *Old Churches, Ministers and Families of Virginia* (Philadelphia, PA: J. B. Lippincott, 1900) I, 20–1; and *Appletons' Cycl.* IV, 454.

11. Otto Lohrenz, 'The Virginia Clergy and the American Revolution, 1774–1799,' (unpublished PhD diss., University of Kansas, 1970), 193–9, 207–10; William Sydnor, 'David Griffith – Chaplain, Surgeon, Patriot,' *HMPEC* 44 (1975), 247–56; his 'Doctor Griffith of Virginia: Emergence of a Church Leader, March 1779–June 3, 1786,' *HMPEC* 45 (1976), 5–24 and his 'Doctor Griffith of Virginia: The Breaking of a Church Leader, September 1786–August 3, 1789,' *HMPEC* 45 (1976), 113–32.

12. On American civil religion, see: Robert N. Bellah, 'Civil Religion in America,' *Daedalus* 96 (1967), 1–21; and Russell E. Richey and Donald G. Jones, eds, *American Civil Religion* (New York: Harper & Row, 1974), *passim.*

13. Catherine L. Albanese, *Sons of the Fathers: The Civil Religion of the American Revolution* (Philadelphia, PA: Temple University Press, 1976), 148; and Robert N. Bellah, 'The Revolution and the Civil Religion,' in *Religion and the American Revolution*, Jerald C. Brauer, ed. (Philadelphia, PA: Fortress Press, 1976), 55–73.

14. On the rituals of Revolution, see Peter Shaw, *American Patriots and the Rituals of Revolution* (Cambridge, MA: Harvard University Press, 1981), 177–231, esp. 203.

15. Nathan O. Hatch, *The Sacred Cause of Liberty: Republican Thought and the Millennium in Revolutionary New England* (New Haven, CT: Yale University Press, 1977), 57–8; and Ruth Bloch, *Visionary Republic: Millennial Themes in American Thought, 1756–1800* (Cambridge: Cambridge University Press, 1988, orig. publ. 1985), 93.

16. John F. Berens, '"A God of Order and Not of Confusion": The American Loyalists and Divine Providence, 1774–1783,' *HMPEC* 47 (1978), 211–19; and his '"Good News From a Far Country": A Note on Divine Providence and the Stamp Act Crisis,' *CH* 45 (1976), 308–15.

17. Sacvan Bercovitch, *The American Jeremiad* (Madison: University of Wisconsin Press, 1976), esp. 132–41; Hatch, *The Sacred Cause of Liberty*, 89; and Bloch, *Visionary Republic*, 77–84.

18. On the development of British nationalism in the eighteenth century, see Linda Colley, *Britons: Forging the Nation 1707–1837* (New Haven, CT: Yale University Press, 1992), 11–145, esp. 18.
19. Dorothy Colburn, 'No More Passive Obedience and Non-Resistance,' *HMPEC* 46 (1977), 455; and Reading to SPG, 18 March 1776, *Hist. Coll.* II, 481–2.
20. Reading to SPG, March 15, 1775, *Hist. Coll.* II, 469.
21. David Griffith, 'Passive Obedience Considered: in a Sermon Preached at Williamsburg, December 31st, 1775,' with an introduction by G. M. Brydon, *HMPEC* 44 (1975), 76–93.
22. David Curtis Skaggs, 'The Chain of Being in Eighteenth Century Maryland: The Paradox of Thomas Cradock,' *HMPEC* 45 (1976), 156–7; and William Jeffrey Welsh, David Curtis Skaggs and Donald K. Enholm, 'In Pursuit of the "Golden Mean": A Case Study of Mid-Eighteenth Century Frontier Anglican Preaching,' *AEH* 57 (1988), 184; and John Calam, *Parsons and Pedagogues: The S.P.G. Adventure in American Education* (New York: Columbia University Press, 1971), 96–8.
23. Citation from John Hurt, *The Love of our Country. A Sermon, Preached Before the Virginia Troops in New-Jersey* (Philadelphia, PA: Styner & Cist, 1777), 9. See also Charles Inglis, *The Christian Soldier's Duty Briefly Delineated: In a Sermon Preached at King's Bridge, September 7, 1777, Before the American Corps Newly Raised for His Majesty's Service* (New York: Hugh Gaine, 1777), 12–13.
24. Charles Inglis, *The Duty of Honouring the King, Explained and Recommended: in a Sermon, Preached in St. George's and St. Paul's Chapels, New-York, on Sunday, January 30, 1780; Being the Anniversary of the Martyrdom of King Charles I* (New York: Hugh Gaine, 1780), 12, 20.
25. Isaac Campbell, *A Rational Enquiry Into the Origin, Foundation, Nature and End of Civil Government, Shewing it to be a Divine Institution, Legitimately Deriving Its Authority from the Law of Revelation only, and not from the Law of Nature, as Hath Heretofore Been Generally Held by Writers, from Time Supposed Immemorial* (1784) in *Pamphlets* XI, No. 3, Maryland Diocesan Library, 5, 11; James F. and Jean H. Vivian, 'The Reverend Isaac Campbell: An Anti-Lockean Whig,' *HMPEC* 39 (1970), 71–89; and Jonathan Boucher, *A View of the Causes and Consequences of the American Revolution* (London: G.G. & J. Robinson, 1797), lvii, 521, 523–4.
26. Samuel Seabury, *St. Peter's Exhortation to Fear God and Honor the King, Explained and Inculcated: in a Discourse Addressed to his Majesty's Provincial Troops, in Camp at King's-Bridge, on Sunday the 28th Sept. 1777* (New York: H. Gaine, 1777), 15.
27. Boucher, *A View of the Causes*, 508.
28. Jacob Duché, *The American Vine, A Sermon, Preached in Christ-Church, Philadelphia, Before the Honourable Continental Congress, July 20, 1775* (Philadelphia, PA: James Humphreys Junior, 1775), 10.
29. James Madison, *A Sermon Preached in the County of Botetourt, On the 13th of December, 1781. Being the Day Appointed By Congress to Be Observed With Prayer and Thanksgiving* (Richmond, VA: Nicholson & Prentis, [1781]), 7–8.

30. John Bracken, *The Duty of Giving Thanks for National Blessings, A Sermon, Preached in the Parish Church of Bruton, Williamsburg; on Thursday February 19th, 1795. Being the day appointed to be kept as a General Thanksgiving to Almighty God throughout the United States of America* (Richmond, VA: Thomas Nicolson, 1795), 6–8, 23, 26.

31. Charles Inglis, *The True Interest of America Impartially Stated, in Certain Sticture [sic] On a Pamphlet Intitled Common Sense. By an American* (Philadelphia, PA: James Humphreys, 1776), 22.

32. Samuel Seabury, *A Discourse on II Timothy III.6* (New York, 1774), 11, as quoted in Glenn T. Miller, 'Fear God and Honor the King: The Failure of Loyalist Civil Theology in the Revolutionary Crisis,' *HMPEC* 47 (1978), 224–5.

33. Samuel Seabury, 'A View of the Controversy,' *Letters of a Westchester Farmer*, 112; and Seabury, *St. Peter's Exhortation to Fear God and Honor the King*, 17.

34. Inglis, *The Christian Soldier's Duty Briefly Delineated*, 18–19.

35. Walter Herbert Stowe, 'A Study in Conscience: Some Aspects of the Relations of the Clergy to the State,' *HMPEC* 19 (1950), 303; and Miller, 'Fear God and Honor the King,' 225.

36. Inglis, *The Duty of Honouring the King*, 14.

37. Chandler, *A Friendly Address to All Reasonable Americans*, 51.

38. Charles Inglis, *A Sermon on Philip III. 20, 21. Occasioned by the Death of Samuel Auchmuty, D.D. Rector of Trinity Church, New-York, Preached March 9, 1777* (New York: H. Gaine, 1777), 20. See also Samuel Andrews, *A Sermon Preached at Litchfield, in Connecticut, Before a Voluntary Convention of the Clergy of the Church of England of Several Provinces in America, June 13, 1770* (New Haven, CT, 1770), 3.

39. Minutes of a Convention or Voluntary Meeting of the Episcopal Clergy of Pennsylvania, 30 April, 2–5 May 1760, *Hist. Coll.* II, 297.

40. John Beach to SPG, 13 April 1767, *Doc. Hist.* II, 108–9; and Roger Viets to SPG, *Doc. Hist.* II, 103–4.

41. Leaming to SPG, 30 September 1765, *Doc. Hist.* II, 82–3. See also John Beach to SPG, 2 October 1765, *Doc. Hist.* II, 83; Rev. Lamson to SPG, 2 April 1766, *Doc. Hist.* II, 86; Samuel Peters to SPG, 12 May 1766, *Doc. Hist.* II, 87–9; James Scovil to SPG, 8 July 1766, *Doc. Hist.* II, 92–3; and Edward Winslow to SPG, 29 September 1768, *Hist. Coll.* III, 542.

42. Clergy of Massachusetts and Rhode Island to Bishop Terrick, 15 May 1766, Fulham Papers VI, 62–3. See also Edward Winslow to Secretary, SPG, 8 January 1766, *Hist. Coll.* III, 521.

43. William Agar to Richard Terrick, 20 April 1766, Fulham Papers VI, 58. See also Bela Hubbard to SPG, 30 January 1767, *Doc. Hist.* II, 106–7; and Joseph Harrison to Bishop Terrick, 12 May 1768, Fulham Papers VI, 66–7.

44. Richard Terrick, Bishop of London, to William Smith, 3 September 1774, Smith Mss in Hawks Coll., AEC, S, II, 5-7-19.

45. James L. Adams, *Yankee Doodle Went to Church* (Old Tappan, NJ: Fleming H. Revell, 1989), 75–81.

46. Inglis, *The Duty of Honouring the King*, 6–7.

47. Inglis, *The Duty of Honouring the King*, 7.

48.   Boucher, *Reminiscences*, 118; his *A View of the Causes*, lxviii, lxxi; and James C. Spalding, 'Loyalist as Royalist, Patriot as Puritan: The American Revolution as a Repetition of the English Civil Wars,' *CH* 45 (1976), 339.

49.   Gordon Rupp, *Religion in England, 1688–1791* (New York: Oxford University Press, 1986), 5–6.

50.   Rupp, *Religion in England*, 5–7, 29–33, 53–6.

51.   William Smith, *A Sermon on the Present Situation of American Affairs. Preached in Christ Church, June 23, 1775. At the Request of the Officers of the Third Battalion of the City of Philadelphia, and District of Southwark* (Philadelphia, PA: James Humphreys Jr, 1775), 20–1. Emphasis his.

52.   Inglis, *The True Interest of America Impartially Stated*, 31; Samuel Seabury, 'The Congress Canvassed,' in *Letters of a Westchester Farmer*, 90. Emphasis his.

53.   John Walton, 'Tradition of the Middle Way: The Anglican Contribution to the American Character,' *HMPEC* 44 (1975) No. 5 (Extra), 7; and Rupp, *Religion in England*, 53; and Henry May, *The Enlightenment in America* (New York: Oxford University Press, 1976), 67.

54.   Micklejohn, *On the Important Duty of Subjection to the Civil Powers. A Sermon Preached Before His Excellency William Tryon, Esquire, Governor, and Commander in Chief of the Province of North-Carolina, and the Troops Raised to Quell the Late Insurrection at Hillsborough in Orange County, on Sunday September 25, 1768* (Newbern, NC, 1768), 15. Emphasis his. See also Durward T. Stokes, 'Different Concepts of Government Expressed in the Sermons of Two Eighteenth Century Clergymen,' *HMPEC* 40 (1971), 82–8.

55.   Micklejohn, *On the Important Duty of Subjection to the Civil Powers*, 8.

56.   Boucher, *A View of the Causes*, lxxxv. Anne Young Zimmer and Alfred H. Kelly note that the texts of those sermons probably did not survive Boucher's flight into exile. See Zimmer and Kelly, 'Jonathan Boucher: Constitutional Conservative,' *JAH* 58 (1972), 899, 905–10; Zimmer, *Jonathan Boucher: Loyalist in Exile* (Detroit, MI: Wayne State University Press, 1978), 268–312; and James B. Bell, 'Anglican Quill-Drivers in Eighteenth Century America,' *HMPEC* 44 (1975), 34.

57.   Zimmer and Kelly, 'Jonathan Boucher: Constitutional Conservative'; Ralph Emmett Fall, 'The Rev. Jonathan Boucher, Turbulent Tory (1738–1804),' *HMPEC* 36 (1967), 323–56; and Moses Coit Tyler, *The Literary History of the American Revolution: 1763–1783*, 2 vols (New York, 1897) I, 325.

58.   Clinton Rossiter, *Seedtime of the Republic: The Origin of the American Tradition of Political Liberty* (New York: Harcourt Brace, 1953), 241; and Jonathan Boucher, *A View of the Causes*, 593. Emphasis his.

59.   Boucher, *A View of the Causes*, 545.

60.   Boucher, *A View of the Causes*, 543–4.

61.   Boucher, *A View of the Causes*, 508, 546.

62.   Seabury, *St. Peter's Exhortation to Fear God and Honor the King*, 12.

63.   Seabury, *St. Peter's Exhortation to Fear God and Honor the King*, 11.

64.   Seabury, 'Congress Canvassed,' in *Letters of a Westchester Farmer*, 93.

65.   Seabury, *St. Peter's Exhortation to Fear God and Honor the King*, 20.

66.   John Lewis, *Naboth's Vineyard, a Sermon, Preached at the Parish Church of St. Paul, Stono, on the Last General Fast Day, and at St. Philip's Church*

in *Charles-Town, on Sunday the First of June, 1777 by the Reverend John Lewis, Rector of St. Paul, Stono, and Chaplain to Capt. John Huger's Company of Volunteers* (Charles-Town, SC: Peter Timothy, 1777), 10–16, esp. 14–15.

67. Lewis, *Naboth's Vineyard*, 16, 19–20.
68. Jacob Duché, *The Duty of Standing Fast in Our Spiritual and Temporal Liberties, a Sermon, Preached in Christ-Church, July 7, 1775. Before the First Battalion of the City and Liberties of Philadelphia* (Philadelphia, PA: James Humphreys Jr, 1775), 9–10. Emphasis his.
69. Boucher, *A View of the Causes and Consequences*, 504–5.
70. Duché, *The Duty of Standing Fast in our Spiritual and Temporal Liberties*, 13–14.
71. David Griffith, 'Passive Obedience Considered,' 84. For similar themes, see William White's sermon of 5 November 1775, later published as *A Sermon on the Duty of Civil Obedience, as Required in Scripture. Delivered in Christ Church and St. Peter's, April 25, 1799, Being a Day of General Humiliation, Appointed by the President of the United States* (Philadelphia, PA: John Ormrod, 1799), iii–iv, 7–10.
72. Griffith, 'Passive Obedience Considered,' 86–8, 89.
73. Griffith, 'Passive Obedience Considered,' 84–5.
74. Seabury, *St. Peter's Exhortation to Fear God and Honor the King*, 11. That particular passage is quoted at length above.
75. Griffith, 'Passive Obedience Considered,' 90–1.
76. Otto Lohrenz, 'The Virginia Clergy and the American Revolution,' 143; and Sandra Ryan Dresbeck, 'The Episcopalian Clergy in Maryland and Virginia, 1765–1805' (unpublished PhD diss., University of California, Los Angeles, 1976), 167.
77. William Smith, *The Christian Soldier's Duty; the Lawfulness and Dignity of his Office; and the Importance of the Protestant Cause in the British Colonies, Stated and Explained. A Sermon Preached April 5, 1757 in Christ-Church, Philadelphia, to the First Battalion of His Majesty's Royal American Regiment; At the Request of Their Colonel and Officers* (Philadelphia, PA: James Chattin, 1757), 14–15. See also William Currie, *A Treatise on the Lawfulness of Defensive War. In Two Parts* (Philadelphia, PA: B. Franklin and D. Hall, 1748), iv–xiv.
78. William W. Rankin, 'Anglican Attitudes and Behaviors Concerning War,' *The Anglican Moral Choice*, 221–50, esp. 221–3; and George Marsden, 'The American Revolution,' in *The Wars of America: Christian Views*, Ronald A. Wells, ed. (Macon, GA: Mercer University Press, 1991), 13–31, esp. 15.
79. John Hurt, *The Love of Our Country*, 14–15.
80. Thomas Coombe, *A Sermon Preached Before the Congregations of Christ Church and St. Peter's, Philadelphia, on Thursday, July 20, 1775* (Philadelphia, PA: John Dunlap, 1775), 5.
81. Robert Cooper, *Courage in a Good Cause, or the Lawful and Courageous Use of the Sword. A Sermon, Preached Near Shippensburg, in Cumberland County, on the 31st of August, 1775* (Lancaster, PA: Francis Bailey, 1775), 8–9, 13. See also William Smith, *An Oration in Memory of General Montgomery, and of the Officers and Soldiers, Who Fell With Him,*

December 31, 1775, Before Quebec; Drawn Up (And Delivered February 19, 1776) At the Desire of the Honorable Continental Congress (Philadelphia, PA: John Dunlap, 1776), 23.

82. Daniel Batwell, *A Sermon, Preached at York-Town, Before Captain Morgan's and Captain Price's Companies of Rifle-Men, on Thursday, July 20, 1775* (Philadelphia, PA: John Dunlap, 1775), 16–17.

83. Boucher, *A View of the Causes*, xli–xlii.

84. Caner to Governor Wentworth, 8 November 1773, extract in *The Price of Loyalty: Tory Writings from the Revolutionary Era* Catherine S. Crary, ed. (New York: McGraw-Hill, 1973), 19.

85. Charles Inglis, *The Letters of Papinian: in which the Conduct, Present State and Prospects of the American Congress, Are Examined* (New York: Hugh Gaine, 1779), 107.

86. Jonathan Boucher, *A View of the Causes*, 1; and Boucher, *A Letter from a Virginian, to the Members of the Congress to be Held at Philadelphia on the first of September, 1774* (Boston, MA: reprinted by Mills and Hicks, 1774), 9–10, 30–1. See also excerpts from John Wiswall's letterbook, as quoted in Robert McCluer Calhoon, *The Loyalists in Revolutionary America, 1760–1781* (New York: Harcourt Brace Jovanovich, 1973, orig. publ. 1965), 258; and Charles Inglis, *The True Interest of America Impartially Stated*, v–vi.

87. Ebenezer Thompson to SPG, 25 April 1769, *Hist. Coll.* III, 546. See also William McGilchrist to SPG, 7 December 1770 in *Hist. Coll.* III, 555.

88. Samuel Andrews, *A Sermon Preached at Litchfield, in Connecticut, Before a Voluntary Convention of the Clergy of the Church of England of Several Provinces in America, June 13, 1770* (New Haven, CT: 1770), 13. See also Boucher, *A Letter From a Virginian*, 8.

89. William Clark to SPG, 1 October 1770, *Hist. Coll.* III, 552–3; Seabury, 'The Congress Canvassed,' in *Letters of a Westchester Farmer*, 96–7; and Seabury, 'A View of the Controversy,' in *Letters of a Westchester Farmer*, 123–4.

90. Samuel Peters to Samuel Huntington, Lieutenant Governor of Connecticut, 6 December 1784, Peters Mss in Hawks Coll., AEC, PII, 24-9-24.

91. Seabury, 'Free Thoughts, on the Proceedings of the Continental Congress,' in *Letters of a Westchester Farmer*, 61. Emphasis his. See also his 'An Alarm to the Legislature,' in *Letters of a Westchester Farmer*, 156.

92. Seabury, 'The Congress Canvassed,' in *Letters of a Westchester Farmer*, 84, 95.

93. Samuel Andrews, *A Sermon Preached at Litchfield*, 9–10.

94. Jonathan Odell, 'The Times: A Poem Written During the American Revolution,' Mss booklet, Subject File, (Rev.) Wm. Duke, EDLM. See also Cynthia Dubin Edelberg, 'The Shaping of a Political Poet: Five Newfound Verses of Jonathan Odell,' *Early American Literature* 18 (1983), 45–70.

95. Chandler, *What Think Ye of the Congress Now?*, 14.

96. Charles Inglis, *The Letters of Papinian*, Letter V to the People of North-America, 48.

97. John Patterson to Governor and Council, 18 March 1778, Maryland State Papers (Black Books), MSA, 4363-94. See also earlier letters by Patterson (4363-85, 4363-86, 4363-88, 4363-93) and John Pattern and W. H. Wright to Governor and Council of Maryland, Baltimore Gaol, 3 December 1777, Maryland State Papers (Red Books), MSA, 4580A-73.

98. William Clark to SPG, 5 January 1778, SPG Ser B, XXII, 150.
99. Chandler, *What Think Ye of the Congress Now?*, 25.
100. Chandler, *A Friendly Address to All Reasonable Americans*, 26.
101. Seabury, 'The Congress Canvassed,' in *Letters of a Westchester Farmer*, 99. See also Charles Inglis, *Letters of Papinian*, 125.
102. Chandler, *A Friendly Address*, 7, 10–11, 14–16, 24; Seabury, 'The Congress Canvassed,' in *Letters of a Westchester Farmer*, 94.
103. Chandler, *A Friendly Address*, 15–16.
104. Boucher, *A Letter From a Virginian*, 20–1.
105. Seabury, 'A View of the Controversy,' in *Letters of a Westchester Farmer*, 130–4; and his 'Free Thoughts,' in *Letters of a Westchester Farmer*, 49, also 54, 59–60.
106. Seabury, 'A View of the Controversy,' in *Letters of a Westchester Farmer*, 127–8.
107. Batwell, *A Sermon, Preached at York-Town*, 16. See also Duché, *The Duty of Standing Fast*, 14–15.
108. Inglis to SPG, New York, 31 October 1776 in SPG Ser B, II, 68.
109. Duché, *The Duty of Standing Fast*, 14–15. On dissenters' perspective on this issue, see Hatch, *The Sacred Cause of Liberty*, 81–2.
110. Hurt, *The Love of our Country*, 20.
111. Inglis, *The Christian Soldier's Duty Briefly Delineated*, 17.
112. William Currie, *A Sermon, Preached in Radnor Church, on Thursday, the 7th of January, 1747. Being the Day Appointed by the President and Council of the Province of Pennsylvania, to be Observed as a General Fast* (Philadelphia, PA: Benjamin Franklin and David Hall, 1748), 4. See also Robert Cooper, *Courage in a Good Cause*, 28–9.
113. Duché, *The American Vine*, iv, 26–9.
114. Samuel Magaw, *A Discourse Preached in Christ-Church, Philadelphia, on Sunday, October 8th, 1775* (Philadelphia, PA: Story and Humphreys, 1775), 14. Emphasis his. See also Thomas Coombe, *A Sermon Preached Before Congregations of Christ Church and St. Peter's*, 26.
115. Duché, *The American Vine*, 16, 21.
116. Thomas Coombe, *A Sermon Preached Before the Congregations of Christ Church and St. Peter's*, 24.
117. Paul Turquand Sermons (3 vols), SCHS, II, sermon dated 12 November 1775.
118. Cooper, *Courage in a Good Cause*, 19–20.
119. Madison, *A Sermon Preached in the County of Botetourt*, 11–12.
120. Boucher, *Letter from a Virginian*, 29, 30–1.

CHAPTER 5 THE DEPOLITICIZATION OF THE COLONIAL ANGLICAN CLERGY

1. Emery Elliott, 'The Dove and Serpent: The Clergy in the American Revolution,' *American Quarterly* 31 (1979), 194–7. On New England Congregationalism, see: George B. Kirsch, 'Clerical Dismissals in Colonial and Revolutionary New Hampshire,' *CH* 49 (1980), 160–77, esp. 167–75;

and Donald M. Scott, *From Office to Profession: The New England Ministry 1750–1850* (Philadelphia, PA: University of Pennsylvania Press, 1978), xi, 1–35.

2. Robert W. Prichard, *A History of the Episcopal Church* (Harrisburg, PA: Morehouse Publishing, 1991), 78–9; and David L. Holmes, 'The Episcopal Church and the American Revolution,' *HMPEC* 47 (1978), 265–8; William Warren Sweet, 'The Role of the Anglicans in the American Revolution,' *Huntingdon Library Quarterly* 11 (1948), 52; Leonard W. Labaree, 'The Nature of American Loyalism,' *Proceedings of the American Antiquarian Society* 54 (1945), 29; and William H. Nelson, *The American Tory* (Boston, MA: Beacon Press, 1964, orig. publ. 1961), 90–1.

3. Prichard, *A History of the Episcopal Church*, 78–9; George MacLaren Brydon, *Virginia's Mother Church and the Political Conditions Under Which It Grew*, 2 vols (Richmond, VA: Virginia Historical Society, 1947) II, 415–22; Otto Lohrenz, 'The Virginia Clergy and the American Revolution, 1774–1799' (unpublished PhD diss., University of Kansas, 1970), *passim*, esp. 400. On Maryland and the Carolinas, see: Sandra Ryan Dresbeck, 'The Episcopalian Clergy in Maryland and Virginia, 1765–1805' (unpublished PhD diss., University of California, Los Angeles, 1976), *passim*; Nelson Waite Rightmyer, *Maryland's Established Church* (Baltimore, MD: Church Historical Society for the Diocese of Maryland, 1956), esp. 155–221; S. Charles Bolton, *Southern Anglicanism: The Church of England in Colonial South Carolina* (Westport, CT: Greenwood Press, 1982), 63–85, 170–4; Michael T. Malone, 'Sketches of the Anglican Clergy Who Served in North Carolina During the Period, 1765–1776,' *HMPEC* 39 (1970), 137–61, 399–429; and Durward T. Stokes, 'The Clergy of the Carolinas and the American Revolution' (unpublished PhD diss., University of North Carolina, 1968), *passim*. I estimate that there were 130 clergymen in Virginia, 58 in Maryland, 22 in South Carolina, 11 in North Carolina, and four in Georgia between 1775 and 1783.

4. On New York, New Jersey, Pennsylvania and Delaware, see: John Paul Jordan, 'The Anglican Establishment in Colonial New York, 1693–1783' (unpublished PhD diss., Columbia University, 1971), esp. 545; Nelson R. Burr, *The Anglican Church in New Jersey* (Philadelphia, PA: Church Historical Society, 1954), 373–415; Edgar L. Pennington, 'The Anglican Clergy of Pennsylvania in the Revolution,' *The Pennsylvania Magazine of History and Biography* 63 (1939), 401–31; and Nelson W. Rightmyer, *The Anglican Church in Delaware* (Philadelphia, PA: Church Historical Society, 1947), 167–71. I consider the two New Jersey and New York patriots to be Robert Blackwell and Samuel Provoost respectively. I estimate that there were 19 clergymen in New York, 11 in New Jersey, and 16 in Pennsylvania/Delaware between 1775 and 1783.

5. Holmes, 'Episcopal Church and the Revolution,' 266; William Wilson Manross, *A History of the American Episcopal Church* (New York: Morehouse-Gorham, 1950), 175. On Connecticut and New England, see: Hector G. Kinloch, 'Anglican Clergy in Connecticut 1701–1785' (unpublished PhD diss., Yale University, 1959); and Charles Mampoteng, 'The New England Anglican Clergy in the American Revolution,' *HMPEC* 9 (1940), 267–304, esp. 270. I estimate that there were 23 ministers in

Connecticut, 16 in Massachusetts, two in New Hampshire, four in Rhode Island, and two in Maine between 1775 and 1783.

6. William Meade, *Old Churches, Ministers and Families of Virginia* (Philadelphia, PA: J.B. Lippincott, 1900), II, 285–6; George J. Cleaveland, 'The Church of Virginia Established and Disestablished,' in *Up From Independence: The Episcopal Church in Virginia*, George J. Cleaveland et al., eds (Orange, VA: Green Publishers, 1976), 35; Lohrenz, 'Virginia Clergy,' 174; Dresbeck, 'The Episcopalian Clergy in Maryland and Virginia,' 160.

7. Patricia U. Bonomi and Peter R. Eisenstadt, 'Church Adherence in the Eighteenth Century British American Colonies,' *WMQ* 39 (1982), 245–86, esp. 275.

8. On Anglican authorship see: James B. Bell, 'Anglican Quill-Drivers in Eighteenth-Century America,' *HMPEC* 44 (1975), 23–45. See also Cynthia Dubin Edelberg, 'The Shaping of a Political Poet: Five Newfound Verses of Jonathan Odell,' *Early American Literature* 18 (1983), 45–70; and Ray Palmer Baker, 'The Poetry of Jacob Bailey, Loyalist,' *New England Quarterly* 2 (1929), 58–92.

9. Harry S. Stout, *The New England Soul: Preaching and Religious Culture in Colonial New England* (New York: Oxford University Press, 1986), 6.

10. Thomas Barton, *The Conduct of the Paxton-Men, Impartially Represented: With Some Remarks on the Narrative* (Philadelphia, PA: Andrew Steuart, 1764). On election sermons and New England dissenting clergy, see Alice M. Baldwin, *The New England Clergy and the American Revolution* (Durham, NC: Duke University Press, 1928), 3–7.

11. William W. Rankin, 'Anglican Attitudes and Behaviors Concerning War,' in Paul Elmen, ed., *The Anglican Moral Choice* (Wilton, CT: Morehouse-Barlow, 1983), 223.

12. Edmund S. Morgan, 'The Revolution Considered as an Intellectual Movement,' in his *The Challenge of the American Revolution* (New York: W.W. Norton, 1976), 61, 75.

13. *Appletons' Cycl.*, II, 241.

14. Jonathan Boucher, *Reminiscences of an American Loyalist, 1738–1789. Being the Autobiography of the Reverend Jonathan Boucher, Rector of Annapolis in Maryland and Afterwards Vicar of Epsom, Surrey, England*, Jonathan Bouchier, ed. (Boston, MA: Houghton Mifflin, 1925), 92; Anne Y. Zimmer, *Jonathan Boucher: Loyalist in Exile* (Detroit, MI: Wayne State University, 1978), 90, 106.

15. Joan R. Gundersen, *The Anglican Ministry in Virginia 1723–1766: A Study of A Social Class* (New York: Garland, 1989), 256; Lohrenz, 'Virginia Clergy,' 26, 138–9; Dresbeck, 'Episcopalian Clergy in Maryland and Virginia,' 103; Frederick Dalcho, *An Historical Account of the Protestant Episcopal Church, in South-Carolina, From the First Settlement of the Province, to the War of the Revolution* (Charleston, SC, 1820), 220; and Michael T. Malone, 'Sketches of the Anglican Clergy Who Served in North Carolina,' 145.

16. George MacLaren Brydon, 'The Clergy of the Established Church in Virginia and the Revolution,' *VMHB* 41 (1933), 16, xiv. On William Bland's sermon of 1769 or Thomas Davis Sr's service as chairman of a committee opposing the Stamp Act, see Lohrenz, 'Virginia Clergy,' 121, 179.

17. Catherine S. Crary, ed., *The Price of Loyalty: Tory Writings from the Revolutionary Era* (New York: McGraw-Hill, 1973), 24–5; Jordan, 'Anglican Establishment in Colonial New York,' 510; and on Boston's reaction to the Solemn League and Covenant, see Colin Bonwick, *The American Revolution* (Charlottesville, VA: University of Virginia Press, 1991), 79–80.
18. William L. Saunders, ed., *The Colonial Records of North Carolina*, I–X (Raleigh, NC, 1886–90), IX, 1037; Malone, 'Sketches of the Anglican Clergy Who Served in North Carolina,' 153; Sarah McCulloh Lemmon, 'The Decline of the Church, 1776–1816,' *The Episcopal Church in North Carolina, 1701–1959* (Raleigh, NC: Episcopal Diocese of North Carolina, 1987), 64.
19. Stokes, 'The Clergy of the Carolinas and the American Revolution,' 75; Malone, 'Sketches of the Anglican Clergy Who Served in North Carolina,' 404; Jordan, 'Anglican Establishment in Colonial New York,' 547; and Lohrenz, 'Virginia Clergy,' 83.
20. E. Clowes Chorley, 'Samuel Provoost: First Bishop of New York,' *HMPEC* 2 (1933), 9. Samuel Provoost held patriotic opinions which differed from those of his loyalist colleagues.
21. G. MacLaren Brydon, 'The Clergy of the Established Church in Virginia and the Revolution,' *VMHB* 41 (1933), 140; Lohrenz, 'Virginia Clergy,' 203; and Walter H. Stowe et al., 'The Clergy of the Episcopal Church in 1785,' *HMPEC* 20 (1951), 273.
22. Jacob Duché, *The Duty of Standing Fast in our Spiritual and Temporal Liberties, a Sermon, Preached in Christ-Church, July 7th, 1775* (Philadelphia, PA: James Humphreys Jr, 1775), ii, 18; and Emery Elliott, 'The Dove and Serpent,' 190.
23. Daniel Batwell, *A Sermon, Preached at York-Town, Before Captain Morgan's and Captain Price's Companies of Rifle-men, on Thursday, July 20, 1775* (Philadelphia, PA: John Dunlap, 1775), 19–20; and James Wetmore to SPG, New York, 10 January 1777, in SPG Ser B, III, 248.
24. Charles Inglis, *The True Interest of America Impartially Stated, in Certain Strictures on a Pamphlet Intitled Common Sense. By an American*, 2nd edn (Philadelphia, PA: James Humphreys Junior, 1776), 70.
25. Thompson to SPG, 25 March 1766, *Hist. Coll.* III, 523. See also John Beach to SPG, 22 April 1766, *Doc. Hist.* II, 87.
26. Crary, *The Price of Loyalty*, 104.
27. Pennsylvania Clergy to State Assembly, 20 May 1778, *Hist. Coll.* II, 492.
28. Reed to SPG, Newbern, 19 July 1774, in SPG Ser B, V, 151 or Saunders, ed., *Colonial Records of North Carolina*, IX, 1015.
29. William Smith to SPG, 10 July 1775, *Hist. Coll.* II, 477.
30. William Smith to Bishop Terrick, 8 July 1774, Fulham Papers VIII, 62–3.
31. Richard Peters, William Smith, Jacob Duché, Thomas Coombe, William Stringer, William White to the Bishop of London, 30 June 1775, *Hist. Coll.* II, 471–2.
32. Philadelphia clergy to Bishop of London, 30 June 1775, *Hist. Coll.* II, 470.
33. Daniel Batwell, *A Sermon, Preached at York-Town*, 12.
34. Thomas Jefferson to the Parish of Saint Anne, 15 August 1779, VSLA, Acquisition 21143. Jefferson contrasts that questionable behavior with the more respectable patriotism of Rev. Charles Clay.

35. Thomas Barton to SPG, 16 December 1777, SPG Ser B, III, 350. See also T. B. Chandler to SPG, 28 January 1774, Elizabeth Town, SPG Ser B, XXIV, 100.
36. Robert Andrews to John Page, 25 May 1769, AL, Acc. 2493. See also Brydon, *Virginia's Mother Church* II, 434; and Lohrenz, 'Virginia Clergy,' 191–3.
37. Avery to SPG, Rye, 25 June 1776, SPG Ser B, III, 247; and Rev. Newton to SPG, 10 December 1766, *Doc. Hist.*, 104–5.
38. John Beach to SPG, 31 October 1781, Newtown, CT, SPG Ser B, XXIII, 50; Thomas Barton to SPG, Lancaster, 1 March 1775, SPG Ser B, XXI, 26; Samuel Magaw to SPG, Dover, 31 August 1775, SPG Ser B, XXI, 157; and David Griffith to Hannah Griffith, Williamsburg, 19 April 1776 and 8 December 1776, David Griffith Papers, 1760–89, 1823, VHS, Mss2 G8755b.
39. William Selden, Memorandum Book, 1771–83, AL, Acquisition 38-564.
40. St Paul's Church, Chowan County, Vestry Minutes 1701–79, NCSA, R024.04001.
41. Vestry Journal, St Philip's Church, 1761–95 (Columbia, SC: Works Progress Administration, 1939), 133 (228 of original), 163 (260 of original), typescript, and Minutes of the Vestry of St Stephen's Parish, Berkeley Co., 1754–1885 (Columbia, SC: Works Progress Administration, 1940), 29–34 (or 35–43 of original) in Manuscript Division, South Caroliniana Library, Columbia, SC. See also *Minutes of the Vestry of St. Matthew's Parish, South Carolina 1767–1838*, A. S. Salley, ed. (Columbia, SC, 1939), 19–21; Northampton County, St George's Parish Wardens' Records, 1773–1814, NCSA, 4, CR071.927.1; Lemmon, 'The Decline of the Church, 1776–1816,' 65; and Vestry Book 1730–85, St Mark's Parish, Spotsylvania Co., 427–8, VSLA, Acc. 19771.
42. Samuel Auchmuty et al. to SPG, New York, 8 February 1777, SPG Ser B, III, 343. See also Thomas Barton to SPG, 24 August 1775, SPG Ser B, XXI, 29.
43. Abraham Beach, 6 December 1775, New Brunswick, New Jersey, SPG Ser B, XXIV, 307.
44. Charles Woodmason to Bishop Terrick, 16 September 1776, *Hist. Coll.* I, 535 or Fulham Papers XIV, 215–16; Philip Reading to SPG, 18 March 1776, *Hist. Coll.* II, 482; and Lohrenz, 'Virginia Clergy,' 177. Smith, who died in 1785, must have been unsure about the ultimate success of the republican experiment.
45. Instructions of General Meeting of 11 March 1756 in SPG Journals XIII, 123–7, esp. 126. See also Alfred W. Newcombe, 'The Appointment and Instructions of SPG Missionaries,' *CH* V (1936), 352–8.
46. Roger Viets to SPG, 25 June 1774, Simsbury, SPG Ser B, XXIII, 395.
47. Pennsylvania Clergy to Pennsylvania Assembly, 20 May 1778, *Hist. Coll.* II, 492.
48. Philip Reading, *The Protestant's Danger, and the Protestant's Duty. A Sermon on Occasion of the Present Encroachments of the French. Preached at Christ-Church, Philadelphia, on Sunday June 22, 1755* (Philadelphia, PA: B. Franklin and D. Hall, 1755), 27–8.
49. Thomas Barton, *Unanimity and Public Spirit. A Sermon Preached at Carlisle, and Some Other Episcopal Churches, in the Counties of York and*

Cumberland, Soon After General Braddock's Defeat ... To which is Prefixed, a Letter from the Reverend Mr. Smith, Provost of the College of Philadelphia, Concerning the Office and Duties of a Protestant Ministry, Especially in Times of Public Calamity and Danger (Philadelphia, PA: B. Franklin and D. Hall, 1755), 4, 9–10, 14. See James P. Myers Jr, 'Thomas Barton's *Unanimity and Public Spirit* (1755): Controversy and Plagiarism on the Pennsylvania Frontier,' *Pennsylvania Magazine of History and Biography* 119 (1995), 225–48.

50. William Smith in preface to Thomas Barton, *Unanimity and Public Spirit*, vi, xii, xvii.
51. Jonathan Boucher, *A View of the Causes and Consequences of the American Revolution, in Thirteen Discourses* (London: G.G. and J. Robinson, 1797), 501n.
52. Jonathan Boucher, *A View of the Causes*, 499. Boucher is probably responding to the poem which appeared in the *Maryland Gazette* on 18 March 1773 which told him to stick to souls instead of politics. This poem is discussed in Rightmyer, *Maryland's Established Church*, 163.
53. C. J., *A Letter to the Rev. Dr. Auchmuty* (New York, 1775), Evans Early American Imprint 14131, 3–4, 8.
54. Samuel Tingley to SPG, 5 March 1782, New York, *Hist. Coll.* V, 139. On the political dimension of enthusiasm, see David S. Lovejoy, *Religious Enthusiasm in the New World: Heresy to Revolution* (Cambridge, MA: Harvard University Press, 1985), 222–7.
55. See Joshua Wingate Weeks to SPG, 21 June 1768, *Hist. Coll.* III, 539; and Weeks to SPG, 2 April 1770, *Hist. Coll.* III, 549.
56. Samuel Johnson to SPG, 25 November 1776, *Hist. Coll.* II, 489.
57. Samuel Peters, *General History of Connecticut, From Its First Settlement Under George Fenwick to its Latest Period of Amity With Great Britain Prior to the Revolution* (New York: D. Appleton, 1877, orig. publ. London, 1781), 237. See also Richard Mansfield to SPG, 29 December 1775, *Doc. Hist.*, II, 199.
58. William McGilchrist to SPG, 28 June 1768, *Hist. Coll.* III, 540.
59. Samuel Seabury to SPG, New York, 29 December 1776, SPG Ser B, II, 190.
60. Charles Inglis to SPG, New York, 31 October 1776, SPG Ser B, II, 68.
61. Crary, *Price of Loyalty*, 104–5.
62. Samuel Seabury to SPG, Westchester, 30 May 1775 in SPG Ser B, II, 187. See also Jacob Bailey to SPG, 8 July 1775, Falmouth, SPG Ser B, XXII, 68.
63. William McGilchrist to SPG, Salem, 27 June 1769, *Hist. Coll.* III, 547.
64. Citation from Pennington, 'Anglican Clergy of Pennsylvania,' 427.
65. *Appletons' Cycl.* IV, 454.
66. Duché, *The Duty of Standing Fast*, 2.
67. Henry Caner, *The Great Blessing of Stable Times, Together With the Means of Procuring It. A Sermon Preached at King's Chapel in Boston, August 11, 1763. Being a Day of Thanksgiving Appointed by Public Authority on Occasion of the General Peace* (Boston, MA: Thomas and John Fleet, 1763), i–ii.
68. Thomas Barton, *The Conduct of the Paxton-Men*, 3.
69. John Sayre, *From the New-York Journal. 'Mr. Holt, Sir, The letter which the Reverend Mr. Sayre sent unto the Committee, I here send you, as he is very Desirous of having it Published, to Shew the World Why he did not Sign the*

Association; and the Committee have agreed it may be (Philadelphia, 1775/6), Evans Early American Imprints 15078, 2, 5–6.
70. Ebenezer Dibblee to SPG, 5 April 1775, *Doc. Hist.* II, 198.
71. Thomas Barton to SPG, Lancaster, 20 October 1775 in SPG Ser B, XXI, 27; and Matthew Graves to General Washington at Camp at Cambridge, Chatham, 5 February 1776, photostat in 'Matthew Graves' biographical file, EADC.
72. Little Abraham (Tyorhansera), Mohawk sachem of Canajohare, petitioned that Rev. John Stuart be permitted to continue his ministrations to the Mohawks at Fort Hunter, New York. See John Wolfe Lydekker, 'The Reverend John Stuart, D.D. (1740–1811), Missionary to the Mohawks,' *HMPEC* 11 (1942), 32.
73. Charles Inglis to SPG, New York, 6 May 1782 in SPG Ser B, II, 74. See also Thomas Barton to SPG, New York, 25 October 1779, *Hist. Coll.* V, 134 or SPG Ser B, XXI, 37; and Henry Caner to Bishop Terrick, 3 December 1770 in Fulham Papers, VI, 76–7; and Gerald J. Goodwin, 'The Anglican Reaction to the Great Awakening,' *HMPEC* 35 (1966), 343–71.
74. Dibblee to SPG, 10 October 1775, Stamford, CT, SPG Ser B, XXIII, 122. See also Joshua Wingate Weeks, *A Sermon Preached before the Worshipful Society of Ancient Freemasons on the Festival of St. John Baptist, June 24, 1782 In St. Paul's Church, Halifax* (1782), 11, American Antiquarian Society Library, Worcester, MA.
75. Mary Beth Norton, *The British-Americans: The Loyalist Exiles in England 1774–1789* (Boston, MA: Little, Brown, 1972), 171–2, *passim*; Samuel Andrews to Samuel Peters, Wallingford, CT, 6 March 1786, EADC; Charles Mampoteng, 'The Reverend Samuel Peters, M.A., Missionary at Hebron, Connecticut, 1760–1774,' *HMPEC* 5 (1936), 73–91; and Wayne N. Metz, 'A Connecticut Yankee in King George III's Court: A Loyalist Anglican Clergyman in England, 1774–1804,' *HMPEC* 52 (1983), 29–41, esp. 33–5.
76. Barton to SPG, 25 November 1776 in Crary, *Price of Loyalty*, 88. See Samuel Johnson to SPG, 25 November 1776, *Hist. Coll.* II, 488–9.
77. See Stuart to SPG, Montreal, 13 October 1781, SPG Ser B, II, 204; Thomas Barton to SPG, New York, 15 December 1778, SPG Ser B, XXI, 35; and Karen Guenther, ' "A Faithful Soldier of Christ": The Career of the Reverend Dr. Alexander Murray, Missionary to Berks County, Pa., 1768–1778,' *HMPEC* 55 (1986), 14.
78. Charles Inglis, *True Interest of America Impartially Stated*, 50; James Madison, New York, to John Norton, London, 30 July 1776 in Sm. Coll. Madison, James, Bp (1749–1812), Special Collections, SL; and Thomas Barton to SPG, Lancaster, PA, 24 August 1775, SPG Ser B, XXI, 29. See also Manross, *A History of the American Episcopal Church*, 172.
79. Samuel Magaw to SPG, 7 October 1776, Philadelphia, SPG Ser B, XXI, 158. See also David Love to Horatio Sharpe, Londontown, Maryland, 23 May 1774, in James High, ed., 'Letters from the Reverend David Love to Horatio Sharpe, 1774–1779,' *HMPEC* 19 (1950), 361.
80. Clergy of Boston in Convention to SPG, 22 September 1768, *Hist. Coll.* III, 541.
81. Philip Reading to SPG, 18 March 1776, *Hist. Coll.* II, 481; and Wallace Brown, *The King's Friends: The Composition and Motives of*

186 Notes

the *American Loyalist Claimants* (Providence, RI: Brown University Press, 1965), 188.

82. Matthew Graves to SPG, 2 November 1775, New London, CT, SPG Ser B, XXIII, 163.
83. William Clark to SPG, 17 April 1775, *Hist. Coll.* III, 578; Crary, *Price of Loyalty*, 25; Charles Mampoteng, 'The Reverend William Clark (1740–1815), S.P.G. Missionary to Massachusetts,' *HMPEC* 16 (1947), 199–216.
84. Jonathan Odell to SPG, 7 January 1777, SPG Ser B, XXIV, 147.
85. C. H. Van Tyne, 'Influence of the Clergy, and of Religious and Sectarian Forces, on the American Revolution,' *AHR* 19 (1913), 44–64; Frank Dean Gifford, 'The Influence of the Clergy on American Politics from 1763–1776,' *HMPEC* 10 (1941), 104–23; and Harry P. Kerr, 'Politics and Religion in Colonial Fast and Thanksgiving Sermons, 1763–1783,' *Quarterly Journal of Speech* 46 (1960), 372–6.
86. Luke Babcock to SPG, 22 March 1776, Philipsborough, SPG Ser B, III, 21.
87. On Georgia's provincial fast day of 29 July 1775, see Haddon Smith to Bishop Terrick, Fulham Papers, II, 45.
88. William Clark to William Fisher, 6 August 1774, in Crary, *Price of Loyalty*, 26.
89. Philadelphia Clergy to Bishop of London, 30 June 1775, *Hist. Coll.* II, 470.
90. William Smith to SPG, 10 July 1775, *Hist. Coll.* II, 475.
91. Luke Babcock to SPG, 22 March 1776, Philipsborough, SPG Ser B, III, 21.
92. Inglis to SPG, New York, 31 October 1776, SPG Ser B, II, 68.
93. Samuel Andrews, *A Discourse, Shewing the Necessity of Joining Internal Repentance, with the External Profession of it. Delivered upon the General Fast, July 20th, 1775* (New Haven, CT: T. and S. Green, 1775), iii–iv, 6–18.
94. The text of the oath appears in Walter Herbert Stowe, 'A Study in Conscience: Some Aspects of the Relations of the Clergy to the State,' *HMPEC* 19 (1950), 303.
95. Prichard, *A History of the Episcopal Church*, 74–5; David Holmes, 'The Episcopal Church and the American Revolution,' 288–91; and Philip Reading to SPG, 25 August 1776, *Hist. Coll.* II, 484.
96. Stowe, 'A Study in Conscience,' 309. On English clerical incomes, see: James Francis Godwin, 'Clerical Incomes in Eighteenth Century England,' *HMPEC* 18 (1949), 311–325, esp. 314.
97. E. Edwards Beardsley, *The History of the Episcopal Church in Connecticut from the Settlement of the Colony to the Death of Bishop Seabury*, 2 vols (New York: Hurd & Houghton, 1865), I, 319; and Clark's Address, March 1777, *Hist. Coll.* III, 591.
98. Tingley to SPG, 5 March 1782, New York, *Hist. Coll.* V, 135–6.
99. G. MacLaren Brydon, 'The Clergy of the Established Church in Virginia and the Revolution,' 13; William Waller Hening, ed., *The Statutes at Large: Being a Collection of All the Laws of Virginia, From the First Session of the Legislature, in the Year 1619*, 13 vols (Richmond, 1809–23), IX, 281–3; George J. Cleaveland, 'The Church of Virginia Established and Disestablished,' 33.
100. Guenther, 'Alexander Murray,' 14; and J. William Frost, *A Perfect Freedom: Religious Liberty in Pennsylvania* (University Park, PA: Pennsylvania State University Press, 1993, orig. publ. Cambridge University Press, 1990), 67.

101. Henry Caner to SPG, 18 April 1775, *Hist. Coll.* III, 578–9.
102. Samuel Tingley to SPG, 5 March 1782. New York, *Hist. Coll.* V, 135.
103. Barton to SPG, Lancaster, 25 November 1776 in SPG Ser B, XXI, 30. See also Philip Reading to SPG, 30 September 1778, Apoquiniminck, *Hist. Coll.* II, 494.
104. William Clark to SPG, 23 February 1781, SPG Ser B, XXII, 154.
105. Clark to SPG, 23 February 1781, SPG Ser B, XXII, 154.
106. Edward Winslow to SPG, 1 January 1777, *Hist. Coll.* III, 589 or SPG Ser B, XXII, 295.
107. Abraham Beach to SPG, 4 January 1782, New Brunswick, New Jersey, SPG Ser B, XXIV, 310.
108. Beardsley, *History of the Episcopal Church in Connecticut* I, 318; Henry Caner to SPG, Halifax, 20 May 1776, SPG Ser B, XXII, 136; and Mampoteng, 'New England Clergy in the American Revolution,' 270. As discussed earlier, the 1777 decree imposed a £50 penalty on those who prayed for the king.
109. Clark to SPG, 23 February 1781, SPG Ser B, XXII, 154; and Clark to Samuel Peters, 8 December 1786, Peters Mss in Hawks Coll., AEC, PII 125-10-16.
110. Parker to SPG, 26 December 1778, SPG Ser B, XXII, 198; and Parker to Samuel Peters, 19 May 1787, Peters Mss in Hawks Coll., AEC, P III 24-10-43. On Parker, see also: William Clark to SPG, 23 February 1781, SPG Ser B, XXII, 154; Roger Viets to SPG, 1 November 1781, SPG Ser B, XXIII, 396; and J. W. Weeks to SPG, 21 July 1779, SPG Ser B, XXII, 261.
111. Jordan, 'Anglican Establishment in Colonial New York,' 612–13; and William Walter to SPG, New York, 23 December 1778, SPG Ser B, III, 346.
112. Jonathan Odell to SPG, New York, 25 January 1777, SPG Ser B, XXIV, 148; Walter Herbert Stowe, 'The Reverend Abraham Beach, D.D. 1740–1828,' *HMPEC* 3 (1934), 78; Nelson R. Burr, *The Anglican Church in New Jersey*, 586; and James McLachlan, 'Robert Blackwell,' *Princetonians, 1748–1768: A Biographical Dictionary* (Princeton, NJ: Princeton University Press, 1976), 632.
113. Samuel Johnston to SPG, 25 November 1776, York Town, Pennsylvania, *Hist. Coll.* II, 488; and Pennington, 'Anglican Clergy of Pennsylvania,' 426.
114. George MacLaren Brydon, 'Clergy of the Established Church in Virginia,' 15; and John R. Wennersten, 'The Travail of a Tory Parson: Reverend Philip Hughes And Maryland Colonial Politics 1767–1777,' *HMPEC* 44 (1975), 415.
115. Clifton E. Olmstead, *History of Religion in the United States* (Englewood Cliffs, NJ: Prentice-Hall, 1960), 211–15.
116. In Virginia, 58 out of 130; in Maryland, 21 out of 58; in South Carolina, nine out of 22; and in North Carolina four out of 11 officially relinquished their posts.
117. Philip Reading to SPG, 26 August 1776, Apoquiniminck, *Hist. Coll.* II, 486. Full text in SPG Ser B, XXI, 211.
118. Inglis to SPG, New York, 31 October 1776 in SPG Ser B, II, 68. See also Thomas Barton to SPG, 25 November 1776, Lancaster, *Hist. Coll.* II, 489–91.
119. Samuel Seabury to SPG, New York, 29 December 1775 in SPG Ser B, II, 190.

120. Philip Reading to SPG, 25 August 1776, SPG Ser B, XXI, 211. See also Thomas Barton to SPG, 25 November 1776, *Hist. Coll.* II, 490.
121. Thomas Barton to SPG, New York, 8 January 1779, *Hist. Coll.* V, 130.
122. Clark to SPG, 5 January 1778, Dedham, SPG Ser B, XXII, 150.
123. John Sayre to SPG, 8 November 1779, Flushing, Long Island, SPG Ser B, XXIII, 233.
124. Miles Selden, 'The Great Duty of Publick Worship' (August 1758), in Heth-Selden manuscripts, AL, Acc. 5071, 10–11, 17–18. See also John Tyler, *The Sanctity of a Christian Temple: Illustrated in a Sermon, at the Opening of Trinity-Church in Promfret, on Friday, April 12, 1771* (Providence, RI: John Carter, 1771), 4, 11–12, 17–18.
125. Roger Viets, *A Serious Address and Farewell Charge to the Members of the Church of England in Simsbury and Adjacent Parts* (Hartford, CT: Hudson and Goodwin, 1787), 10; John Tyler, *The Sanctity of a Christian Temple*, 10; and William Walter to SPG, New York, 18 May 1780 in SPG Ser B, III, 348.
126. William Smith to SPG, 10 July 1775, Philadelphia, *Hist. Coll.* II, 476.
127. Robert Blackwell to SPG, 26 June 1775, Gloucester, New Jersey, SPG Ser B, XXIV, 17.
128. Beardsley, *History of the Episcopal Church in Connecticut* I, 320.
129. Abraham Beach to SPG, 4 January 1782, New Brunswick, New Jersey, SPG Ser B, XXIV, 310; Thomas Bradbury Chandler to Samuel Seabury, London, 4 February 1779, photostat, EADC; and William Ayers to SPG, 29 May 1782, Freehold, New Jersey, SPG Ser B, XXIV, 13.
130. Samuel Cooke to SPG, New York, 7 May 1782, SPG Ser B, XXIV, 121.
131. William Frazer to SPG, 4 January 1782, Amwell, New Jersey, SPG Ser B, XXIV, 247; Abraham Beach to SPG, 4 January 1782, New Brunswick, SPG Ser B, XXIV, 310; and David L. Holmes, 'The Episcopal Church and the American Revolution,' *Episcopal Churches in a Revolutionary Era*, C. Fitzsimons Allison, ed. (Cincinnati, OH: Forward Movement Publications, 197–), 15.
132. Thomas Bradbury Chandler, *A Sermon Preached Before the Corporation for the Relief of the Widows and Children of Clergymen, in Communion of the Church of England in America; at their Anniversary Meeting on October 2d, 1771, at Perth-Amboy* (Burlington, NJ: Isaac Collins, 1771), 18; and C. J., *A Letter to the Rev. Dr. Auchmuty* (New York, 1775), 8.

CHAPTER 6   DIVIDED ALLEGIANCES AND DISESTABLISHMENT

1. Charles Inglis to SPG, New York, 31 October 1776, in SPG Ser B, II, 68.
2. Nathan Hatch, *The Democratization of American Religion* (New Haven, CT: Yale University Press, 1989), 17–46; William G. McLoughlin, 'The Role of Religion in the Revolution: Liberty of Conscience and Cultural Cohesion in the New Nation,' in *Essays on the American Revolution*, Stephen G. Kurtz and James H. Hutson, eds (New York: W.W. Norton, 1973), 208.

3. Clara O. Loveland, *The Critical Years: The Reconstitution of the Anglican Church in the United States of America, 1780–1789* (Greenwich, CT: Seabury Press, 1956), *passim*; William Wilson Manross, *A History of the American Episcopal Church* (New York: Morehouse-Gorham, 1950), 172–201; Frederick V. Mills, Sr, *Bishops by Ballot: An Eighteenth-Century Ecclesiastical Revolution* (New York: Oxford University Press, 1978), 182–287.
4. Jean Paul Jordan, 'The Anglican Establishment in Colonial New York, 1693–1783' (unpublished PhD diss., Columbia University, 1971), 601; Loveland, *The Critical Years*, 23–9; Thomas J. Curry, *The First Freedoms: Church and State in America to the Passage of the First Amendment* (New York: Oxford University Press, 1986), 140–1, 148–52; Sydney E. Ahlstrom, *A Religious History of the American People* (New Haven, CT: Yale University Press, 1972), 380; and Mills, *Bishops by Ballot*, 172–6. On disestablishment in Virginia, see also Otto Lohrenz, 'The Virginia Clergy and the American Revolution' (unpublished PhD diss., University of Kansas, 1970), 282–399; and Thomas E. Buckley, *Church and State in Revolutionary Virginia, 1776–1787* (Charlottesville, VA: University Press of Virginia, 1977).
5. For a nineteenth-century analysis, see Samuel Wilberforce, *A History of the Protestant Episcopal Church in America* (New York: Stanford and Swords, 1849), 139–41.
6. Samuel Seabury, *Bishop Seabury's Second Charge, to the Clergy of His Diocess [sic], Delivered at Derby, in the State of Connecticut, on the 22d of September, 1786* (New Haven, CT: Thomas and Samuel Green, 1786), 4. See also Joshua Bloomer to SPG, Jamaica, Long Island, 3 October 1785, SPG Ser C, II, unnumbered.
7. John Tyler to SPG, Norwich, 15 May 1783, SPG Ser C, III, 87. See also Ebenezer Dibblee to SPG, Stamford, Connecticut, 3 May 1785, SPG Ser C, III, 68; Abraham Jarvis to SPG, New York, 6 May 1783, SPG Ser C, III, 92.
8. Richard Clarke to SPG, New Milford, Connecticut, 25 September 1785, SPG Ser C, III, 72. On the possible creation of a voluntary society to replace the SPG, see Roger Viets to Bela Hubbard, 9 December 1785, Peters Mss in Hawks Coll., AEC, PII 66-9-66.
9. Bruce E. Steiner, *Samuel Seabury, 1729–1796: A Study in the High Church Tradition* (Oberlin, OH: Ohio University Press, 1971), 189–224.
10. Raymond W. Albright, *A History of the Protestant Episcopal Church* (New York: Macmillan, 1964), 130–3; Manross, *A History of the American Episcopal Church*, 194–8.
11. James Thayer Addison, *The Episcopal Church in the United States, 1789–1931* (Hamden, CT: Archon Books reprint, 1969, orig. publ., 1951), 65–73, esp. 69–71; Robert W. Prichard, *A History of the Episcopal Church* (Harrisburg, PA: Morehouse Publishing, 1992), 86; S.D. McConnell, *History of the American Episcopal Church, 1600–1915*, 11th edn (Milwaukee, WI: Morehouse Publishing, 1916, orig. publ. 1890), 244–47; and Raymond W. Albright, *A History of the Protestant Episcopal Church*, 135, 140.
12. Thomas Bradbury Chandler, *A Sermon Preached Before the Corporation for the Relief of the Widows and Children of Clergymen, in Communion of the*

Church of England in America; at their Anniversary Meeting on October 2d, 1771, at Perth-Amboy (Burlington, NJ: Isaac Collins, 1771), 26, 28–30; and Samuel Auchmuty, *A Sermon Preached Before the Corporation for the Relief of the Widows and Children of Clergymen; at their Anniversary Meeting in Trinity-Church, New-York, on Tuesday, October the 2d, 1770* (New York: H. Gaine, 1771), 22–4. See also John Tyler, *The Sanctity of a Christian Temple: Illustrated in a Sermon, at the Opening of Trinity-Church in Pomfret, on Friday, April 12, 1771* (Providence, RI: printed by John Carter, 1771), 10.

13. Thomas Barton to SPG, New York, 15 December 1778, *Hist. Coll.* V, 129–30. See also Philip Reading to SPG, Apoquiniminck, 30 September 1778, *Hist. Coll.* II, 495.

14. Samuel Cooke to SPG, New York, 5 October 1782, SPG Ser B, XXIV, 122; and Abraham Beach to SPG, New Brunswick, 4 January 1782, SPG Ser B, XXIV, 310.

15. John Sayre to SPG, New York, 8 November 1781 in SPG Ser B, II, 125; and Mather Byles to SPG, Halifax, 30 September 1776, SPG Ser B, XXV, 209.

16. John Rutgers Marshall to SPG, New York, 24 April 1782, SPG Ser B, III, 351. See also William Clark to SPG, Newport, Rhode Island, 6 July 1778, *Hist. Coll.* III, 597; and Samuel Andrews to SPG, Wallingford, 10 February 1784, SPG Ser C, III, 37.

17. James Scovil to SPG, Waterbury, 26 March 1783, SPG Ser C, III, 58; Scovil to SPG, 25 May 1785, SPG Ser C, III, 59; and Scovil to SPG, 20 August 1785, SPG Ser C, III, 60.

18. Roger Viets, *A Serious Address and Farewell Charge to the Members of the Church of England in Simsbury and the Adjacent Parts* (Hartford, CT: Hudson and Goodwin, 1787), 5.

19. Doty to SPG, Montreal, 20 May 1775 in John W. Lydekker, 'The Reverend John Doty, 1745–1841,' *HMPEC* 7 (1938), 293.

20. Samuel Tingley to SPG, Somerset County, Maryland, 11 May 1784, SPG Ser C, IV, 70.

21. Philip Reading to SPG, Apoquiniminck, 18 March 1776, *Hist. Coll.* II, 482.

22. Edward Winslow to SPG, Braintree, 5 August 1775 and 1 January 1777, *Hist. Coll.* III, 582, 588–90.

23. G. MacLaren Brydon, 'The Clergy of the Established Church in Virginia and the Revolution,' *VMHB* 41 (1941), 15; Cumberland County to General Assembly, 3 November 1779 and 23 November 1780, Legislative Petitions, Religious Petitions to the General Assembly of Virginia, 1774–1802, VSLA, Miscellaneous Reel 425.

24. Lohrenz, 'The Virginia Clergy and the American Revolution,' 32; Brydon, 'The Clergy of the Established Church,' 132.

25. Josephine Fisher, 'Bennet Allen, Fighting Parson,' *Maryland Historical Magazine* 28 (1943), 299–322; 29 (1944), 49–72, esp. 57, 59, 61; and James A. Allen, *The Allen Chronicle: A Family in War and Peace* (Braunton, Devon: Merlin Books, 1988), 34–43, esp. 34.

26. William Douglas to John Martin, 1 September 1778, original at VSLA, 20318, photostat at AL, 437-X.

27. J. Graves to Episcopal Church and Congregation in Providence, Providence, 13 July 1776; Graves to J. Jenkins, churchwarden, 23 December 1778;

Graves to Members of the church meeting, 19 April 1781; and Graves to SPG, 12 February 1782; Graves to Episcopal Church in Providence, 15 April 1783; and Churchwardens at Providence, RI to J. Graves, 26 April 1783; SPG Ser C, IX, 160, 162, 164, 168, 169, 171.

28. Edward Bass to SPG, Newbury Port, New England, 9 January 1784, *Hist. Coll.* III, 631, 632. For opinions on Bass's conduct see Col Frye to SPG, 24 May 1783, *Hist. Coll.* III, 628–9 and other letters, 611–38.

29. Bailey to J. W. Weeks, 10 October 1777 in William S. Bartlett, ed., 'The Frontier Missionary: A Memoir of the Life of the Rev. Jacob Bailey, A.M. Missionary at Pownalborough, Maine, Cornwallis and Annapolis, N.S.,' *Collections of the Protestant Episcopal History Society* II (New York: Stanford and Swords, 1853), 114.

30. Daniel Fogg to SPG, Pomfret, 24 January 1783, SPG Ser C, III, 31.

31. Edwin G. Burrow and Michael Wallace, 'The American Revolution: The Ideology and Psychology of National Liberation,' *Perspectives in American History* 6 (1972), 167–306; J. M. Bumsted, ' "Things in the Womb of Time": Ideas of American Independence, 1633–1763,' *WMQ* 3rd Ser., 31 (1974), 533–64; John M. Murrin, 'A Roof Without Walls: The Dilemma of American National Identity,' in Richard Beeman et al., eds, *Beyond Confederation: Origins of the Constitution and American National Identity* (Chapel Hill, NC: Institute of Early American History and Culture, 1987), 333–48; and Linda Colley, *Britons: Forging the Nation 1707–1837* (New Haven, CT: Yale University Press, 1992), esp. 101–45.

32. G. MacLaren Brydon, ed., 'Letter of the Rev. James Ogilvie to Colonel John Walker of Belvoir, Virginia, April 26, 1771,' *HMPEC* 1 (1932), 34–5.

33. Thomas Coombe Jr to Thomas Coombe Sr, London, 6 June 1770 and 8 October 1770, Coombe Family Papers, HSP, MSS 1993.

34. William Smith to SPG, Philadelphia, 28 August 1775, *Hist. Coll.* II, 479.

35. Thomas Bradbury Chandler, *A Friendly Address to All Reasonable Americans, on the Subject of Our Political Confusions: in Which the Necessary Consequences of Violently Opposing the King's Troops, and of a General Non-Importation are Fairely Stated* (Boston, MA: Mills and Hicks, 1774), 7; and his, *What Think Ye of the Congress Now? Or, An Inquiry, How Far the Americans are Bound to Abide By and Execute the Decisions of, the Late Congress?* (New York: James Rivington, 1775), 48.

36. Jonathan Boucher, *A View of the Causes and Consequences of the American Revolution, in Thirteen Discourses* (London: G.G. and J. Robinson, 1797), 592–3.

37. Henry P. Ippel, 'British Sermons and the American Revolution,' *Journal of Religious History* 12 (1982), 197.

38. George Bisset, *Honesty the Best Policy in the Worst of Times, Illustrated and Proved From the Exemplary Conduct of Joseph of Arimathea, and its Consequent Rewards; With an Application to the Case of Suffering Loyalists, A Sermon Intended to have been Preached at Newport, Rhode Island, on the Sunday preceding the Evacuation of that Garrison by his Majesty's Troops. And afterwards preached at St. Paul's and St. George's Chapels, New York, On Sunday, October 8th, 1780* (London: W. Richardson, 1784), 16. Sermon located at American Antiquarian Society Library, Worcester, MA.

39. Thomas Bradbury Chandler to SPG, Elizabeth Town, New Jersey, 3 October 1785, SPG Ser C, II, unnumbered.
40. Ebenezer Dibblee, 'Letters of the Reverend Doctor Ebenezer Dibblee, of Stamford, to the Reverend Doctor Samuel Peters, Loyalist Refugee in London,' *HMPEC* 1 (1932), 63.
41. See David Griffith to Hannah Griffith, Williamsburg, 2 July 177[6?] and Griffith to Hannah Griffith, Elizabeth Town, 17 November 1778 in David Griffith Papers, 1760–89, VHS, Acc. Mss2 G8755 b.
42. John Hurt, *The Love of our Country. A Sermon, Preached before the Virginia Troops in New-Jersey* (Philadelphia, PA: Styner & Cist, 1777), 7.
43. James Madison, *A Sermon Preached Before the Convention of the Protestant Episcopal Church in the State of Virginia, on the Twenty Sixth of May, 1786* (Richmond, VA: Thomas Nicolson, 1786), 3.
44. Madison, *A Sermon Preached Before the Convention* (1786), 4–6.
45. John Tyler, *An Eulogy on the Life of General George Washington, Late Commander in Chief of the Armies of the United States of America, Who Died Dec. 14, 1799. Delivered Before the Inhabitants of the Parish of Chelsea, in Norwich, on the 22d of Feb. 1800* (Norwich, CT: Thomas Hubbard, 1800), 13.
46. Daniel Fogg to Mr Parker, Pomfret, Connecticut, 1 August 1783, *Doc. Hist.* II, 213; and Richard Mansfield to Samuel Peters, 3 June 1788, Peters Mss in Hawks Coll., AEC, PIII 90-11-1.
47. William Currie to SPG, Radnor, 1 October 1784 and 30 March 1785, SPG Ser C, IV, 65, 66.
48. Abraham Jarvis (for the Clergy of Connecticut) to SPG, New York, 6 May 1783, SPG Ser C, III, 92.
49. Viets to SPG, Simsbury, 4 August 1785, SPG Ser C, III, 55.
50. J. Wiswall to SPG, Boston, 1 December 1775, SPG Ser C, VI, 54A.
51. Mather Byles to SPG, Boston, 29 April 1775, SPG Ser B, XXII, 90.
52. Bartlett, 'Frontier Missionary: A Memoir of the Life of the Rev. Jacob Bailey,' 143.
53. Ranna Cossit to SPG, Boston, 18 October 1785, SPG Ser C, VI, 85; and Fogg to SPG, Pomfret, 23 May 1785, SPG Ser C, III, 35.
54. Viets, *A Serious Address and Farewell Charge*, 7.
55. Richard Samuel Clarke to Samuel Peters, Gagetown, New Brunswick, 19 January 1791, photostat in EADC, original in the Samuel Peters Papers, AEC.
56. Curtis Fahey, *The Anglican Experience in Upper Canada, 1791–1854* (Ottawa: Carleton University Press, 1991), xv; Judith Fingard, *The Anglican Design in Loyalist Nova Scotia* (London: SPCK, 1972), esp. 1–5; William Knox to William Pitt, 1786, Fulham Papers, I, 102. See also Charles Inglis to William White, 7 August 1788, Hawks Mss in Hawks Coll., AEC, RG 117.65.Misc, unidentified 39.
57. J. Wiswall to SPG, Cornwallis, Nova Scotia, 12 December 1783, SPG Ser C, VI, 55.
58. Inhabitants of Digby, Nova Scotia to SPG, 1 August 1785, SPG Ser B, VI, 222.
59. Bartlet 'The Frontier Missionary: A Memoir of the Life of the Rev. Jacob Bailey,' 150. Bailey's opinions later changed, and Mather Byles Jr also described Halifax as an 'American Siberia' rather than Canaan. See also

Bailey to Samuel Peters, 11 May 1780, Peters Mss in Hawks Coll., AEC, PI 45-8-46; and Byles to Samuel Peters, 10 May 1782 and 22 October 1782, Peters Mss in Hawks Coll., AEC, PI 63-8-64 and PI 70-8-71.

60. Matthew Graves to SPG, New York, 29 September 1779, *Doc. Hist.* II, 204.
61. Philip Reading to SPG, Apoquiniminck, 25 August 1776, SPG Ser B, XXI, 211.
62. William to Bishop John Henry Hobart, 1 September 1819, as quoted in Jennifer Clark, ' "Church of Our Fathers": The Development of the Protestant Episcopal Church Within the Changing Post-Revolutionary Anglo-American Relationship,' *The Journal of Religious History* 18 (1994), 27.
63. Edward Winslow to SPG, New York, 4 January 1779, SPG Ser B, XXII, 296.
64. John Sayre to SPG, New York, 14 August 1782, SPG Ser B, III, 359.
65. Uzal Ogden, *A Letter, From the Reverend Uzal Ogden, Rector of Trinity Church in Newark, and President of the Convention of the Protestant Episcopal Church in the State of New-Jersey – Addressed to the Several Congregations of this Church, in Said State. Written and Published at the Request of the Convention of the Church Aforesaid, Held in the City of Trenton, June 8, 1797* [Circular], (Newark, NJ: Pennington and Dodge, 1798), 3.
66. Bela Hubbard to SPG, New Haven, 3 April 1783, SPG Ser C, III, 98.
67. William Duke, *Observations on the Present State of Religion in Maryland* (Baltimore, MD: Samuel and John Adams, 1795), 46–7.
68. Duke, *Observations on the Present State of Religion in Maryland*, 14, 15, 19.
69. Bennet Allen, *A Reply to the Church of England Planter's First Letter Respecting the Clergy* (Annapolis, MD: Anne Catherine Green, 1770), 7.
70. Allen, *A Reply to the Church of England Planter's First Letter*, 11.
71. Joshua Bloomer to SPG, Jamaica, Long Island, 6 February 1784, SPG Ser C, II, unnumbered.
72. Clergy of the Established Church to the General Assembly, 8 November 1776, in Legislative Petitions, Religious Petitions 1774–1802 presented to the General Assembly of Virginia, VSLA, Miscellaneous Reel 425.
73. Shield to David Griffith, Caroline, 20 December 1784, in David Griffith Papers, 1760–89, VHS, Acc. Mss2 G8755b.
74. Abraham Beach to SPG, New Brunswick, New Jersey, 30 October 1783, SPG Ser C, II, 74. Emphasis his. See also Roger Viets to SPG, Simsbury, 4 August 1785, SPG Ser C, III, 55.
75. Daniel Earl to SPG, 1 June 1784, Edenton, North Carolina, SPG Ser C, VIII, 115; and Earl to SPG, 22 April 1779, SPG Ser B, V, 131.
76. Uzal Ogden, *A Sermon Delivered in St. Peter's Church, in the City of Perth-Amboy, May 16, 1786 Before a Convention of Clerical and Lay Delegates, of the Protestant Episcopal Church, in the state of New-Jersey* (New York: Samuel & John Loudon, 1786), 28.
77. Charles Edward Taylor to SPG, Bertie County, North Carolina, 13 October 1783, SPG Ser C, VIII, 118.
78. Of the 20 ministers residing in Connecticut in 1783 (two had died during the Revolution and one had exiled in late 1774), seven left for Canada between 1783 and 1789. At least one who remained, Christopher Newton, expressed misgivings about the new church. On Newton, see Hector G. Kinloch, 'Anglican Clergy in Connecticut 1701–1785' (unpublished PhD diss., Yale University, 1959), 88.

79. Henry Purcell, *Strictures on the Love of Power in the Prelacy; Particularly in a Late Claim of a Complete Veto, on all the Proceedings of the Clergy and Laity in Legal Convention Assembled. As set Forth in a Pamphlet, Published Prior to their Meeting in New-York* (Charleston, SC: W.P. Young, 1795), 46.

80. Griffith to William White, 26 July 1784, White Mss in Hawks Coll., AEC, WI, 37-1-39. See also John Tyler to Samuel Peters, 9 January 1784, Peters Mss in Hawks Coll., AEC, PII 2-9-2.

81. Duché to William White, 11 August 1783, White Mss in Hawks Coll., AEC, WI, 22-1-24; and Parker to Samuel Peters, 7 May 1785, Peters Mss in Hawks Coll., AEC, PII 39-9-39.

82. Uzal Ogden, *A Sermon Delivered in St. Peter's Church, in the City of Perth-Amboy, May 16, 1786*, 25–6; and Abraham Jarvis, *A Discourse Delivered Before a Special Convention of the Clergy, and Lay Delegates, of the Episcopal Church in the State of Connecticut, in Trinity Church, New-Haven, on the Fifth Day of May, 1796: Occasioned by the Death of the Right Reverend Samuel Seabury, D. D. Bishop of Connecticut and Rhode Island* (New Haven, CT: T. & S. Green, 1796), 22.

83. William White, *A Sermon, on the Due Celebration of the Festival, Appointed as a Thankgiving for the Fruits of the Earth; Preached in Christ-Church and St. Peter's, by the Rev. William White, D.D. and Rector of the Said Churches, October 29, 1786, the Day Preceding his Departure for England, to Obtain Episcopal Consecration* (Philadelphia, PA: Hall & Sellers, 1786), 15–16.

84. Parker to Samuel Peters, 15 December 1788, Peters Mss in Hawks Coll., AEC, PIII 128-11-39; Parker to William White, 10 September 1784, White Mss in Hawks Coll., AEC, WI 143-1-44; and Parker to Peters, 23 October 1786, Peters Mss in Hawks Coll., AEC, PII 113-10-14.

85. Tyler to Peters, 9 January 1784, Peters Mss in Hawks Coll., AEC, PII 2-9-2; and Bela Hubbard to Samuel Peters, 21 January 1784, Peters Mss in Hawks Coll., AEC, PII 3-9-3.

86. James Madison, *A Discourse on the Death of General Washington, Late President of the United States, Delivered on the 22d of February, 1800, In the Church in Williamsburg*, 2nd edn (New York, 1800), 6, 40; Madison, *A Sermon Preached Before the Convention of the Protestant Episcopal Church in the State of Virginia, on the Twenty Sixth of May, 1786*, 16. For a similar message, see Samuel Magaw, *A Sermon Delivered in St. Paul's Church, on the 4th of July, 1786* (Philadelphia, PA, 1786), 14–18.

87. James Madison, *An Address to the Members of the Protestant Episcopal Church, in Virginia* (Richmond, VA: printed by T. Nicolson, 1799), 4–5, 23.

88. Samuel Parker, *A Sermon, Preached Before His Honor the Lieutenant-Governor, the Honorable the Council, and the Honorable the Senate, and House of Representatives, of the Commonwealth of Massachusetts, May 29, 1793; Being the Day of General Election* (Boston, MA: Thomas Adams, 1793), 10–11, 31–2. See also John Tyler, *The Blessing of Peace: A Sermon Preached at Norwich, on the Continental Thanksgiving, February 19, 1795* (Norwich, CT: John Trumbull, 1795), 17–18.

89. Roger Viets, *A Sermon, on the Duty of Attending the Public Worship of God. Preached at Digby in Nova-Scotia, April 19th, 1789* (Hartford, CT: Hudson

and Goodwin, 1789), 14. On religion's role in supporting republican governments, see also William White, *A Sermon, on the Reciprocal Influence of Civil Policy and Religious Duty. Delivered in Christ Church, in the City of Philadelphia, on Thursday, the 19th of February, 1795* (Philadelphia, PA: Ormrod & Conrad, 1795), 13–14, 17, 22; and John Andrews, *An Address to the Graduates in Medicine: Delivered at a Medical Commencement, in the University of Pennsylvania, Held May 12, 1797* (Philadelphia, PA: Ormrod & Conrad, 1797), 18.

90. Uzal Ogden, *A Letter, from the Reverend Uzal Ogden* [Circular], 3–6.
91. William Smith, *A Sermon Preached in Christ-Church, Philadelphia, on Friday, October 7th, 1785, Before the General Convention of the Protestant Episcopal Church, in the States of New-York, New-Jersey, Pennsylvania, Delaware, Maryland, Virginia, and South-Carolina* (Philadelphia, PA: Robert Aiken, 1785), 12–13.
92. William Duke, *Thoughts on Repentance. By a Minister of the Protestant Episcopal Church of Maryland* (Baltimore, MD: William Goddard, 1789), 6.
93. Samuel Magaw, *A Sermon Delivered in Christ-Church, Philadelphia, on Monday in Whitsun-Week, the 28th of May, 1787; at the First Ordination Held by the Bishop of the Protestant Episcopal Church, in the State of Pennsylvania* (Philadelphia, PA: Prichard & Hall, 1787), 8–9.
94. Samuel Seabury, *Bishop Seabury's Second Charge*, 8.
95. Samuel Magaw, *A Sermon Delivered in Christ-Church, Philadelphia, on Monday in Whitsun-Week, the 28th of May, 1787*, 27.
96. John Tyler to SPG, Norwich, 1 December 1784, SPG Ser C, III, 88.
97. Bela Hubbard to SPG, New Haven, 17 March 1784, SPG Ser III, 99.
98. On temperament, see Philip J. Greven, *The Protestant Temperament: Patterns of Child-Rearing, Religious Experience, and the Self in Early America* (Chicago, IL: University of Chicago Press, 1988, orig. publ. New York: Knopf, 1977), 337.
99. Dibblee to Samuel Peters, Stamford, 5 February 1793, in 'Letters of the Reverend Doctor Ebenezer Dibblee,' 76–7.
100. Coombe to Vestry of Christ Church, Philadelphia, 7 July 1778, excerpt in Edgar Legare Pennington, 'The Anglican Clergy of Pennsylvania in the American Revolution,' *Pennsylvania Magazine of History and Biography* 63 (1939), 422. See also Arthur Pierce Middleton, 'The Bestowal of the American Episcopate – A Bicentennial Remembrance,' *HMPEC* 53 (1984), 323.
101. William White, *Memoirs of the Protestant Episcopal Church in the United States of America, From Its Organization Up to the Present Day*, 2nd edn (New York: Swords, Stanford, 1836), 23.
102. Samuel Parker to SPG, Boston, 10 May 1783, SPG Ser C, V, 116A.
103. Clergy of Connecticut, signed by Abraham Jarvis, to Archbishop of York, New York, 21 April 1783, *Doc. Hist.* II, 214.
104. Dibblee to Samuel Peters, Stamford, Connecticut, 3 May 1785 and 20 March 1786, in 'Letters of the Reverend Doctor Ebenezer Dibblee,' 63–4, 72–3.
105. White, *Memoirs of the Protestant Episcopal Church*, 21. See also Loveland, *Critical Years*, 195–6.
106. See Loveland, *The Critical Years*, 21–61; and John F. Woolverton, 'Philadelphia's William White: Episcopalian Distinctiveness and Accomodation in the Post-Revolutionary Period,' *HMPEC* 43 (1974), 279–96.

107. William White, *The Case of the Episcopal Churches in the United States Considered* (Philadelphia, PA: David C. Claypoole, 1782), 6–7, 17, 33.
108. Seabury, *Bishop Seabury's Second Charge, to the Clergy of His Diocess*, 11, 15. See also John Hamilton Rowland, *A Sermon Before the Convention of the Protestant Episcopal Church, at New Brunswick, In the State of New-Jersey, on Thursday, 7th July, 1785* (New York: Hugh Gaine, 1785), 6, 9. On primitivism, see also Peter Doll, 'The Idea of the Primitive Church in High Church Ecclesiology from Samuel Johnson to J. H. Hobart,' *AEH* 65 (1996), 6–43.
109. Samuel Seabury, *Bishop Seabury's Second Charge*, 15.
110. Hubbard to Samuel Peters, 29 November 1785, Peters Mss in Hawks Coll., AEC, PII 60-9-60.
111. Chandler to SPG, Elizabeth Town, New Jersey, 3 October 1785, SPG Ser C, II, unnumbered.
112. John Bowden, *An Address from John Bowden, A.M. to the Members of the Episcopal Church in Stratford. To Which is Added, a Letter to the Rev'd Mr. James Sayre* (New Haven, CT: T. & S. Green, 1792), 11, 16–17, 18.
113. Clark, 'Church of Our Fathers,' 40.
114. Viets, *A Serious Address and Farewell Charge*, 10, 12.
115. Roger Viets to SPG, Simsbury, 29 October 1785, SPG Ser C, III, 53. See also Dibblee to SPG, Stamford, 27 September 1790, SPG Ser C, III, 69.
116. William White, *A Sermon, Delivered in Christ-Church, on the 21st of June, 1786, at the Opening of the Convention of the Protestant Episcopal Church, in the States of New-York, New-Jersey, Pennsylvania, Delaware, Maryland, Virginia, and South-Carolina* (Philadelphia, PA: Hall & Sellers, 1786), 25, 29, 30.
117. William Smith, *A Sermon Preached in Christ-Church, Philadelphia, on Friday, October 7th, 1785*, 22.
118. William Smith, *A Sermon Preached in Christ-Church, Philadelphia, on Friday, October 7th, 1785*, 24–28, citation 28.
119. Henry Purcell, *Strictures on the Love of Power in the Prelacy*, 5, 8, 33–4, 46–8.

EPILOGUE

1. Sydney E. Ahlstrom, *A Religious History of the American People* (New Haven, CT: Yale University Press, 1972), 381–3.
2. Walter B. Posey, 'The Protestant Episcopal Church: An American Adaptation,' *Journal of Southern History* 25 (1959), 8; William Wilson Manross, *A History of the American Episcopal Church* (New York: Morehouse-Gorham, 1950), 199; Lawrence L. Brown, 'The Americanization of the Episcopal Church,' *HMPEC* 44 (1975), No. 5 (Extra), 45; and Robert W. Prichard, *A History of the Episcopal Church* (Harrisburg, PA: Morehouse Publishing, 1991), 95.
3. Prichard, *A History of the Episcopal Church*, 95–6; Ahlstrom, *A Religious History of the American People*, 370.

4.   Ahlstrom, *A Religious History of the American People*, 370; and Raymond W. Albright, *A Religious History of the Protestant Episcopal Church* (New York: Macmillan, 1964), 136–7.

5.   Prichard, *A History of the Episcopal Church*, 97–8; Manross, *A History of the American Episcopal Church*, 208; and Albright, *A Religious History of the Protestant Episcopal Church*, 149, 162–3, 193.

6.   Manross, *A History of the American Episcopal Church*, 202, 213, 238–43, 252–3; Albright, *A History of the Protestant Episcopal Church*, 178–80. Both Hobart and Griswold were consecrated in 1811. In 1824 the Virginia Theological Seminary opened in Alexandria, Virginia.

Index